PROPAGANDA AND RHETORIC IN DEMOCRACY

PROPAGANDA  RHETORIC IN DEMOCRACY

HISTORY, THEORY, ANALYSIS

EDITED BY
GAE LYN HENDERSON AND M. J. BRAUN
With a foreword by Charles Bazerman

SOUTHERN ILLINOIS UNIVERSITY PRESS
CARBONDALE

Southern Illinois University Press
www.siupress.com

19 18 17 16   4 3 2 1

Library of Congress Cataloging-in-Publication Data

Names: Henderson, Gae Lyn, editor. | Braun, M. J. (Mary Jean) editor.
Title: Propaganda and rhetoric in democracy : history, theory, analysis / edited
    by Gae Lyn Henderson, M. J. Braun ; contributions by Laural Lee Adams ;
    foreword by Charles Bazerman ; contributions by Catherine Chaput ; con-
    tributions by Patricia Dunmire ; contributions by Sharon Kirsch ; contribu-
    tions by Lanette Grate ; contributions by Jayson Harsin ; contributions by
    Thomas Huckin ; contributions by Robert Jensen ; contributions by Meg
    Kunde ; contributions by John Oddo ; contributions by Stefania Porcelli ;
    contributions by Gary Thompson.
Description: Carbondale : Southern Illinois University Press, 2016. |
    Includes bibliographical references and index.
Identifiers: LCCN 2016010037 | ISBN 9780809335060 (paperback) |
    ISBN 9780809335077 (ebook)
Subjects: LCSH: Propaganda. | Rhetoric—Social aspects. | Democracy. |
    BISAC: LANGUAGE ARTS & DISCIPLINES / Rhetoric.
Classification: LCC HM1231 .P756 2016 | DDC 303.3/75—dc23 LC record
    available at http://lccn.loc.gov/2016010037

Printed on recycled paper. ♻

CONTENTS

FOREWORD

CHARLES BAZERMAN

Propaganda and Rhetoric in Democracy: History, Theory, Analysis presents important insights into the deep role of ideas in the formation of societies and in the ways people contend for the control of those ideas. In its exposure of the history and contemporary cases of malicious manipulation of the ideas of the populace, it helps us understand how the dark arts of propaganda have evolved in the last century. In delving into these dark arts it gives a frightful picture, but actually it is a picture I find filled with hope because analysis exposes the manipulations of mind-clouding magic. The episodes reported in this volume also remind us of the larger progressive contexts within which modern propaganda grew: the increasing democracy and dependence of even authoritarian states on assent of the populace; the rapid and continuing expansion of media; and the growth of ways of reporting on, knowing, and understanding the world apart from the interests of religions, states, and corporations. These positive forces are the very reason interested organizations have to work so hard and creatively to bend public opinion. These forces fracture the hegemony of closed cultural, political, and economic systems. They bring more knowledge and more voices to bear on matters of opinion and to contest assertion. They also offer conditions for increasing sophistication in querying the ideas by which the powerful attempt to forge assent. The essays in this volume continue the struggle to contest the means by which ideologies of acquiescence are spread and democracy is undermined to serve the interests of the few.

Propagating ideas that reinforce assent to power has always required work, and that work has increased as power has extended over great distances and larger groups of people. In particular, writing has been the primary means of extending ideas that boost commitment to ruling social organizations beyond the face-to-face relations of the tribe and the assertion of power at the point of a spear. The earliest recorded epic, the *Epic of Gilgamesh*, spread fame of the accomplishments, beneficence, and wisdom of the fifth king of Uruk. Another early major text was Hammurabi's Code, which is actually only one example of several written laws distributed through the ancient Middle East. While we may most remember the code for its eye-for-an-eye harshness, it was also the means of extending allegiance to a state over widespread domains through the promise of uniform laws inscribed on stele and clay tablets distributed in cities throughout the Babylonian Empire. Above the laws on one surviving stele is a bas-relief of the king providing a ruling to a compliant citizen, sending the message even to those who could not read that adherence to the reign of the king and his written law brought justice and prosperity.

The Hebrew scriptures contained the history of a people represented as preserved by the will of God, an enumeration of God's law, and promises of the prosperity to come from adhering to the law. These scriptures and attendant practices of study and regulation held the people together, even in the Diaspora. Equally, the hegemony of the Chinese Empire rested on the spread of ideology through Confucian texts, the selection of government officials for their Confucian learning, and an educational and examination system based on knowledge of the same texts that inculcated Confucian values.

So while the role of ideology in fostering support for states is nothing new, our current concern for the propagation of beliefs that serve dominant social, political, and economic powers arises within particular trends in more recent history. Part of those trends go back to the eighteenth and nineteenth centuries, with the ascent of nation-states based on romantic ideologies of the unity and genius of the peoples who made up those states. This romantic nationalism was coincident with the rise of capitalism as an explicit ideology and its connection with the wealth and well-being of nations—along with its dialectical ideological opposite of state ownership. Ideas of state, people, and economy and their relation became important to maintaining allegiance at the same time as democratic movements, competing states, competing economic models, and competing ideologies became more available. The growth of a print-based public sphere, facilitated by new lower-cost paper and print technologies, as well as expanding education, provided means for these ideologies to be purveyed and contested. In the twentieth century, conflicts, saturated with ideological meanings, became global, even as now-pervasive print was supplemented by radio, movies, television, and other mass media.

As the stakes and threats increased, it became urgent for those holding economic, political, and social power to spread beliefs to maintain mass allegiance to existing institutions and policies that brought high costs with few benefits to most citizens: misdistribution of wealth, wars, and despoiling of the planet. Yet at the same time, new resources became available to contest the official or dominant stories and ideas that reinforced current arrangements of power and privilege. The rise of sciences and social sciences provided standards of truth, methods of attaining facts, and increasingly large bodies of knowledge distinct from the interests of state, church, or financial institutions—though funding, regulation, and other forms of influence have not always kept lines of distinction clean. Nonetheless, the growth of a research culture and of research institutions has provided more and more grounds on which to contest official stories and standpoints from which to identify misrepresentations. The rise of the modern press, developing professional standards over the last century or so, has also provided some degree of independent representation of events—despite the many limits and perversions arising from the press's ties to corporate and government interests. Nor should we forget the escalation of a popular entertainment industry that seeks attention of citizen audiences by articulating its perceptions and desires in pleasurable ways. Representing previously unexposed contradictions in society, articulating skeptical attitudes toward public figures, finding satiric comedy in exposing duplicity—all have turned out to be good business for at least niche markets. Realist social problem dramas, musicals with progressive themes, idealistic stories of social visionaries and contributors to the common good, documentaries, and political comics have served to deflate propaganda and establish alternative views, even as they contribute to the wealth of interested corporations. Subversive art, as long as it is profitable, finds its sponsors.

The availability of facts, reasoning, and ideas somewhat independent of large institutions propagating their views has given rise to the modern assessment of propaganda as malicious manipulation, as there are widespread alternatives by which to compare and evaluate official stories. When official stories in the twentieth century did attempt to recover a good name for propagation of their ideas, it was often through assertion of independent truth as a fundamental value of their organization in contrast with the obfuscations of others.

Sources of somewhat independent knowledge have also been taken up by citizen groups in their pursuit of policies that favor citizens over factions of entrenched power, as with the mid-twentieth-century antinuclear testing campaigns and the nascent environmental movements. These groups drew their membership and leadership from the increasing numbers of people with higher education, disposing them to look toward independent research and scientific knowledge to evaluate ideas in the public sphere. Finally, into this mix we must add new communicative media, including the Internet, that further add the number of voices, standpoints, and sources of knowledge that can contest official stories, even as the more complex communicative landscape becomes harder to evaluate and sort out.

Contesting propaganda requires critiques of the sources and means by which malicious manipulation is created and spread. Contesting propaganda also requires alternate representations based on more credible evidence, facts, and reasoning—appealing to more profound emotions. There is no foreseeable end to this struggle when all tricks will be exposed and without effect, for there is no foreseeable end to interests that motivate new tricks. Further, while some will find their way out of obfuscations, others will still be entranced. But through efforts such as in this volume, we can keep sweeping away the fog and clearing the field for serious democratic deliberation. We should be thankful for the peacemaking work that the rhetoricians contributing to this volume accomplish.

ACKNOWLEDGMENTS

We acknowledge the contributors to this volume for their provocative work and insights into historical and contemporary propagandas. They have taught us a great deal about the rhetorical production of economic and political realities in managed democracy. We also acknowledge two student research assistants at Utah Valley University: Jennifer Gallagher, for her help in research and copyediting, and Mat Sillito, for his help in research. We appreciate the input of our reviewers and are grateful to Kristine Priddy at Southern Illinois University Press for her assistance and encouragement. Finally, we acknowledge members of Rhetoricians for Peace who inspired us to initiate this project.

PROPAGANDA AND RHETORIC IN DEMOCRACY

INTRODUCTION: A CALL FOR RENEWED ATTENTION TO PROPAGANDA IN WRITING STUDIES AND RHETORIC

GAE LYN HENDERSON AND M. J. BRAUN

> Paradoxically, it is easier to construct a coherent story when you know little, when there are fewer pieces to fit into the puzzle. Our comforting conviction that the world makes sense rests on a secure foundation: our almost unlimited ability to ignore our ignorance.
> —Daniel Kahneman, *Thinking, Fast and Slow*

> Comprehension, in short, means the unpremeditated attentive facing up to, and resisting of, reality—whatever it may be.
> —Hannah Arendt, *The Origins of Totalitarianism*

Margarethe von Trotta's 2012 film *Hannah Arendt* depicts the philosopher's struggle reporting for the *New Yorker* on the 1961 trial of Adolf Eichmann, an ex-Nazi accused of war crimes. Arendt came under attack for her analysis of Eichmann as a cog in the military machine, a bureaucrat who followed orders, culminating in her famous phrase "the banality of evil" to describe his (shared) guilt. The film dramatizes the controversy and suspicion directed toward Arendt for her dispassionate analysis of Eichmann's actions. Arendt's point about collective responsibility was prefigured by Kenneth Burke in *A Rhetoric of Motives* when he says that a "technical expert," working on weapons of destruction, for example, may believe he has no moral responsibility: "The extreme division of labor . . . [has] made dispersion the norm" (30–31). But by 1961, popular entrenched views of the subhuman, criminal Nazis had been constructed through more than two decades of newsreels, newspaper stories, movies, political

1

speeches, and powerful wartime rhetoric. Burke himself, in perhaps his best-known essay, "The Rhetoric of Hitler's Battle," condemned Hitler's propaganda campaign targeting the Jewish people. The American public, long accustomed to associating Nazis with dastardly evil, were ill-prepared and unwilling to assess Arendt's logic on its merits. Arendt protested at the time that people were not reading or responding to her actual argument, an argument that offers substantive insight into how ordinary German citizens could perpetrate horrendous atrocities. At the end of the film, Arendt, played by Barbara Sukowa, passionately defends her ideas in a crowded lecture hall. To win over a contemporary audience to material still emotionally charged today, von Trotta staged Arendt's philosophical argument as a speech performed for enthralled students, faculty, and the public. Sukowa won critical acclaim for her performance; her speech powerfully argues that humanity itself is defined by our ability to reason, to think, and that the evils of the Holocaust resulted when Nazis systematically denied that humanity. Film critics responded positively; Mick LaSalle comments that the film shows that Arendt's "dedicated work in trying to unravel the causes of Europe's moral collapse was worthy of study." The film suggests, however, that because Arendt's main assignment was to "cover" Eichmann's trial for the *New Yorker* audience, perhaps she erred rhetorically by including in her article series a critique of German Jewish leaders. The outrage that her articles elicited (in film and in life) prompts us to acknowledge that rhetorical obstacles, such as identifications, emotions, and loyalties, continually impede and complicate the reception of rational argument and democratic deliberation.

This collection invites conversation among writing studies and rhetoric scholars about obstacles to democratic deliberation, focusing on two concepts that we suggest remain undertheorized: the notion of *managed democracy*, with its wide-ranging implications for public, political, and academic discourse, and the genre of *propaganda*, with its troubled and complex relationship to democracy. Scholars in multiple disciplines employ theories of managed democracy to describe the transnational and globalized financial power that increasingly influences and even determines U.S. domestic and foreign policy.[1] Princeton political philosopher Sheldon Wolin warns in *Democracy Incorporated: Managed Democracy and the Specter of Inverted Totalitarianism* that today's globalized corporations wield an interdependent weaponry of "science, technology, and capital" to achieve aims that serve only the most elite class. Corporate "superpower" manages democracy to "redefine the citizenry as respondents rather than actors, as objects of manipulation rather than as autonomous" (132). Such manipulation—ubiquitous, deceptive, mass-mediated, and highly motivated—represents an insidious version of propaganda with widespread consequences for humanity.

Rhetoricians focusing on public discourse echo Wolin's concerns. In *Deliberative Acts: Democracy, Rhetoric, and Rights*, Arabella Lyon describes a globalized propaganda culture: "new technologies of mass media and manipulation, the erosion of state power and the ideal of communitarian democracy, the invidious spread of consumer capitalism, and the vilification of democracy in its (neo)liberal guise" (9). Donald Lazere asserts that "the pervasiveness and elaborate engineering of both political and commercial propaganda in our time far exceed that in any past period of history" (*Reading* 10). Mourning the publication end of NCTE's *Quarterly Review of Doublespeak* in 2000, Nancy McCracken worries that "readers have lost their capacity for outrage along with the expectation that civic discourse represent an attempt at clarity and accuracy. When terms like 'managed news' and 'managed care' are used comfortably in common discourse, it is more of a challenge to find examples of, for example, actual news reporting, than examples of doublespeak" (2). Manipulative public discourse may be labeled as doublespeak,[2] logical fallacies (ad hominem, *ad ignorantiam*, *ad populum*, and so on), corporate-funded public relations, political spin, demagoguery, or by numerous other pejoratives. While the term *propaganda* has been defined in multiple ways (as essays in this collection explore), we find it appropriate nomenclature for identifying rhetorics that secure a political/economic system that renders citizens governable rather than governing. Our inquiry, then, is focused on a specific discursive practice of managed democracy—propaganda—that hinders or closes down discussion, response, inquiry, education, information, and deliberation. We call for renewed attention to propaganda because studying its uses in modern democracy opens up important theoretical questions that may challenge normative rhetorical practices. Further, gaps in scholarship may provoke promising research and much-needed rhetorical interventions in public discourse and education.

THEORETICAL QUESTIONS

Examining the relationship between propaganda and democracy elicits provocative and difficult questions; here we focus on three particularly vexed examples, later suggesting possible answers to prompt further discussion.

This collection problematizes and explores these and similar questions in ways we hope contribute broadly to rhetorical theory and to ongoing scholarship in democratic deliberation.

First: Is there a value-free rhetoric? Do we judge rhetoric based on its inherent or underlying ideology, the hegemony that may prompt or motivate it? Is rhetoric (or propaganda) ethically neutral? Do we evaluate rhetoric solely upon whether it works (is persuasive)? Or can we legitimately assess it using some sort of rubric, as a more or less fair or honest rhetorical performance? Is it true that "propaganda as a mere tool is no more moral or immoral than a pump handle" (Lasswell 21)? The film *Hannah Arendt* poses questions not only about the ethics of obedience within systems of power but also about the morality of war propaganda and how rhetorical performance complicates determinations of justice. The film's multiethnic points of view may prompt us to ask: In a globalized culture, what transnational ethical values are deployed to compete with traditional nation-state loyalties?

Second: How can one determine facticity, accuracy, and truth? Poststructuralist language theory, social constructionism, cultural relativism, and multiculturalism all complicate attempts to determine meaning, define terms, and establish common ground among interlocutors. Do we know propaganda when we see it? If propaganda is often described as misinformation, misleading manipulation, or bullshit (to use the title of Harry Frankfurt's essay and Penn & Teller's Showtime series), when do we have enough information to evaluate any instance of rhetoric as essentially or predominantly deceptive? More troubling is propaganda's deliberate (or even unintentional) blend of fact and fiction. Fictions of course include artistic genres; in our film example, then, why are rhetorical strategies of image, dialogue, and music so essential in communicating the filmmakers' (and Arendt's) message? Is it accurate or theoretically productive to label artistic genres as anti-propaganda education, or is art simply propaganda for alternative ideologies?

Third: Do any circumstances justify misrepresentation? When is less than full disclosure justified? Or, to put the question more simply, when do the ends justify the means? In "War Rhetoric, Defensible and Indefensible," Wayne Booth asks, "If I can save the world by lying effectively, is not the lie more honorable than truth-telling that leads to massive disaster?" (235). Does the very notion of "saving the world" (one that often comes up in war propaganda) suggest politically troubled and highly motivated rhetorical performance? Can scholarly disinterest be summoned to thoughtfully analyze instances of propaganda, or will such evaluations derive from outgroup versus ingroup–determined perspectives? The film's rather heroic presentation of Hannah Arendt—as honest, clear-thinking, and thoughtful analyst—poses a question we repeatedly encounter as we study propaganda: Must we challenge propaganda (and its effects), even when that propaganda is directed against our enemies?

These questions are not new, and such questions about the ethics of persuasion have troubled rhetoricians since the inception of democracy in Athens. Because rhetorical performance determined governance, power, and policy, class interests became intrinsically tied to rhetorical expertise. It is certainly true that not only in ancient Greece but also throughout history, rhetoric has contributed to repression, but at the same time, rhetorical analysis and performance has provided a means to counter repression and fight manipulation. Thus, this collection joins conversations among contemporary scholars who, responding to prevalent *effects* of propaganda—its cultural and sociological fallout of entrenched political polarization, adversarial politics, loss of civility, manipulative journalism, and corporate-managed policy—reimagine normative rhetorical practices to reinvigorate the ideal of deliberative democracy.

Sharon Crowley, in *Toward a Civil Discourse: Rhetoric and Fundamentalism*, focuses on problems—carefully tracing the intransigence of fundamentalisms—but she also suggests possible solutions. Rhetors must acknowledge their opponents' values while arguing for competing ones, deploy stories (myths) as well as emotional appeals, and carefully "disarticulate" beliefs from their commonplace associations (198–201). She cautions that the strategy of disarticulation "depends on the relations between rhetors and audiences because it requires time and patience from both parties" (201). In *Hannah Arendt*, the philosopher's attempt to disarticulate a theory of social responsibility from her audience's deepest racial and religious affiliations ultimately failed. Many of Arendt's friends, in both the film and in life, disavowed their relationship. If a (storied) film may enable today's audiences to appreciate Arendt's points, then a similar strategy emerges in Lyon's *Deliberative Acts*. She constructs a theory of *performative* deliberation, recasting democratic practices outside "normative commitments to institutionalized, rational deliberation" (9). Summarizing Arendt, Lyon warns that too often "the performative nature of healthy deliberation is displaced by a tightening system of lies, itself a dramatic performance laboring to construct a symbolic system deaf to other constituting forces" (135). Thus, alternative "dramatistic" performances become crucial. Just as audiences who view

Hannah Arendt may recognize the problematic nature of black-and-white categorizations of guilt, Lyon posits that clashing voices of interlocutors in media and artistic genres perform conflicting claims for justice that demand attention (7–8). Theories of rhetorical intervention (Crowley, Lyon), then, suggest remediation for problems of conflicted social communication.

Patricia Roberts-Miller, in her detailed analysis of six models of the public sphere, *Deliberate Conflict: Argument, Political Theory, and Composition Classes,* asserts that rhetorical training provides the opportunity to consciously practice adopting other perspectives (182–88). Public debate ensures exposure to conflicting values; she notes the historical example of Adolf Eichmann and Rudolf Hoess, who carried out the Final Solution based on duty and loyalty but were never exposed to "Jewish arguments against it" (185). As in Lyon's advocacy of performatives, Roberts-Miller argues that nuanced rhetorical analyses may reveal complex motives and reasoning processes within opposing arguments (204–7). Following Roberts-Miller, we suggest that the painful conflict portrayed in the film between Arendt and her audience opens up valuable space for discussion. In *The Origins of Totalitarianism,* published in 1951 before the Eichmann controversy, Arendt explains that a key propaganda technique is the (false) construction of an unconflicted history: "Stalin decided to rewrite the history of the Russian Revolution; the propaganda of his new version consisted in destroying, together with the older books and documents, their authors and readers" (341–42).

Rhetorical (anti-propaganda) education, therefore, would expose existing social conflicts, particularly between majority and underrepresented voices. Christian Kock and Lisa Villadsen warn in *Rhetorical Citizenship and Public Deliberation* that exponentially growing diversity in global cultures threatens the very possibility of democracy as leaders orchestrate and sustain majority consensus: "As diverse cultures increasingly seek access and acceptance in modern democracies, it is natural that concerns over collective identity, social cohesion, and the difficulties of intersegmental communication (if any) come to the fore" (3). In another influential example, Krista Ratcliffe argues in *Rhetorical Listening: Identification, Gender, Whiteness* that listening across difference is taxing, but with high-stakes consequences: "Though individually we may each have moments when listening appears too great an effort to imagine or enact, culturally we have no such excuse. Lives and psyches, indeed fates of nations, frequently depend on such efforts" (94). If, as Ratcliffe explains, cultural logics, or shared beliefs, warrant the validity of claims that other groups may dismiss, then it becomes imperative to investigate the affective bases of how and why such persuasion (labeled by some as propaganda) is effective.

In her culminating study, *Trust in Texts: A Different History of Rhetoric*, the late Susan Miller rereads the history of rhetoric through the lens of emotion, provocatively situating persuasion as a pedagogical interaction dependent on trust. In the face of "uncertainty," humans seek for and tend to trust discourse that promises to teach or to reveal new information (3). The possibility of concealed truth is key to the way propaganda functions, offering simplistic information that portends more detail is available, just not (yet) conveyed. As Arendt describes Nazi propaganda, "Everything hidden, everything passed over in silence, became of major significance" (351). Miller further explains that uncertainty is remediated not "logically or analytically" but "symbolically and charismatically" (31).[3] For Miller, persuasion becomes a process of enculturation into what she calls "knowledge of knowledge systems" (31). This sense of knowledge—just out of reach but yet existent—gives propaganda enormous symbolic power that appeals to our most basic sense of knowing:

> We are not persuaded by argumentative proofs, nor by signs of expertise, knowledge, and fairness in their sources. We trust discourse we perceive to contain unknown, secreted if not secret content, when we feel that there is more to be known, yet that we already know more by virtue of our teachers' access to a metadiscourse whose very existence promises that the unknown is not unknowable. (31)

Miller provides insight not only broadly for theories of composition and rhetoric but also for how and why the most basic human emotions seem to underlie our allegiances, choices, and continuing loyalties, or what Miller calls "our ways of imagining ourselves as occupants of good or bad stories" (31). Ultimately, propaganda is the base appeal to such stories and to emotional extremes that structure our most immediate reactionary responses. Miller cites Catullus (Poem 85) with a definition of reality that we suggest clearly encapsulates the simple emotional reality that propaganda accesses: "I hate and I love" (32). Arendt describes the effects of propaganda similarly when she says the masses "do not trust their eyes and ears but only their imaginations, which may be caught by anything that is at once universal and consistent in itself. What convinces masses are not facts, and not even invented facts, but only the consistency of the system of which they are presumably part" (351). Propaganda activates the human desire for consistency, for trust in universals.

By citing Arendt's observations about human predispositions, however, we do not necessarily agree with historical assertions by Gustave Le Bon,[4] Edward Bernays,[5] Walter Lippmann,[6] and others[7] who argue not only that a democratic public sphere is a hopeless ideal but also that "public relations" specialists must manage and control mass communication practices for the unthinking herd. Nor by situating emotion and trust as basic conditions of propaganda reception do we suggest that rational discourse, or simple "debunking," provides a neat solution. As Miller and others mentioned above assert, argumentation, expertise, and fairness do not always persuade, but practices of inclusion, listening, analysis, teaching, and performative deliberation offer rhetorical rather than rationalist/ontologically-realist solutions. Given the widespread concern with democratic discourse and deliberation, we pose a further question: Has the specific topic of propaganda been recently neglected in writing studies and rhetoric, and if so, why and how?

PROMISING TRENDS AND GENERATIVE GAPS

Rhetoric and writing scholars of course reside in multiple academic disciplines, but most work in communication and English departments. Certainly communication scholars have made impressive contributions to history and analysis of propaganda, including recent books by Nancy Snow, J. Michael Sproule, and Garth S. Jowett and Victoria O'Donnell. English scholars, engaged with a belletristic tradition and a historical literary subject matter, are at times stereotyped as ivory-tower intellectuals who shy away from issues of public discourse. As John Ackerman and David Coogan describe the field, "Our disciplinary achievements have not been earned through everyday contact with publics, but through a hard-earned insularity from them" (2). An important exception to this generalization shows up in the NCTE Doublespeak Award, which we discuss later. But certainly scholars in writing studies belie this characterization with decades of research in socialized theories of writing instruction, civic literacy, community and public writing, multimodal composition, writing in the disciplines, and critical pedagogy. Donald Lazere, for example, has repeatedly argued that because the stakes are so high both for democracy and for the welfare of global citizens, both writing instruction and the larger field of English studies should be reconceived as training in national public rhetoric and civic literacy ("Postmodern"; *Reading*).

Further, the topic of propaganda has recently been taken up among rhetoricians and compositionists critiquing U.S. war rhetoric. Daphne Desser's "Teaching Writing in Hawaii after Pearl Harbor and 9/11: How to 'Make Meaning' and 'Heal' Despite National Propaganda" discusses the difficulties of teaching writing when students have been heavily exposed to dominant war rhetoric. Wayne Booth's previously mentioned essay examines the "rhetrickery" present in justifications for war set forth by media and government. Hilton Obenzinger examines narratives justifying war as well as the pejorative labeling of dissent in "On Being a Traitor." One of our contributors, Catherine Chaput, coauthored with Karen Powers "'Anti-American Studies' in the Deep South: Dissenting Rhetorics, the Practice of Democracy, and Academic Freedom in Wartime Universities," which explores dissenting rhetoric in current wartime discourse. Communication scholar Robert L. Ivie's *Democracy and America's War on Terror* argues that since 9/11 the United States has become "an aggressive republic of fear" (5) and makes the point that we, and our political leaders, cannot choose between rhetoric and reality; rather, "our choices are always between one kind of rhetoric and another" (4). And Gerard Hauser's award-winning *Prisoners of Conscience: Moral Vernaculars of Political Agency* juxtaposes a "thick moral vernacular of human rights" against elite rhetorics of power (43–45). Those in power, such as the Bush administration after 9/11, "disseminate information, opinions, and decisions while evading direct interrogation" (43). Hauser identifies the Abu Ghraib prisoner images and subsequent scandal as challenging "the rationale for the war in Iraq" and shows how new media play a prominent role in "defining public understanding of war and sustaining or eroding its public support" (185). These texts represent only a sampling of research in the field that tackles war propaganda since 9/11, the war on terror, and the wars in Iraq and Afghanistan.

This collection builds on this scholarship; we further suggest that renewed attention in writing studies[8] to the rich history of propaganda analysis may generate intriguing intersections among theories of composing, the history of rhetoric, and, more broadly, philosophy and critical theory. In *Propaganda and Democracy*, Sproule discusses two historical gaps in research. First, in the 1930s through the 1950s, as social science research burgeoned to investigate how the public could be influenced and managed through new techniques of opinion polling and the fast-growing public relations industry, corporations and scientists collaborated in exciting projects of mass persuasion. In the humanities, scholars continued to be concerned about increasing government and corporate reliance on propaganda, but Sproule argues such critique lacked a "large-scale theoretical framework and a compelling vocabulary of analysis" (89). The painful irony was that the history of rhetoric could have provided such a frame but was virtually ignored because English composition had replaced training in oratory/rhetoric since the late nineteenth century: "The theory and practice of rhetoric had become so obscure and antiquarian that it went completely undiscovered in the giant bibliography of propaganda studies prepared by Lasswell et al. for the Social Science Research Council" (89). Lasswell's 1934 article "Propaganda," first published in the *Encyclopedia of the Social Sciences*, represents the era's academic consensus on the topic by classifying propaganda's functions, sources, techniques, and power, concluding that "the task of the propagandist is that of inventing goal symbols that serve the double function of facilitating adoption and adaptation. The symbols must induce acceptance spontaneously and elicit those changes in conduct necessary to bring about permanent adoption" (24–25). The gap that existed in the 1930s, between the techniques of the "skilled manipulator" (17) and sustained scholarly critique grounded in the history of rhetoric, continues today; this collection begins to address it.

The second example shows up in the early 1970s when English scholars seemed oblivious to academic study of propaganda, even when aroused to enter public debate about deceptive public discourse. Responding to political crises that intruded onto campus (civil rights, protests against the Vietnam War, Watergate), in 1971 the NCTE formed the Doublespeak Committee to present an annual award for an egregious public example of language that George Orwell warned against: "grossly deceptive, evasive, euphemistic, confusing, or self-centered" ("Doublespeak Award"). The Doublespeak Award elicited controversial pushback from politicized sources; Sproule recounts that the committee "clearly was searching widely and somewhat desperately for theoretical models" (264). Of course English teachers primarily drew on literary and semantic sources (such as Orwell and S. I. Hayakawa). However, "references cited (and not cited) . . . showed that academicians had forgotten much about propaganda critique in the thirty years since the closure of the IPA's New York office" (264). The Institute for Propaganda Analysis was formed in 1937 by concerned intellectuals Kirtley Mather, Edward Filene, and Clyde Miller; Robert Jackall explains that the institute regularly circulated a newsletter to warn the public about propaganda sources ranging from "the Catholic fascist, Father Coughlin, to the public relations campaigns of Henry Ford" (5).

Newsletters included instruction about logical fallacies—the propaganda devices that "sway us to be 'for' or 'against' nations, races, religions, ideals, economic policies and practices, and so on through automobiles, cigarettes, radios, toothpastes, presidents, and wars" (Institute 217). Where the Doublespeak Award drew on sources from literature and language theory, the IPA tried to warn the general public about public relations techniques. Even if Sproule's observation is correct, that some scholars were less familiar with the history of the IPA, we suggest it is also possible, given the newsletter's articles (Institute), that English teachers equated propaganda analysis with exposing logical fallacies. Again, we notice that a similar perception, that a one-to-one correspondence exists between logical errors and propaganda, continues today and may explain in part why some researchers place less focus on propaganda.

In addition to examples cited by Sproule, another Internet-era scholarly intervention occurred in 2003. At that time, academics participating in the e-mail list H-Rhetor discussed their deep misgivings about discourse promulgated by the Bush administration and by media sources to solidify public opinion about Saddam Hussein readying weapons of mass destruction and the necessity for launching a preemptive strike. As participants on the e-mail list complained about blatant instances of war propaganda, Charles Bazerman (author of our preface here) asked, "Where are the rhetoricians?" He wondered whether rhetoric teachers and scholars were challenging misinformation, engaging in public debate, and acting as public intellectuals, both in media sources and in the classroom. His question and subsequent intense discussion provoked the forming of Rhetoricians for Peace (RFP), "a community of writing teachers dedicated to the exploration of opportunities in civil and academic discourse for promoting nonviolence."[9] Members of RFP approached NCTE with the idea of the *1984+* project, which was instituted in secondary schools and in colleges across the United States. English students read and wrote about Orwell's novel during the 2004 school year; the project was unique in its national scope and in inviting college and secondary classrooms to consider issues in twenty-first-century public discourse. Since 2003, RFP members interact primarily on an e-mail list but also meet annually at the Conference on College Composition and Communication, sponsoring workshops and special events, forming panels for national and regional conferences, and creating public initiatives toward peace and away from violence and war. After the *1984+* project, RFP workshops focused on the issue of propaganda, as members shared their research showing how public opinion continues to be swayed on multiple sides of the political spectrum by media pundits, campaign rhetoric, and political speeches. (Some RFP-instigated research is included here.) RFP is an example of how academics can work collaboratively via the Internet to challenge contemporary propagandas.

One difficulty that public intellectuals still face is the charge of polemics, but as Walker Gibson argues, "No single activity of English teachers has ever aroused such attention nationally as the annual Doublespeak Award" (11). Perhaps another reason some writing teachers have steered clear of propaganda as a research focus stems from controversy surrounding the awards.[10] The irony is that our divisive public sphere is the result of what French social-psychologist Jacques Ellul calls "sociological propaganda," which pervades the ideology, beliefs, and structure of society itself: "*It is the penetration of an ideology by means of its sociological context*" (63). Thus, challenges to normative states may be labeled as progressive propaganda. Nonetheless, research in this volume shows that propaganda crosses political party lines; we agree with Ellul's analysis that endemic sociological propaganda creates not only the answers to politicized questions but also the questions themselves. Ellul seemed to predict, as did Orwell, the increasing saturation of propaganda into all aspects of our lives, the propaganda culture we now inhabit. But as George Lipsitz reminds us, "Principled people in an unprincipled world always confront problems that seem too complex to solve; they always find themselves pitted against powers that seem too strong to defeat" (30). In that spirit, the scholars in this collection imagine a unique opportunity and obligation to challenge propaganda culture.

RHETORICAL ANALYSIS OF PROPAGANDA

Questions posed earlier—about how to ascertain any given rhetoric's neutrality, truth, and motive—make this challenge particularly daunting, but here we propose possible answers while inviting readers' critical responses. While theorists may disagree about the feasibility of evaluating a particular rhetoric as good, bad, or neutral, we find provocative Wayne Booth's argument in *The Rhetoric of Rhetoric*. Booth points out that in our contemporary culture, the development of rhetorical judgment is paramount for ethical human interaction and for a functioning democracy. Thus, he argues that persuasive means vary intrinsically on ethical grounds and subdivides rhetoric into categories to highlight such distinctions:

Rhetoric: The whole range of arts not only of persuasion but also of producing or reducing misunderstanding.

Listening-rhetoric (LR): The whole range of communicative arts for reducing misunderstanding by paying full attention to opposing views.

Rhetrickery: The whole range of shoddy, dishonest communicative arts producing misunderstanding—along with other harmful results. The arts of making the worse seem the better cause.

Rhetorology: The deepest form of LR: the systematic probing for "common ground." (10–11)

Booth includes propaganda in his category of rhetrickery, along with other questionable rhetorics: "*propaganda, bombast, jargon, gibberish, rant, guff, twaddle, grandiloquence, purple prose, sleaze, crud, bullshit, . . . harangue, tirade, verbiage, balderdash, rodomontade, flapdoodle, nonsense; 'full of sound and fury, signifying nothing'*" (11–12).

For Booth, rhetoric is not a neutral tool. Rather, each rhetorical act, each persuasive event or text, can be analyzed to assess the ethics of its construction and deployment. Does a specific rhetorical construction attempt to produce or reduce misunderstanding? What attention does it give to those with opposing views? Does it try to listen and find common ground? Booth advises, "The history of rhetoric teaches that learning to listen, and encouraging our opponents to listen, can *sometimes* yield moments of sheer illumination: a trustful pursuit of truth replacing what had appeared to be a hopeless battle" (172). Booth's recommendation for listening-rhetorics echoes Ratcliffe and other scholars of democratic deliberation who evaluate not just specific arguments but also the quality of subsequent discursive interaction. Roberts-Miller contends that "public deliberation leads to better and more just political decisions only if there is equal access on the part of people with genuinely different points of view, the opportunity to make arguments (rather than simply assertions), the time for exploration of different options, and a cultural milieu that values listening" (*Deliberate* 186). She further points out that these same goals may apply to classroom discussion (186). We agree that democratic values align with learned skills of good education: discussing thoughtfully, thinking critically, searching for broad background information, using logic, and probing for answers through scientific methodology. Ethical assessment of the rhetorical act helps us decide whether it is fundamentally an example of blatant rhetrickery or of honest, good-faith communication.

Thus, Booth's categories directly counter a common academic judgment about propaganda, which would categorize it, as well as rhetoric, as ethically neutral. If propaganda is neutral, then our judgment of it depends only on what side of the war (or issue) we take up—propaganda becomes a phenomenon scholars may examine but not challenge. Philosopher Stanley Cunningham points out that this view of propaganda as a neutral tool "has become widely entrenched, especially in the social sciences, to the point that it is now virtually universal" (129). Historically, as the essays in this volume show, this view has well served government and corporate agencies that conflate instrumental propaganda with information. Cunningham protests, as do we: *the neutrality thesis appears to arise in direct proportion to the distance between propaganda, conceived as an artifact, and the phenomenological epicenter of communicative behavior—perception, judgment, decision, choice. The more that propaganda is distanced from human choice and acting, the easier it is to assume its moral indifference"* (131, emphasis in original). Rhetoricians may see such separation as wrongheaded—precisely because rhetorical education from its inception in ancient Greece has been directly tied to human choice and action. The purpose of this volume, then, is not only to analyze propaganda but also to expose its rhetrickery and educate human beings in how to resist and challenge it.

Any attempt to expose the deceptiveness of propaganda requires us to acknowledge ongoing debate, given antifoundational sensibilities, about whether and how truth claims can be evaluated. Truth questions, however, are the precise location where propaganda analysis may draw on the rich history of rhetoric. Joe Sachs, as he introduces his translation of Plato's *Gorgias* and Aristotle's *Rhetoric*, observes that these texts reveal "the emergence of political life itself" (3). Plato's deep suspicions about rhetoric no doubt spurred his student Aristotle to tackle the problem directly in the *Rhetoric*. But Aristotle makes a key, differential point in his definition of rhetoric. Students and even scholars sometimes cite his definition as simply "all the available means of persuasion," but they miss a critical element. Aristotle defines rhetoric as "a power of *theorein*, of recognizing or beholding" (Sachs 18). Rhetoric is a theoretical ability, a power, an insight, a judgment of all of the ways, both ethical and unethical, through which human beings can be persuaded; rhetorical education and judgment, then, may counter the dangers of deceptive persuasion in democratic societies.

Many theorists across disciplines of course have grappled with the "Truth problem"; in Michael Bernard-Donals and Richard Glejzer's collection *Rhetoric in an Antifoundational World*, Patricia Roberts[-Miller] critiques a well-known model for public discourse, Jürgen Habermas's "rational-critical sphere," concluding that although his model presents an appealing ideal, it presupposes false reliance on authority that undermines its applicability in pluralistic societies that lack agreement on a priori principles ("Habermas's Rational-Critical Sphere"). In several of his later essays, in *The Inclusion of the Other: Studies in Political Theory*, Habermas responds to issues of pluralistic societies, arguing that both majority and minority voices must engage in deliberation: "The affected persons themselves first articulate and justify in public debate those aspects that are relevant to equal or unequal treatment" (264). The question then becomes how such voices gain an audience or enter public debate, because for Habermas, rhetoric itself is an example of what he labels *strategic action*: sophistry motivated by unitary interest focused on instrumental goals (Lyon 14). Only his discourse model of *communicative action*, "oriented to achieving, sustaining and reviewing consensus," would lead to "intersubjective recognition of criticisable validity claims" (Habermas, *Theory* 17). Intersubjective recognition thus creates the possibility of a universal ethics, one in which validity claims are critiqued and evaluated. Perhaps citizens need a baseline level of rhetorical awareness to successfully assess the validity of competing claims, but Habermas does not suggest how they may achieve it: "Habermas's highly idealized and formal model hardly does justice to the substantive richness of the rhetorical tradition" (Bohman and Rehg par. 38). Rhetoricians, then, as previous examples suggest, continue to draw on that substantive tradition in analyzing and further developing models for deliberation, inclusive public discourse, and pedagogy.[11] Lyon, for example, argues that deliberation is not just procedural: "Moments of radical courage, innovation, transformation and constitution [that is, rhetoric] need deliberative theory's attention. Characterizing deliberation as a reasoned procedure leading to agreements, unitary outcomes, or consensus deeply damages the concept itself, for the model is inadequately descriptive" (16). Stakes are high: democracy needs creative rhetorical invention integrating theory and practice to move truth problems beyond philosophical limitations and toward dialogic and pluralistic solutions.

Finally, we acknowledge that questions about motive and intention pose evaluative difficulties, as essays in this volume explore. Kenneth Burke, for example, advocated socialist propaganda as a corrective for the effects of ingrained capitalist discourse that structured American values during the Depression and World War years. Although Jane Addams fiercely resisted widely supported World War I propaganda, Elizabeth Bowen was recruited along with many other artists to propagandize during World War II. Evaluation of these and other examples hinges not only on careful analysis of the rhetorical situation but also on one's definition of propaganda. While Thomas Huckin's chapter cites common definitions and stipulates a new one, chapters here examine propaganda from time-bound prevailing definitions to grapple with challenging ethical (and rhetorical) questions that propaganda analysis repeatedly elicits. In sum, essays in this collection suggest that propaganda is a rhetorical strategy—the principal strategy through which the contradictions of capitalism are rhetorically allayed and managed in modern democratic societies. Managed democracy, then, is integral to capitalist societies that claim to be democratic; propaganda is the default rhetoric of managed democracy. We argue that careful attention to this rhetorical reality is essential work for rhetoric and writing scholars and for the students whom they teach. As Hannah Arendt posits, comprehending history requires attentive and critical attention: "examining and bearing consciously the burden ... [history] has placed on us—neither denying its existence nor submitting meekly to its weight" (viii).

ORGANIZATION OF THE VOLUME

The essays in this volume are divided into two parts. Part 1 examines the historical development of the theory of propaganda during the rise of industrialism, the expansion of democracy, and the growth of mass-mediated society. Part 2 offers case studies of the deployment of propaganda today.

Part 1, "Historical and Theoretical Studies of Propaganda," begins with Sharon J. Kirsch's chapter, "Democracy and Disclosure: Edward Bernays and the Manipulation of the Masses," examining the figure most identified as the father of propaganda. Unlike Walter Lippmann, who concerned himself with the problem propaganda posed for citizens in democracy, Bernays celebrated propaganda as a form of secret governance that allows democracy to function smoothly. The chapter examines the role Bernays played in shifting our cultural conceptions of "propaganda" to the seemingly more palatable practice of "public relations" (PR). Kirsch explores the discursive stranglehold PR gained in the early twentieth century and exposes the dangerous PR recuperation of Muammar Gadhafi's Libya. She calls for marshaling "intellectual and interdisciplinary resources for thinking through the continued political power of PR messaging" and the necessity for communicative transparency in the democratic public sphere.

Chapters 2 and 3 continue to trace the history of propaganda through the eyes of citizens embroiled in historical moments that forced them to confront propaganda. In chapter 2, "Jane Addams: A Foe of Rhetorics of Control," Lanette Grate challenges the belief that the study of propaganda as a means of social control did not appear until after World War I. Jane Addams, the twentieth-century social activist and Nobel Peace Prize winner who founded and directed Hull-House in Chicago, observed the way war propaganda was used to coerce consent and stifle dissent as early as the Spanish-American War. Grate explores Addams's unrecognized contributions to propaganda studies, revealing the conscious political forces and unconscious social responses that cause democracy to shut down in the very name of democracy. In chapter 3, "The Psychological Power of Propaganda: From Psychoanalysis to Kenneth Burke," Gae Lyn Henderson examines the conflicts that Burke experienced during the Great Depression as he was adjured to take up the propaganda fight against a failing capitalist system. Ultimately Burke rejected propaganda in his World War II analyses of Hitler's writing, as well as in his warnings about Cold War rhetoric. Burke's heuristics provide essential insight into the power and pervasiveness of propaganda, as well as rhetorical tools to counter its insidious force.

In chapter 4, "Elizabeth Bowen's Wavering Attitude toward World War II Propaganda," Stefania Porcelli explores the scope and effects of British propaganda on the neutral country of Ireland. Bowen, an Anglo-Irish writer, reported on Ireland for the British Ministry of Information. Her reports may have contributed to Winston Churchill's decision not to invade Ireland. Both Bowen's political reports and her short fiction shed new light on British propaganda during the Second World War, especially with regard to Irish neutrality, as well as testifying to the strong link between writers and propaganda in wartime.

Part 1 concludes with two chapters focusing on definition. In chapter 5, "Propaganda Defined," Thomas Huckin traces how the meaning of propaganda shifted from a parochial to a rhetorical practice in the beginning of the twentieth century. Through dictionary and expert definitions and random samplings of actual usage, he constructs a composite definition that clarifies the basis of its negative connotation. He also proposes that the effect of propaganda multiplies as it is unwittingly taken up in general discourse. Following Sheldon Wolin's notion of inverted totalitarianism, Huckin argues that "propaganda . . . is most typically disseminated collectively and unconsciously." While this view is explored in some of the analytical essays in part 2, others demonstrate how the conscious production of propaganda has become a normalized global business practice. In chapter 6, "A Taxonomy of Bullshit," Gary Thompson defines various rhetorics that are often associated with propaganda, arguing that while some forms of bullshit may be innocuous, other forms may function as propaganda and be corrosive to public discourse. Democratic societies depend upon informed consent, which is not possible when bullshit supplants information. Bullshit may be thought of as semantic malpractice, unchallenged because omnipresent, and can best be countered by granular attention to meaning.

Part 2 of the collection, "Propaganda's Challenge to Democracy: Sites and Mechanisms of Social Control," features specific analyses of propaganda production and distribution. In chapter 7, "Popular Economics: Neoliberal Propaganda and Its Affectivity," Catherine Chaput views propaganda through the lens of affect theory. After reviewing neoliberal economic thinking and its historical trajectory and exploring the role that the book *Freakonomics* played in normalizing neoliberal ideology, Chaput shows (citing Robert H. Frank) how today's reading public has been molded into "economic naturalists" who see "'every feature of human and animal behavior' in terms of cost-benefit analysis."

The public's perception of U.S. policy often is mediated through network news broadcasts. In chapter 8, "Privatized Propaganda and Broadcast News: Legitimizing the Call to Arms," John Oddo and Patricia Dunmire study news broadcasts of the major call-to-arms address by George W. Bush prior to the Iraq War. Oddo and Dunmire show that television news enhanced the salience and authority of the president's arguments, even adding visual images that displayed the "threat" posed by Saddam Hussein and his "weapons of mass destruction." Meanwhile, opponents to war generally were not represented, were represented as marginal, or were represented as obstacles to be overcome by the administration.

Jayson Harsin also confronts the propagandistic nature of media journalism in chapter 9, "Attention! Rumor Bombs, Affect, and Managed Democracy." Harsin describes how political communication techniques create and proliferate "rumor bombs" that misinform the public. Harsin surveys a variety of rumor bomb episodes over the last decade (Saddam

Hussein had "links" to Al Qaeda, John Kerry is French, Barack Obama is a Muslim). Rumor bombs demonstrate ongoing professionalization of political communication in conjunction with the tabloidization of news and culture in a new period of information explosion. An ecology of new media complicates traditional theories of propaganda through techniques of distraction, noise, distrust, and confusion.

Meg H. Kunde, in chapter 10, "The *Contract with America*: A Legal, Social, and Rhetorical Contractual Obligation," analyzes the 1994 election document released by the Republican Party. Kunde reveals that the *Contract with America* was, indeed, more than a "promise" and both more and less than a "detailed agenda": it was a tool of propaganda that gained depth and power from the conceptual, structural, and stylistic layering of generic form. The contract employed an iconic structure and style, making arguments about legislation, Republican legislators, and policy.

The final chapter of part 2 will be of particular interest to educators who view with growing concern the systematic reshaping of higher education according to corporate business models. Laural Lea Adams, in chapter 11, "Propagandist Management: 'Sustainability' in the Corporatized Public University," analyzes the increasingly privatized academy as a unique sector of the knowledge economy. Adams interrogates the construct of "sustainability" in the administrative discourse of higher education to demonstrate that the privatized university carefully veils its aims and intentions, including globalization and the micromanagement of faculty, via manipulative discursive mechanisms, such as university websites and sustainability certification processes. She argues that these mechanisms function in an economy of legitimization to enable universities to operate like for-profit entities while appearing to many stakeholders to retain their traditional role in fostering the public good.

The conclusion to our collection is Robert Jensen's personal retrospective on his career as an activist-scholar, "Writing Dissent in the Propaganda Flood." Given the realities of managed democracy and propaganda this volume exposes, Jensen speaks to both academics and students to provide a pragmatic model for action. He both discusses the troubling challenges of countering contemporary propaganda culture and envisions potential for intervention and future change.

The editors hope that this volume, by exploring histories, theories, and practices of propaganda, offers both new students of propaganda and those who have long examined it insights into why propaganda is integral to the study of rhetoric, argument, and representation.

Notes

1. See McChesney, *Political Economy of Media*; Chomsky and Herman, *Manufacturing Consent*; and Carey, *Taking the Risk Out of Democracy*.

2. Gibson reports that the original Resolutions Committee used the term *public lying*, but to come up with something less aggressive, Executive Committee member Virginia Reid combined George Orwell's *newspeak* and *doublethink* in 1972 to create the term *doublespeak* (8). The original resolutions aimed to "propose techniques for preparing children to cope with commercial propaganda," as well as to "combat semantic distortion by public officials, candidates for office, political commenters" (6). Lutz defines doublespeak as "language which makes the bad seem good . . . negative appear positive . . . unpleasant appear attractive, or at least tolerable. It is language which avoids or shifts responsibility. . . . It is language which conceals or prevents thought" (17).

3. Miller's extensive research in affect/emotion is helpful in understanding an audience's reception of propaganda (12–21). She labels Gross's *Secret History of Emotion* as "the landmark study of rhetoric and emotion from a contemporary perspective" (14). She cites Worsham's essays "Going Postal" and "Eating History, Purging Memory, Killing Rhetoric" as well as research linking emotion with the history of rhetoric, writing studies, and philosophy.

4. According to Le Bon, even education cannot supplant the psychological power of crowd mentality: "As soon as a few individuals are gathered together they constitute a crowd, and, though, they should be distinguished men of learning . . . the faculty of observation and the critical spirit possessed by each of them individually at once disappears" (43).

5. In *Propaganda*, Bernays states that "the voice of the people expresses the mind of the people, and that mind is made up for it by the group leaders in whom it believes and by those persons who understand the manipulation of public opinion. It is composed of inherited prejudices and symbols and clichés and verbal formulas applied to them by the leaders" (109).

6. In *The Phantom Public*, Lippmann argues that democracy has not given the U.S. citizen adequate education: "It has merely given him a hasty, incomplete taste of what he might have to know if he meddled in everything. The result is a bewildered public and a mass of insufficiently trained officials" (52–53). Of course, Lippmann in his extensive writing also argues for solutions: improved public education, investigative journalism, and informed political debate.

7. Doob explains, in his analysis of Nazi minister Joseph Goebbels's principles for executing propaganda, that Goebbels channeled aggressive tendencies of the masses toward Bolsheviks and Jews to "foment suspicion, distrust, and hatred" (213–14). See also Zeman's analysis in "The State and Propaganda" of how the German people gradually and almost inevitably submitted to Hitler's will.

8. From 1939 to 1970, a series of articles appeared in journals discussing the teaching of propaganda analysis and logical fallacies. In the college section of *English Journal*, Miller warns against "hysterias and phobias caused by propaganda . . . to make us hate and fear Catholics, Jews, foreigners, and various other racial and religious groups" (821). In *College Composition and Communication*, Oliver reports on Harold Allen's Conference on College Composition and Communication workshop in which Allen explains possible dangers of teaching propaganda analysis in freshman English: "Given a fuller knowledge of propaganda techniques, [some] may simply put that knowledge to work for cynical and selfish purposes" (4). More typical is a teaching report in *CCC* by Dempsey, Maurer, and Pisani of Florissant Valley Community College describing four propaganda units they created, which led to analysis of a pair of films: "*Operation Abolition*, produced by the House Un-American Activities Committee on the San Francisco riots in 1963; and *Operation Correction*, which is the American Civil Liberties Union's answer" (336–37). Subsequent ongoing (even obligatory) attention to logical fallacies in writing textbooks likely emerges from this early work.

9. See the Rhetoricians for Peace Facebook page.

10. One of the early critics, A. M. Tibbetts, criticized not only the committee's "liberal, even radical" attitude toward language but also (chair) Hugh Rank's assertion that "language manipulation is a natural, neutral human activity" (qtd. in 408). Rank later responded that despite criticisms of the committee as politicized, the diverse committee included "semanticists, rhetoricians, Aristotelians, anti-Aristotelians, politically Left, Right, Center" (231). In 2001, Bushman reviewed twenty years of recipients; Reich's 2013 dissertation offers a recent history. The 2013 award went to Democratic Chicago mayor Rahm Emanuel for the rhetoric he used to justify closing over fifty public schools for "underutilized" space. The NCTE committee ironically noted that Mayor Emanuel "deserves this prestigious award for his embodiment of Orwell's vision of a rhetorically fraudulent society" ("Past Recipients").

11. See Hansen's "Deliberative Democracy" and other essays in Kock and Villadsen's collection. Henderson's dissertation, "Intersubjectivity," also works toward this goal.

Works Cited

Ackerman, John M., and David J. Coogan. Introduction. *The Public Work of Rhetoric: Citizen-Scholars and Civic Engagement.* Ed. Ackerman and Coogan. Columbia: U of South Carolina P, 2010. 1–16. Print.

Arendt, Hannah. *The Origins of Totalitarianism.* 1951. New York: Harcourt, 1973. Print.

Bernard-Donals, Michael, and Richard R. Glejzer, eds. *Rhetoric in an Antifoundational World: Language, Culture and Pedagogy.* New Haven: Yale UP, 1998. Print.

Bernays, Edward. *Propaganda.* New York: Ig, 1928. Print.

Bohman, James, and William Rehg. "Jürgen Habermas." *The Stanford Encyclopedia of Philosophy.* Ed. Edward N. Zalta. Summer 2007 ed. Web. 12 May 2016.

Booth, Wayne. *The Rhetoric of Rhetoric: The Quest for Effective Communication.* Malden, Mass.: Blackwell, 2004. Print.

———. "War Rhetoric, Defensible and Indefensible." *JAC* 25.2 (2005): 221–44. Web. 10 May 2016.

Burke, Kenneth. "The Rhetoric of Hitler's Battle." *The Philosophy of Literary Form.* Baton Rouge: Louisiana State UP, 1941. New York: Vintage, 1957. 164–89. Print.

———. *A Rhetoric of Motives.* 1950. Berkeley: U of California P, 1969. Print.

Bushman, John H. "Honesty in Language: Is This the Way to Achieve Power?" *English Journal* 90.4 (March 2001): 17–19. Web. 16 June 2014.

Carey, Alex. *Taking the Risk Out of Democracy: Corporate Propaganda versus Freedom and Liberty.* Champaign: U of Illinois P, 1996. Print.

Chomsky, Noam, and Edward S. Herman. *Manufacturing Consent: The Political Economy of Mass Media.* New York: Pantheon, 2002. Print.

Crowley, Sharon. *Toward a Civil Discourse: Rhetoric and Fundamentalism.* Pittsburgh: Pittsburgh UP, 2006. Print.

Cunningham, Stanley B. *The Idea of Propaganda: A Reconstruction.* Westport, Conn.: Praeger, 2002. Print.

Dempsey, Ann, Mary Lou Maurer, and Rosemary Pisani. "English: Everything from an Experimental Film to *Esquire* Cartoons." *College Composition and Communication* 19.5 (December 1968): 336–37. Web. 13 May 2015.

Desser, Daphne. "Teaching Writing in Hawaii after Pearl Harbor and 9/11: How to 'Make Meaning' and 'Heal' Despite National Propaganda." *Trauma and the Teaching of Writing.* Ed. Shane Borrowman. Albany: State U of New York P, 2005. 85–97. Print.

Doob, Leonard W. "Goebbels' Principles of Propaganda." *Public Opinion Quarterly* 14.3 (1950): 419–42. Rpt. in *Propaganda*. Ed. Robert Jackall. New York: New York UP, 1995. 190–215. Print.

"The Doublespeak Award." National Council of Teachers of English. Web. 14 July 2014.

Ellul, Jacques. *Propaganda: The Formation of Men's Attitudes.* New York: Vintage, 1973. Print.

Frankfurt, Harry G. *On Bullshit.* Princeton: Princeton UP, 2005. Print.

Gibson, Walker. "An Introduction to Doublespeak." *Doublespeak: A Brief History, Definition, and Bibliography, with a List of Award Winners, 1974–1990.* Ed. Walker Gibson and William Lutz. Urbana: NCTE, 1991. 5–16. ERIC. Web. 15 May 2016.

Gross, Daniel. *The Secret History of Emotion: From Aristotle's Rhetoric to Modern Brain Science.* Chicago: U of Chicago P, 2006. Print.

Habermas, Jürgen. *The Inclusion of the Other: Studies in Political Theory.* Ed. Ciaran Cronin and Pablo De Greiff. Trans. Ciaran Cronin. Cambridge: MIT P, 1999. Print.

———. *The Theory of Communicative Action.* London: Beacon, 1981. Print.

Hannah Arendt. Dir. Margarethe von Trotta. Perf. Barbara Sukowa. Zeitgeist Films, 2012. Netflix. Web. 15 May 2014.

Hansen, Kasper Møller, "Deliberative Democracy: Mapping Out the Deliberative Turn in Democratic Theory." *Rhetorical Citizenship and Public Deliberation.* Ed. Christian Kock and Lisa Villadsen. University Park: Penn State UP, 2012. 13–27. Print.

Hauser, Gerard A. *Prisoners of Conscience: Moral Vernaculars of Political Agency.* Columbia: U of South Carolina P, 2012. Print.

Henderson, Gae Lyn. "Intersubjectivity: An Ethics for Critical Rhetoric and Writing." Diss. U of Utah, 2007. ProQuest Dissertations and Theses. Web. 10 July 2014.

Institute for Propaganda Analysis. "How to Detect Propaganda." *Propaganda Analysis* 1.2 (1937). Rpt. in *Propaganda*. Ed. Robert Jackall. New York: New York UP, 1995. 217–24. Print.

Ivie, Robert L. *Democracy and America's War on Terror.* Tuscaloosa: U of Alabama P, 2006. Print.

Jackall, Robert. Introduction. *Propaganda*. Ed. Jackall. New York: New York UP, 1995. 1–9. Print.

Jowett, Garth S., and Victoria O'Donnell, eds. *Propaganda and Persuasion.* 6th ed. Los Angeles: Sage, 2014. Print.

Kahneman, Daniel. *Thinking, Fast and Slow.* New York: Farrar, 2011. Print.

Kock, Christian, and Lisa Villadsen, eds. *Rhetorical Citizenship and Public Deliberation*. University Park: Penn State UP, 2012. Print.

LaSalle, Mick. "'Hannah Arendt' Review: Convincing Look at Bold Thinker." *San Francisco Chronicle* 1 August 2013. Web. 20 May 2014.

Lasswell, Harold D. "Propaganda." *Encyclopaedia of the Social Sciences*. Ed. Edwin R. A. Seligman. Vol. 12. London: Macmillan, 1934. Rpt. in *Propaganda*. Ed. Robert Jackall. New York: New York UP, 1995. 13–25. Print.

Lazere, Donald. "Postmodern Pluralism and the Retreat from Political Literacy." *JAC* 25.2 (2005): 257–91. Print.

———. *Reading and Writing for Civic Literacy: The Critical Citizen's Guide to Argumentative Rhetoric*. Boulder: Paradigm, 2005. Print.

Le Bon, Gustave. *The Crowd: A Study of the Popular Mind*. 1960. New York: Viking, 1966. Print.

Lippmann, Walter. "The Phantom Public." Excerpt from *The Phantom Public*. London: Macmillan, 1925. Rpt. in *Propaganda*. Ed. Robert Jackall. New York: New York UP, 1995. 47–53. Print.

Lipsitz, George. *American Studies in a Moment of Danger*. Minneapolis: U of Minnesota P, 2001. Print.

Lutz, William. "Notes Toward a Description of Doublespeak (Revised)." *Doublespeak: A Brief History, Definition, and Bibliography, with a List of Award Winners, 1974–1990*. Ed. Walker Gibson and William Lutz. Urbana: NCTE, 1991. 17–26. ERIC. Web. 15 May 2016.

Lyon, Arabella. *Deliberative Acts: Democracy, Rhetoric, and Rights*. University Park: Penn State UP, 2013. Print.

McChesney, Robert W. *The Political Economy of Media: Enduring Ideas, Emerging Dilemmas*. New York: Monthly Review, 2008. Print.

McCracken, Nancy. "Looking Back with an Eye to the Future." *Quarterly Review of Doublespeak* 26.4 (2000): 1–2. ProQuest Central. Web. 15 June 2014.

Miller, Clyde R. "Propaganda and Press Freedom." *English Journal* 28.10 (1939): 821–27. Web. 1 May 2015.

Miller, Susan. *Trust in Texts: A Different History of Rhetoric*. Carbondale: Southern Illinois UP, 2008. Print.

Obenzinger, Hilton. "On Being a Traitor." *JAC* 25.2 (2005): 245–56. Web. 10 June 2014.

Oliver, Kenneth. "The One-Legged, Wingless Bird of Freshman English." *College Composition and Communication* 1.3 (1950): 3–6. Web. 15 April 2015.

"Past Recipients of the NCTE Doublespeak Award." National Council of Teachers of English. PDF file.

Penn & Teller: Bullshit! Showtime. 2003–10. Television.

Powers, M. Karen, and Catherine Chaput. "'Anti-American Studies' in the Deep South: Dissenting Rhetorics, the Practice of Democracy, and Academic Freedom in Wartime Universities." *College Composition and Communication* 58.4 (2007): 648–81. Web. 1 July 2014.

Rank, Hugh. "A Comment on A. M. Tibbetts on Doublespeak." *College English* 41.2 (1979): 230–32. Web. 15 June 2014.

Ratcliffe, Krista. *Rhetorical Listening: Identification, Gender, Whiteness.* Carbondale: Southern Illinois UP, 2005. Print.

Reich, Pavel. "Doublespeak in Televised Political Debates." Diss. Masaryk U, 2013. Kamenice, Czech Republic. Web. 14 July 2014.

Roberts-Miller, Patricia. *Deliberate Conflict: Argument, Political Theory, and Composition Classes.* Carbondale: Southern Illinois UP, 2004. Print.

———. "Habermas's Rational-Critical Sphere and the Problem of Criteria." *Rhetoric in an Antifoundational World: Language, Culture and Pedagogy.* Ed. Michael Bernard-Donals and Richard R. Glejzer. New Haven: Yale UP, 1998. 170–94. Print.

Sachs, Joe. Introduction. *Plato:* Gorgias; *and Aristotle:* Rhetoric. Trans. Sachs. Newburyport, Mass.: Focus, 2009. 1–27. Print.

Snow, Nancy, ed. *Propaganda and American Democracy.* Baton Rouge: Louisiana State UP, 2014. Print.

———. *Propaganda, Inc.: Selling America's Culture to the World.* New York: Seven Stories, 2010. Print.

Sproule, J. Michael. *Propaganda and Democracy: The American Experience of Media and Mass Persuasion.* New York: Cambridge UP, 1997. Print.

Tibbetts, A. M. "Case of Confusion: The NCTE Committee on Public Doublespeak." *College English* 40.4 (1978): 407–12. Web. 10 June 2014.

Wolin, Sheldon S. *Democracy Incorporated: Managed Democracy and the Specter of Inverted Totalitarianism.* Princeton: Princeton UP, 2008. Print.

Worsham, Lynn. "Eating History, Purging Memory, Killing Rhetoric." *Writing Histories of Rhetoric.* Ed. Victor J. Vitanza. Carbondale: Southern Illinois UP, 1994. 139–55. Print.

———. "Going Postal: Pedagogic Violence and the Schooling of Emotion." *JAC* 18 (1998): 213–45. Print.

Zeman, Z. A. B. "The State and Propaganda." Excerpt from *Nazi Propaganda.* London: Oxford UP, 1964. Rpt. in *Propaganda.* Ed. Robert Jackall. New York: New York UP, 1995. 174–89. Print.

PART 1

HISTORICAL AND THEORETICAL STUDIES OF PROPAGANDA

DEMOCRACY AND DISCLOSURE:
EDWARD BERNAYS AND THE
MANIPULATION OF THE MASSES

SHARON J. KIRSCH

> Men and women who are interested in their civilization
> should have a thorough knowledge of the scope of propa-
> ganda, its functions, and its limitations.
> —Edward Bernays, "Freedom of Propaganda"

Edward Bernays, the self-fashioned "father of public relations," published *Propaganda* in 1928 to define and legitimate a new social, political, and corporate endeavor: the field of public relations. Though practitioners of public relations already existed, they had no professional identity, no self-conscious sense of civic function, no recognition, and little credibility. Bernays sought to change that. The ostensible central purpose of *Propaganda*, as Bernays reports, is "to explain the structure of the mechanism which controls the public mind, and to tell how it is manipulated by the special pleader who seeks to create public acceptance for a particular idea or commodity" (45). Implicit in Bernays's pronouncement is the assumption that the public mind can be controlled en masse and, further, that a well-trained "special pleader" can do so with machine-like precision. To be an effective special pleader, one needs both an understanding of this mechanism and the ability "to tell" how it works. Enter Bernays, special pleader par excellence.

Bernays's claim that propaganda exists in almost every aspect of our lives offered a corrective to those who assumed public relations was limited to corporations, governments, or products. He sought to define public relations as distinct from advertising and as a more important enterprise in a democratic society, so central that "virtually no important undertaking is now carried on without it" (52). Nearly seventy years later, social critic

Stuart Ewen concurred, opening his *PR! A Social History of Spin* with a provocative assertion that "nearly every moment of human attention is exposed to the game plans of spin doctors, image managers, pitchmen, communication consultants, public information officers and PR specialists" (19). Even if this statement were only half true, then understanding the power of public relations, the role it plays in our lives, and its relation to the quality of our public discourse and our democracy is imperative. The pervasiveness of public relations messages in the twenty-first century necessitates that we recognize how they mediate public communication and persuade publics by identifying and shaping beliefs and values.

Surprisingly, rhetoricians have paid little attention to the rise of public relations in the United States, due, in part, to the disciplinary fragmentation of rhetoric toward the end of the nineteenth century, which pulled the study of rhetoric away from its theoretical, multidisciplinary, and civic roots. Steven Mailloux's explication of "disciplinary identities" helps to explain how public relations and the broader functioning of public discourse were lost in this disciplinary shuffle, particularly in the early decades of the twentieth century as the rise of corporate public relations gained momentum in the United States.[1] By the early twentieth century, the realignment of humanities disciplines relegated the study of rhetoric to Departments of English, reduced to the teaching of writing, and to Departments of Speech, reduced to the teaching of public speaking. In an attempt to legitimate their institutional place, scholars in the burgeoning field of speech communication wrote histories of public speaking that dominated rhetorical studies for the first three-quarters of the twentieth century until historians of rhetoric located in English departments began to examine the history of writing instruction and the rise of the modern-day composition. Although pioneering studies by James Berlin, Sharon Crowley, and Nan Johnson, among others, offer important additions to the history of rhetoric, their particular historical and institutional moment required grounding their research in the teaching of writing and classroom practice, not in broader studies of rhetorical theory and practice applicable to public discourse and public relations.

Late twentieth-century communication studies scholarship considers aspects of public relations such as crisis communication and media relations; however, the focus tends to be on image management, practical strategies, and analysis of best practices with little attention given to the social, political, and economic conditions in which particular discursive strategies are employed. Robert L. Heath's 2009 introduction to *Rhetorical and Critical*

Approaches to Public Relations II, a collection of essays geared toward communication studies scholars, identifies "the dawn of a new era" in public relations scholarship, particularly in the United States, where scholars will move beyond social scientific approaches and consider "judgments of meaning and the ways it is formed" (1). This new era incorporates consideration of "the assumptions and principles of the rhetorical heritages, social constructionism, discourse analysis, and critical theory"—topics that have long been addressed in rhetorical scholarship by scholars on the English side of the disciplinary divide (1). To clarify the use of the term *rhetoric* in the title of the book, Heath finds it necessary to explain that rhetorical theory "has its own body of ideas and principles" and means more than manipulation or spin. The fact that his intended audiences—primarily public relations scholars in communication studies—might not be aware of the "rhetorical heritages" mentioned by Heath, let alone their applicability to their work, makes clear how deeply PR is caught in the institutional fragmentation of rhetoric. While contemporary rhetorical theory returns the theory and practice of rhetoric to its multidisciplinary and civic roots, much work remains to close the gap between English and communication studies so that we can better understand the magnitude of the rise of public relations in the early twentieth century and its impact on contemporary public discourse. If we are "interested in [our] civilization," we should, as Bernays himself recommends, "have a thorough knowledge of the scope of propaganda, its functions, and its limitations" ("Freedom of Propaganda" 744).

However, it is not just the splintering of rhetoric in the academy that has led rhetorical scholars to overlook the role public relations and propaganda play in our contemporary world and in our histories of rhetoric. For rhetoricians, no less than for "the masses" imagined by Bernays, PR creates public image "privately," in corporate centers of invention. Those who founded the field of public relations described themselves in Bernays's words as "shrewd persons operating behind the scenes" who constituted an "invisible government" (*Propaganda* 61, 37). Because much of the work of the public relations counsel is strategically hidden, creating circumstances that appear to have occurred naturally, we need a fuller sense of how public relations became what Mark Dowie calls "a communication medium in its own right [and] an industry designed to alter perception, reshape reality and manufacture consent" (2).

Returning to *Propaganda*, the field-defining book of public relations, this chapter examines the discursive stranglehold public relations gained in the early twentieth century and the role Edward Bernays played in shifting our cultural conceptions of "propaganda" to the seemingly more palatable "public relations." The methodology orienting this chapter can be described as a historical and critical mode of analysis that draws on public sphere theory to trace the prevailing logic of the PR industry and its employment in a democracy as a means of statecraft.[2] I begin by examining Bernays's claim for the centrality and necessity of propaganda in a democracy. Next, considering definitions of "the public" and the problem of relying on a behind-the-scenes communication medium that continues to dominate our public discourse, I turn to a contemporary example of the specter of Bernays in Muammar Gadhafi's Libya.[3] I conclude with a call for marshaling the richest intellectual and interdisciplinary resources for thinking through the continued political power of PR messaging and the necessity for transparency in communication in the democratic public sphere.

DEFINING PROPAGANDA AS A NECESSITY OF DEMOCRACY

The provocative opening line of *Propaganda* makes clear how central and far-reaching the work of public relations is in a democratic society: "The conscious and intelligent manipulation of the organized habits and opinions of the masses is an important element in democratic society" (37). Bernays desires much more than securing favorable exposure for clients; he calls for a form of manipulation that is both "conscious" and "intelligent." He thus appeals to the intelligence of *Propaganda*'s audience of readers, particularly those who are, or may be, capable of learning to use propaganda effectively. At the same time, the opening chapter, titled "Organizing Chaos," plays on his audience's fears that we live in an increasingly chaotic world where "we are governed, our minds molded, our tastes formed, our ideas suggested, largely by men we have never heard of" (37). The use of the plural pronoun "we" positions Bernays, at this moment in the text, not as a molder of public opinion but as one who may also be subject to these "invisible governors . . . who pull the wires which control the public mind" (38). He suggests that his readers need to be aware of and participate in "the conscious and intelligent manipulation," lest they become part of the masses who are controlled by the intelligent few. Bernays imagines a democratic mission for public relations as a form of social control by the elites, those intelligent enough to lead. Though Bernays seemingly positions himself as one of the people, he ultimately situates himself not only as one who pulls the wires but also as one who knows how to control the public mind effectively, efficiently, and invisibly. *Propaganda* offers both a defense of these invisible governors, whom Bernays calls "necessary . . . to the orderly functioning of our group life," and an extended advertisement for why readers may require the services of a PR counsel, perhaps even Bernays himself (38).

Acknowledging that the word *propaganda* carries negative connotations, Bernays attempts to salvage the term as "a perfectly legitimate form of human activity" by offering a technical and etymological definition, quoting from the dictionary and from an article in *Scientific American* (49). He observes that even the "well informed" will be surprised by the "extent to which propaganda shapes the progress of affairs" (50). Part of the function of his book *Propaganda* is to convince readers of the pervasiveness of propaganda, so much so that, as Bernays implies, readers who want to be "well informed" better listen up. In fact, if readers wonder who these leaders are who wield the influence of propaganda, Bernays assures them "that anyone with sufficient influence can lead sections of the public," a tantalizing proposition for captains of industry—one of Bernays's intended audiences for *Propaganda*. His well-timed publication of *Propaganda* in 1928 appealed to business leaders who were experiencing unprecedented growth in the boom years of the Roaring Twenties (54).[4]

Bernays himself was hired by many of the leading corporations in the United States, including General Motors, United Fruit Company, the U.S. Department of State, Procter and Gamble, and General Electric, among others. The American Tobacco Company hired Bernays to increase its market share by lifting the taboo against women smoking in public. By linking the emancipation of women, who had won the right to vote earlier in the decade, with smoking cigarettes, Bernays's famous "Torches of Freedom" campaign successfully and quickly changed public attitudes. Working behind the scenes and carefully staging the event, Bernays had his secretary, Bertha Hunt, send a seemingly personal telegram inviting thirty debutantes to "light another torch for freedom" for women by marching in New York City's Easter parade smoking cigarettes, suggesting that if the most feminine and respectable ladies could do it, then any woman could. Although the press had received press releases in advance, the event appeared to happen spontaneously as the women stepped out of the crowd to join the campaign. Bernays, who prepared Hunt to be a spokesperson, created a national sensation and garnered massive national press coverage, which never mentioned that Hunt was Bernays's secretary. Bernays's campaign used many of the strategies still employed by public relations practitioners: working behind the scenes to carefully craft events that appear to be spontaneous; garnering press coverage of these events that portray them as news, not as public relations campaigns; and creating messages that draw on and shape public fears and desires. Although the serious health dangers of smoking were not publicly well known at this time, once the harmful side effects came to light, Bernays no longer accepted tobacco companies as clients.[5]

For Bernays, the Torches of Freedom campaign demonstrated the power of public relations to shape attitudes, beliefs, and buying habits; it also confirmed the link between public relations and democracy. In his defense of the necessity of propaganda in a democratic society, Bernays draws a distinction between theory and practice. While "in theory, every citizen may vote for whom he pleases . . . [and] every citizen makes up his mind on public questions and matters of private conduct," in practice it is simply too difficult "to study . . . abstruse economic, political, and ethical data involved in every question" (38). Therefore, in practice, "we have voluntarily agreed to let an invisible government" narrow our choices to what Bernays calls "practical proportions" (38). "We" in this instance includes Bernays and, perhaps, his readers as well. Furthermore, Bernays offers additional analysis of how the practice of democracy works. If we accept the fact that there is "a vast and continuous effort going on to capture our minds" and agree that we want our society to "make free competition function with reasonable smoothness," then we require, according to Bernays, strong rulers who will gain consent through their "leadership and propaganda" (39). In a tactical maneuver, Bernays offers the suggestion that "it might actually be better to have . . . committees of wise men who would choose our rulers, dictate our conduct, private and public" (39). But, alas, democracy is a system of government by the people, at least in theory, and codified in the Constitution, thus limiting or complicating how "committees of wise men" rule. Bernays's argument that undisclosed social control serves a constitutive function in democratic society is, of course, troubling.

Bernays bemoans open competition because "we" will now need to find a way to make the free market perform with "reasonable smoothness" (39). In other words, the free market and perhaps democracy itself teeters on the brink of chaos, particularly if too much power falls in the hands of the uncontrolled masses. Thus Bernays defines the "New Propaganda," which responds to a shift in cultural power from an aristocratic to a democratic society, where power was taken "away from kings and given . . . to the people," so much so that "even the bourgeoisie stood in fear of the common people" (47). But Bernays offers a solution, noting that the "minority has discovered a powerful help in influencing majorities" (47). Power is regained by "mold[ing] the mind of the masses" so that "they will throw their newly gained strength in the desired direction" (47). For readers with misgivings, Bernays reassures that "this practice is inevitable" and cannot be avoided: "Whatever of social importance is done today, whether in politics, finance, manufacture, agriculture, charity, education, or other fields, must be done with the help of propaganda" (47–48). There is no escaping it. Because "new activities call for new nomenclature," Bernays coined the name "public relations counsel" as the official title for the practitioner of PR.[6] The use of the term "counsel" suggests a level of professionalism and importance on a par with legal counsel, lawyers.

Bernays notes that some may criticize the use of propaganda, for example, "the manipulation of the news, the inflation of personality, and the general ballyhoo by which politicians and commercial products and social ideas are brought to the consciousness of the masses" (39). Interestingly, it is not the people wielding the power of propaganda causing the problems for Bernays; rather it is the "instruments by which public opinion is organized and focused" that may be "misused" (39). Even so, organization and focus "are necessary to an orderly life." Indeed, because "civilization has become more complex," we increasingly "need" this invisible government along with "the technical means . . . by which opinion may be regimented" (39–40). Hardly submerged here is Bernays's massive condescension toward his untrustworthy "masses" and their ostensible inability to understand or function productively in a "complex" society. Though he does not explicitly say so at this point in *Propaganda*, it is not just Bernays's imagined PR counsel who has invented and now exercises these "technical means"; it is Bernays himself. Bernays reportedly charged upward of $1,000 per hour for his services (Ewen 18).[7]

But despite his lifetime practice of highly paid consulting, Bernays denied that public relations was connected with power. Bill Moyers ended an interview with Bernays by asking him about the cultural power wielded by public relations practitioners, including Bernays himself. Bernays responded: "I never thought of it as power. I never treated it as power. People want to go where they want to be led" ("Image Makers").[8] Managing the people in a democracy requires "intelligent minorities . . . to make us[e] of propaganda continuously and systematically" (*Propaganda* 57). In an effort to persuade his readership that they might be able to participate, Bernays played on and cultivated readers' anxiety that they may not be a member of the "intelligent minority." Identifying himself with these anxious readers, Bernays notes, "Small groups of persons can, and do, make the *rest of us* think what they please about a given subject" (57, emphasis added). Bernays seems to position himself as one of the "rest of us," but at the same time, *he* is the one offering analysis of and lessons in effective propaganda.

In case readers remain unconvinced, Bernays provides an overview about why the services of PR counsel are necessary. Because PR counsels hold a special expertise in the systematic study of mass psychology, they are able to understand the potential of the "invisible government" and the ways it manipulates "the motives which actuate man in the group" (71). Thus, a public relations expert knows how to analyze the public and how to make people act in particular ways. In fact, Bernays points out, prosperous companies, especially successful large corporations, employ a PR counsel because "they had come to recognize that they depended upon public good will for their continued prosperity," implicitly suggesting that readers may want and need to do the same (67). In the chapter "Business and the Public," Bernays makes a more overt sales pitch: "Big business, I believe, is realizing this more and more. It is increasingly availing itself of the services of the specialist in public relations. . . . And it is my conviction that as big business becomes bigger the need for expert manipulation of its innumerable contacts with the public will become greater" (91). In this rare instance of speaking in first person, Bernays positions himself as one of the "intelligent few," an expert analyst of culture and trends in business, and he does so with conviction.

In what might be characterized as the "Hire Eddie" chapter, Bernays addresses those whose minds might not be made up or those who might still question the value of retaining PR counsel. To those who might think anyone can do the job of the PR expert, Bernays offers a warning: "He [the PR counsel] cannot afford to be a stunt artist or a freelance adventurer in publicity. He must know his public accurately and modify its thoughts and actions" (107). The work of the public relations counsel—a position requiring much more than the skills of a mere press agent—involves intelligence, knowledge of mass psychology, and constant vigilance. To be successful, "modern business must have its finger continuously on the public pulse. It must understand the changes in the public mind and be prepared to interpret itself fairly and eloquently to changing opinion" (107). Therefore, monitoring the public pulse and shaping the public mind is a full-time job; ensuring success means hiring Bernays. Bernays crafts a PR counsel who offers much more than a press manual. *Propaganda* defines the principles of a necessary mission of social control as an inherent requirement in democracy.

THE CROWD, THE PUBLIC, AND THE
PROBLEM OF DISCLOSURE

Bernays applies lessons learned from his uncle Sigmund Freud and positions the public relations expert as a social scientist. In addition to Freud's studies of the individual psyche, Bernays draws on Gustave Le Bon's *The Crowd: A Study of the Popular Mind*, a work Stuart Ewen calls "a Bible to a growing body of people who were worried by a climate of popular unrest" (64). Le Bon argued that in a crowd, individuals are "a sort of collective mind which makes them feel, think, and act in a manner quite different from that in which each individual of them would feel, think and act" (6). Ewen notes that "Le Bon's book spoke to the deep fears of a world in which the liberal ideal of natural rights had moved beyond its roots in middle-class life and had given rise to more inclusive conceptions of popular democracy" (64–65). Le Bon pointed to what some saw as a troubling shift toward a too-demanding voice of the people: "Today the voice of the masses has become preponderant. . . . The destinies of nations are elaborated at present in the heart of the masses, and no longer in the councils of princes" (xv). Le Bon claimed the middle-class "public" continued to be guided by reason and was capable of rational thought, but the "masses" were not; they were governed by what Freud would later call "unconscious drives," by their passion and their irrational responses. They react; they follow. The "crowd" became something to be both feared and manipulated. *Propaganda* offers a chapter, "The Psychology of Public Relations," full of advice in which Bernays promises, "If we understand the mechanism and motives of the group mind, is it not possible to control and regiment the masses according to our will *without their knowing about it?*" (71, emphasis added). Though in other passages in *Propaganda*, Bernays carefully positions himself as one of the people, here he aligns himself with a "we" that does not constitute but rather understands and controls the group mind. Perhaps more troubling is his promise that this manipulation can be done invisibly, behind the scenes, without the consent, knowledge, or awareness of the group.

In 1929, Bernays engaged in a debate in the pages of *Forum Magazine* on the value and dangers of propaganda with social critic and educator Everett Dean Martin. Martin, best known for *The Behavior of Crowds* and his lectures on modern psychology that drew audiences in the thousands, entered this debate with Bernays ready to unmask "our invisible masters," as he titled his essay.[9] Martin provides a broad definition of propaganda as "the manipulation of the public to the end of securing some specific action" (Martin and Bernays 142). He acknowledges that propaganda *could* be used "to increase general knowledge and keep open in public life an arena in which truth may have a fair deal in its endless contest with ignorance and falsehood" but finds more often that it "does not serve these ends" and is conducted "for profit and power" so much so that "its aim is to 'put something over' on the people, with or without their knowledge and consent" (142). Martin underscores the pervasive power of propaganda in democracy, noting that even the defenders of propaganda acknowledge how powerful and effective their techniques are: "The methods used are so effective that the average person is entirely at the mercy of those now in command of the forces by which he is manipulated" (143). Martin quotes Bernays's discussion of "invisible rulers who control the destiny of millions" and the "invisible government" that "tends to be concentrated in the hands of the few" (143). He then asks, "What are the qualifications of these invisible governors? Who are they that they should command?" (143). Inverting Bernays's argument that democracy requires the rule of the intelligent few to organize the chaos, Martin notes, "If there is to be any stability or order in society, those who rule must at least be known and something must be required of them" (143). Democracy requires transparency and reciprocation, where "the people" have an opportunity to participate in their governance. As an advocate of liberal education and director of the People's Institute, Martin supported "the kind of education which sets the mind free from the servitude of the crowd and from vulgar self-interests" (*Meaning* viii).[10] Thus, as Martin condemns "our invisible masters," he cautions against the conflation of education and propaganda, noting that "education aims at independence of judgment" but "propaganda offers ready-made opinions for the unthinking herd" (145).

In his response to Martin, Bernays examines "our debt to propaganda" and opens by positioning himself as "a truth seeker and a propagandist for propaganda" (146). His opponent does not fare so well. Bernays calls Martin a "propagandist against propaganda" whose "sweeping emotional belief is expressed in a series of unsubstantiated statements" leading to a "distorted point of view" (146). Bernays believes that "propaganda serves a useful purpose" because it "increases general knowledge" and "tends to keep an open arena in public life in which the battle of truth may be fairly fought" (146). Bernays does not deny pernicious uses of propaganda but assures that "the conscientious propagandist . . . will have nothing to do with a product or a cause that is socially vicious" (146). Bernays defends big business's use of propaganda and communication with the public, noting that Martin acts "as if it were impossible to conceive of a bargain in which both parties derived equal profit and advantage" (147). But the use of propaganda is not limited to big business; Bernays claims that "there has hardly been a single new idea, new invention, or new product accepted by the public which was not made available for the public's benefit thought the use of propaganda in one form or another" (147). He uses an example of "scores of minority groups" who used propaganda to "bring their views before the public" (148). From this, Bernays concludes that, "since [propaganda] is available to all, it is an insurance against autocracy in government" (148). Martin offers a brief rebuttal, noting that indeed a wide range of people, including Abraham Lincoln, have used propaganda, but, in the case of Lincoln, there were not hidden, undisclosed, or ulterior motives. To drive home his point, Martin notes that even in advertising, the "advertiser generally sells what he advertises"—indicating that the realm of advertising does not host invisible rulers.

Discussing "propaganda and political leadership," Bernays invokes the newly established discipline of sociology and offers a troubling clarification of his sense of the public mind: "No serious sociologist any longer believes that the voice of the people expresses any divine or specially wise and lofty idea" (*Propaganda* 109). The "voice of the people," according to Bernays, merely "expresses the mind of the people, and that mind is made up for it by the group leaders in whom it believes and by those persons who understand the manipulation of public opinion" (109). Bernays's *Propaganda* stresses the seeming inevitability of "the mind of the people" being shaped by group leaders. This claim runs counter to his earlier assertion that "the public" was not merely at the disposal of the PR expert; rather, "the public has its own standards and demands and habits. You may modify them, but you dare not run counter to them. . . . This public is not an amorphous mass which can be molded at will, or dictated to" (86). Here, the public relations expert, at best, can offer modification, but only working within parameters set by "the public." Bernays offers a warning to those who might see public relations as "fool[ing] or hoodwink[ing] the public" (70). The PR counsel must avoid a bad reputation by ensuring that propaganda material is "clearly labeled as to source" (70). The contradiction between clearly labeling one's sources and functioning as an "invisible government" continues on the following page, where Bernays even goes so far as to wonder that if "we"—presumably now including Bernays and the audience interpellated by his argument—"understand the mechanism and motives of the group mind, is it not possible to control and regiment the masses according to *our* will *without their knowing about it?*" (71, emphasis added). If the masses do not know that their thinking and behaviors are being controlled and regimented to conform to the will of the "invisible government," then the work of the PR counsel certainly could be characterized as a deceitful and a deliberate strategy for keeping the public in check and not in a position to challenge the power of the governing elite.

MONITORING CONTEMPORARY
PROPAGANDA: GADHAFI'S LIBYA

More than eighty years later, Bernays's troubling defense of antidemocratic communication as a central component of democratic governance reverberated in a recent public relations campaign led by the Cambridge, Massachusetts–based Monitor Group, a public relations firm founded by professors from Harvard University, to "enhance" the image of Muammar Gadhafi and Libya. Monitor Group's multiyear, multimillion-dollar efforts to shift international public perception of a dictatorial government and its leader remained behind the scenes until the spring of 2011 when protests broke out across Libya and confidential documents detailing Monitor's campaign were leaked by the National Conference of the Libyan Opposition. The campaign to soften Gadhafi's image and to improve Libya's international reputation occurred when the Bush administration worked to strengthen U.S.-Libyan relations. In 2004, after Libya took responsibility for the Lockerbie bombing, the United States terminated sanctions and opened a liaison office in Tripoli, later upgraded to a U.S. embassy in 2006.[11] Between 2006 and 2008, the Monitor Group agreed to give Muammar Gadhafi an image makeover under a $250,000 a month contract plus an open expense account of up to $3 million. Its plan, paid for by the Libyan government, included a two-hour television program, *Dialogue around the Ideas of Muammar Gadhafi*, representing Gadhafi not as a dictator but as an "individual thinker." The program included interviews conducted by renowned British journalist and interviewer David Frost and was to be followed by a full-length biography, which never materialized. In the Executive Summary titled "Project to Enhance the Profile of Libya and Muammar Qadhafi," the in-house document obtained and leaked by the National Conference of the Libyan Opposition, the Monitor Group listed as a "key outcome" increased media coverage that was "broadly positive and increasingly sensitive to the Libyan point of view" (2).[12]

The Monitor Group clearly considered the media plan to be a "vital component" of its Executive Summary, which identified "high-caliber individuals" who would visit Libya, meet with Gadhafi, and follow their visits with lectures and publications about their experience ("Project" 14, 4). Joseph Nye of Harvard's Kennedy School, for example, published an article in the *New Republic* in 2007 noting that Gadhafi was interested in discussing "direct democracy." Benjamin Barber of Rutgers University and then Senior Fellow at the University of Southern California Center for Public Diplomacy visited Libya three times and wrote in the *Washington Post* of the possibility of Libya becoming "the first Arab state to transition peacefully and without Western intervention to a stable, non-autocratic government."[13] In response to *The Nation*'s request for clarification on payment Barber received, Barber replied, "I did not take money from Qaddafi. The money to Monitor was coming from the Qaddafi Foundation," an organization funded by Gadhafi's son, "who was providing the impetus for reform." Barber continued, "Everyone gets paid. Consultants get paid, and I was paid by Monitor" (Wiener). Barber's statement is certainly true. It is also true that governments, corporations, for-profit and nonprofit agencies, and individuals can and do employ the services of public relations consultants legally and ethically. Without transparency in the process of rehabilitating Gadhafi's image, however, and with the means themselves undisclosed, Bernays's "invisible governors" continued to "pull the wires which control the public mind," leaving the public with little opportunity to understand, let alone form opinions about or respond to, world events. Monitor Group's campaign can be identified as Bernaysian in its obscuring of rhetorical agency.[14]

Attempting to police the ethics of public relations communications has long been complicated and tied to power and politics. The U.S. government intervened in 1938 when it passed the Foreign Agent Registration Act (FARA) to fight Nazi propaganda. FARA provides a disclosure statute that requires U.S. firms who perform "acts in a public relations capacity for a foreign principal" to register their activities with the U.S. government. The Department of Justice makes clear that periodic public disclosures must include "their relationship with the foreign principal, as well as activities, receipts and disbursements in support of those activities" (National Security Division). The Registration Statement, available on the Department of Justice's website, "requires persons acting as agents of foreign principals in a political or quasi-political capacity to make periodic public disclosure of their relationship with foreign principal" (National Security Division). It exempts "persons whose activities are of a purely commercial nature or solely of a religious, scholastic, academic, scientific or fine arts nature." Joseph Nye was under the impression that his contract with the Monitor Group "was to help bring about reform in Libya." Responding via e-mail to *The Nation's* article "Professors Paid by Qaddafi: Providing 'Positive Public Relations,'" Nye wrote, "I was not told the contract was to 'enhance the profile of Qaddafi.'"[15] Lack of knowledge about the extent of the Monitor Group's image makeover campaign provided Nye plausible deniability and may have met the FARA exemption for "persons whose activities are of a purely . . . academic . . . nature."

Just a week before news broke of the Monitor Group's multimillion-dollar lobbying campaign, Harvard professor Robert Putnam recalled in the *Wall Street Journal* his 2007 trip to Libya to meet with Gadhafi. Putnam remembered the initial invitation—through a former student—from Monitor Group requesting him to visit Libya to discuss his research on civil society and democracy with Gadhafi. Putnam noted that "an international consulting firm that was advising the Libyan government on economic and policy reform" would pay his standard consulting fee. He agreed to go, the first time. After his two-hour "lively conversation" with Gadhafi, Putnam wondered if "this was a serious conversation or an elaborate farce." When asked to return for a second visit, Putnam declined, concluding "that the whole exercise was a public-relations stunt." Putnam's narration of events suggests that like Nye, he was ostensibly invited to discuss his research and economic and political reform, not to participate in enhancing the profile of Libya and Gadhafi. The Monitor Group's "Project to Enhance the Profile of Libya and Muammar Qadhafi" tells a different story when it claimed success by "leverag[ing] the reputation of key influencers engaged in conversation with the Leader in highly public forums" (14). These forums included articles by or interviews with Monitor's "international thought-leaders" in *Newsweek*, the *Financial Times*, *National Public Radio*, the *New York Times*, and the *Washington Post*.

Public relations strategies, such as Monitor Group's efforts to establish "a *dialogue* with the international community through the media" by "showcasing and leveraging Libya's links to some of the world's influential thinkers" (emphasis added), are not necessarily problematic in and of themselves ("Project" 13–14). However, a discrepancy exists between the Monitor Group's strategy as stated in the "Project to Enhance the

Profile of Libya and Muammar Qadhafi" and the "high-caliber individuals'" understanding of their role. The Monitor Group makes clear that the
international consulting firm fully understood its lobbying and public
relations role and goal of shifting "the tone of the coverage of the Leader
and Libya." Furthermore, it identified the function of "the world's foremost scholars and influencers" as "*designed to elevate Libya's agenda* to
a more prominent global position" with the media strategy intended to
"elevate and clearly communicate Libya's goals and agenda for the future"
("Project" 3, emphasis added). However, a dialogue, as Monitor suggested
it successfully established, requires a conversation between two or more
people, an exchange of ideas. FARA established its disclosure requirements
in order to facilitate "evaluation by the government and the American
people of the statements and activities of such persons in light of their
function as foreign agents" (National Security Division). Evaluation is not
possible without a clear understanding of what is at stake in the conversation; otherwise, we are left only with what Bernays calls the "intelligent
manipulation . . . of the masses" (*Propaganda* 37).

   Strategies used by Monitor Group in its attempts to revise Gadhafi's
image as a dictator share stark similarities with a campaign led half a
century earlier to topple the Guatemalan government at the request of
one of America's wealthiest corporations, the United Fruit Company. As
Guatemala's primary landowner, employer, and exporter, United Fruit
controlled the country for decades through pliable dictators until the
election in 1951 of democratic socialist Jacobo Arbenz Guzman, who con-
fiscated and returned 200,000 acres of United Fruit's land to the people
of Guatemala. At the corporation's request and for an annual fee of likely
more than $100,000, Bernays orchestrated an image makeover for Ar-
benz by turning his leadership into a threat to American democracy.[16]
To disparage the popularly elected leader as a Communist and to play
on increasing Cold War fears, Bernays organized a trip to Guatemala for
journalists and created a news agency front called the Middle American
Information Bureau, through which he issued cautionary press releases
and stories about the instability in Guatemala. Thomas McCann, United
Fruit's public relations official during this period, commented on the
journalists' visit in his memoirs: "The trips were ostensibly to gather information, but what the press would hear and see was carefully staged
and regulated by the host" (45–46).[17] Though these reporters and editors understood the propagandized nature of their visit, they still wrote
stories echoing the threat of Guatemala's Communist ties to American

democracy. The Guatemalan Human Rights Commission estimates that more than 200,000 people disappeared or were killed in the thirty-six years of military rulers initially installed and kept in power by the United States.[18] Just as Monitor kept in touch with "the high-caliber individuals" they hired to go to Libya through "briefings and debriefings" as well as via "ongoing dialogue," Bernays used what the then-editor of the *New York Times* described as a "subtle and kind of even-handed approach" when he called the *Times'* foreign desk to "keep in touch" (qtd. in Tye 171). By June 1954, Arbenz was branded a Communist and his government was overthrown with, in Bernays's words, an "army of liberation," consisting of two hundred men recruited and trained by the CIA.

Additional details about Bernays's involvement came to light after his death in 1995 when fifty-three boxes of his papers were made public, which, according to Larry Tye, provide "vivid detail [about] his behind the scenes maneuvering and show how, in 1954, he helped to topple" the Guatemalan government (156). Similarly, it was not until the Monitor Group's confidential documents were leaked that the public, including the readership of the media outlets that covered the story, had a clear understanding of the public relations campaign behind Libya's makeover. In response to growing pressure from international media coverage and from continued unrest in Libya, the Monitor Group issued a statement asserting that "much of the recent commentary on our work in Libya does not capture accurately who we are, what we do, and what drives us" ("Statement"). In an effort to recuperate its own image, Monitor reiterated that its work on behalf of Libya occurred during "a period of promise" when Gadhafi "had renounced terror, forfeited nuclear and chemical weapons and programs, and declared himself ready to rejoin the community of nations," claiming to regret the short duration of that moment of promise ("Statement"). Indicating that it would take accusations of lobbying "very seriously," Monitor launched an internal investigation and hired outside counsel that found that Monitor employees saw themselves as "economic analysts and management consultants," not as public relations counselors (Stockman). But a closer look led even the Monitor Group to concur that "some elements" of its work in Libya could be considered lobbying and "should have been registered under FARA" ("Regarding F.A.R.A."). Following textbook crisis communication strategies of ethos-based self-management by acknowledging errors, Monitor took responsibility and action, including "enhanced management training" (Stockman).

CONCLUSION

The place of ethics and enforcement in the field of public relations has a troubled history. The Public Relations Society of America (PRSA), the world's largest organization for public relations professionals, revamped its code of ethics in 2000 from an "enforcement" model to an "inspiration" model. After nearly fifty years of attempting to police ethical violations, the PRSA found that its "high hopes for cleaning up many of the bad practices that sullied the reputation of the profession" were frustrated by a lack of cooperation along with the expensive and time-consuming investigations and lawsuits. These efforts rarely provided a "return on investment," leading the PRSA to revise its code of ethics to focus on "helping practitioners learn how to be ethical" ("About Enforcement"). The PRSA's principles call for practitioners to "protect and advance the free flow of accurate and truthful information" and to "foster informed decision making through open communication," directives notably in line with FARA. Following these guidelines requires practitioners to "be honest and accurate in all communications" and to "reveal sponsors for represented causes and interests." Yet each of these recommendations was violated by the Monitor Group and by Bernays's United Fruit campaign, violations that did not come to light until after the campaigns were complete and documentation became available for public review. These examples suggest at the very least a history of obfuscation in the profession; they are exemplars of the surrender of democratic principle in an age of spin ushered in by Edward Bernays. These principles and guidelines speak to the importance of being transparent with one's audiences so that recipients of PR messaging can make "informed decisions." When PR practitioners like Bernays purport to be just offering the facts, ostensibly allowing journalists and the public with whom they communicate to reach their own conclusions, it is difficult to squarely place the blame. But if public relations strategies include misleading, obfuscating, or deceitful messaging and tactics or if they remain, in Bernays's word, "unseen," the PR industry sharply limits the public's ability to respond effectively and succeeds in "pull[ing] the wires which control the public mind."

There is nothing inherently wrong with using public relations techniques to relate with the public or to tell a story in the best possible light and in the most effective way. However, when corporations, businesses, or individuals present their stories as "news" or rely on an "expert" or "spokesperson" who is being paid to speak or write about an idea, person, or product in a way that may shape beliefs, policy, or global standing, the audience has a right to know, and public relations firms and their clients have a duty to disclose the source and purpose of their efforts. With international "consulting" firms orchestrating the content of so much of our public discourse—in the news, in articles in leading media, in lectures and publications by leading intellectuals, from our politicians, from our government—the state of civic discourse suffers, particularly when these efforts remain behind the scenes. Without transparency in the process of rehabilitating Gadhafi's image, or of the private production of any "public" image, with the means themselves undisclosed, the free flow of accurate and truthful information is deeply hampered. With a multibillion-dollar global industry hard at work spinning our realities, realizing Bernays's claim that "virtually no important undertaking is now carried on without [public relations]," many opportunities remain for scholars of rhetoric across disciplines to pull back the curtain on the special pleader and better understand how the rise of public relations in the United States has altered communication in the democratic public sphere.

Notes

A shorter version of this chapter, "PR Guns for Hire: The Specter of Edward Bernays in Gadhafi's Libya," appeared previously in *Present Tense: A Journal of Rhetoric in Society*, 2.1 (2011), Web.

1. The first chapter of Mailloux's *Disciplinary Identities* offers a detailed account of how "by the middle of the twentieth century, rhetoric as the study of language arts found itself radically fragmented into separate disciplinary domains with faculties that did not, and, for the most part, still do not talk to each other" (32).

2. Early critical theorists like Jürgen Habermas help us to better understand factors contributing to "the structural transformation of the public sphere" and the role of communication between individuals and the state. Well before Habermas and in response to the encroaching culture of widespread public opinion management, John Dewey, Bernays's contemporary, argued for the urgency of analyzing how communication functions in a democratic public sphere and toward what ends. See Dewey's *The Public and Its Problems*, published in 1927, just one year before Bernays's *Propaganda*.

3. Gadhafi's Arabic name can be and is transliterated in many different ways. I have opted to follow the Associated Press with *Muammar Gadhafi*.

4. The transition from a wartime economy led to a period of great economic growth throughout the 1920s with the nation's wealth doubling until the market crashed in 1929. See Dumenil's *Modern Temper.*

5. See Mark Crispin Miller's introduction to *Propaganda* (25) and chapter 2 of Tye's *Father of Spin* (44–50).

6. Bernays first used the phrase "public relations counsel" in his seminal book *Crystallizing Public Opinion,* published in 1923. For extensive histories on public relations, see Cutlip.

7. Though Bernays's wife, Doris Fleischman, was his business partner involved in nearly all aspects of their publicity business, including a contractual fifty-fifty split of all profits, her work remained largely behind the scenes. She explained, "If ideas were considered first in terms of my sex, they might never get around to being judged on their merits" (*Wife* 171). Though she helped to pioneer nearly every significant aspect of the profession, Edward Bernays retains the mantle "father of public relations." See also Henry and Lamme.

8. Bernays figures prominently in "The Image Makers," an episode in Bill Moyers's *Walk through the 20th Century.*

9. Martin and Bernays's "Are We Victims of Propaganda? A Debate" includes "Our Invisible Masters" by Martin and "Our Debt to Propaganda" by Bernays.

10. Founded by Cooper Union in 1897, the People's Institute offered adult education, meetings, and lectures. Martin was the director from 1922 to 1934 and oversaw the development of the School of the People Institute, geared at teaching a great books curriculum to New York City's working-class and immigrant communities.

11. In early March 2011, the U.S. government cut ties with the Libyan government and imposed sanctions on the Gadhafi regime in response to its violent crackdown on protesters.

12. The "Project to Enhance the Profile of Libya and Muammar Qadhafi" is a typical document produced by the PR team for the client and is not intended for public distribution (see http://www.motherjones.com/files /project_to_enhance_the_profile_of_libya_and_muammar_qadhafi.pdf). This eighteen-page document contains a detailed overview of the work completed by the Monitor Group, including "Goals of the Project," "Summary of Outcomes," "Action Plan" (cataloging the "visitors" who met with Gadhafi), and a section detailing Monitor's "ongoing dialogue with leading individuals." The National Conference of the Libyan Opposition released several other documents including the initial proposal for the project and a letter

from Monitor's CEO to Gadhafi's head of military intelligence, Abd Allah al-Sanusi, who oversaw the Monitor campaign. The letter details the visits of leading intellectuals and discusses the financial arrangements, including the $250,000 monthly retainer.

13. In addition to Joseph Nye and Benjamin Barber, other "high-caliber individuals" included the leading British intellectual Anthony Giddens, Harvard professor Robert Putnam, and philosopher and professor of political economy Francis Fukuyama, among others. See Monitor Group, "Project to Enhance the Profile of Libya and Muammar Qadhafi" and Corn and Mahanta, "From Libya with Love."

14. I follow Cooper's sense of rhetorical agency as emergent, enacted, and embodied and distinct from postmodernism's decentered subject. See Cooper's recent "Rhetorical Agency as Emergent and Enacted."

15. See *The Nation* reporter Jon Wiener's "Professors Paid by Qaddafi."

16. See Tye, *Father of Spin*, 165, 178.

17. In 1974 McCann published *The American Company*, in which he described Bernays's engineering of anti-American demonstrations in Guatemala that were followed by coverage in the American press creating the sense that Communists wanted to take over Guatemala. Bernays, then eighty-four, was outraged by the accusations and contacted the publisher and threatened to sue. See Tye, *Father of Spin*, 181–82.

18. See www.ghrc-usa.org/AboutGuatemala/History.htm.

Works Cited

Barber, Benjamin. "Gadafi's Libya: An Ally for America." *Washington Post.* Washington Post, 15 August 2007. Web. 5 May 2011.

Bernays, Doris Fleischman. *A Wife Is Many Women.* New York: Crown, 1955. Print.

Bernays, Edward. "Freedom of Propaganda: The Constructive Forming of Public Opinion." *Vital Speeches of the Day* 24.2 (1936): 744–46. Print.

———. Interview with Bill Moyers. "The Image Makers." *A Walk through the 20th Century.* Dir. Bill Moyers. PBS Video, 1984. Film.

———. *Propaganda.* Brooklyn: Ig, 1928. Print.

Cooper, Marilyn M. "Rhetorical Agency as Emergent and Enacted." *College Composition and Communication* 62.3 (2011): 420–49. Print.

Corn, David, and Siddhartha Mahanta. "From Libya with Love." *Mother Jones.* Foundation for National Progress, 3 March 2011. Web. 5 May 2011.

Crowley, Sharon. *The Methodical Memory: Invention in Current-Traditional Rhetoric.* Carbondale: Southern Illinois UP, 1990. Print.

Cutlip, Scott M. *Public Relations History: From the 17th to the 20th Century.* Hillsdale, N.J.: Erlbaum, 1995. Print.

———. *The Unseen Power: Public Relations, a History.* Hillsdale, N.J.: Erlbaum, 1994. Print.

Dewey, John. *The Public and Its Problems.* New York: Holt, 1927. Print.

Dowie, Mark. Introduction. *Toxic Sludge Is Good for You: Lies, Damn Lies and the Public Relations Industry.* By John Stauber and Sheldon Rampton. Monroe, Maine: Common Courage, 2002. 1–4. Print.

Dumenil, Lynn. *The Modern Temper: American Culture and Society in the 1920s.* New York: Hill and Wang, 1995. Print.

Ewen, Stuart. *PR! A Social History of Spin.* New York: Basic, 1996. Print.

Habermas, Jürgen. *The Structural Transformation of the Public Sphere.* Trans. Thomas Burger and Frederick Lawrence. Cambridge: MIT P, 1989. Print.

Heath, Robert L. Introduction. *Rhetorical and Critical Approaches to Public Relations II.* Ed. Robert L. Heath, Elizabeth Toth, and Damion Waymer. New York: Routledge, 2009. 1–12. Print.

Henry, Susan. "Anonymous in Her Own Name: Public Relations Pioneer Doris Fleischman." *Journalism History* 23.2 (1997): 50–62. Print.

———. "'There Is Nothing in This Profession . . . That a Woman Cannot Do': Doris E. Fleischman and the Beginnings of Public Relations." *American Journalism* 16.2 (1999): 85–111. Print.

Johnson, Nan. *Nineteenth-Century Rhetoric in North America.* Carbondale: Southern Illinois UP, 1991. Print.

Lamme, Margot Opdycke. "Outside the Prickly Nest: Revisiting Doris Fleischman." *American Journalism* 24.3 (2007): 85–107. Print.

Le Bon, Gustave. *The Crowd: A Study of the Popular Mind.* 2nd ed. New York: Macmillan, 1897. Print.

Mailloux, Steven. *Disciplinary Identities: Rhetorical Paths of English, Speech, and Composition.* New York: MLA, 2006. Print.

Martin, Everett Dean. *The Meaning of a Liberal Education.* Garden City, N.Y.: Garden City, 1926. Print.

Martin, Everett Dean, and Edward Bernays. "Are We Victims of Propaganda? A Debate." *Forum Magazine* 81.3 (1929): 142–49. Library of Congress. Web. 27 July 2011.

McCann, Thomas. *On the Inside: A Story of Intrigue and Adventure, on Wall Street, in Washington, and in the Jungles of Central America.* Boston: Quinlan, 1987. Print.

Miller, Mark Crispin. Introduction. *Propaganda.* By Edward Bernays. 1928. Brooklyn: Ig, 2005. 9–33. Print.

Monitor Group. "Project to Enhance the Profile of Libya and Muammar Qadhafi: Executive Summary of Phase 1." Cambridge: Monitor Group, 2007. *Mother Jones*. Web. 20 March 2009.

———. "Regarding F.A.R.A. Registration." *Monitor*. Monitor Group, 6 May 2011. Web. 31 May 2011.

———. "Statement by Monitor Group Concerning Libya." *Monitor*. Monitor Group, 24 March 2011. Web. 24 March 2011.

National Security Division. "Foreign Agent Registration Act." FARA.gov. U.S. Department of Justice, n.d. Web. 6 May 2011.

Nye, Joseph S., Jr. "Tripoli Diarist." *New Republic*. New Republic, 10 December 2007. Web. 5 May 2011.

Public Relations Society of America. "About Enforcement." PRSA.com. Public Relations Society of America, n.d. Web. 21 August 2011.

Putnam, Robert D. "With Libya's Megalomania 'Philosopher King.'" *Wall Street Journal*. Dow Jones & Co., 26 February 2011. Web. 5 May 2011.

Stockman, Farrah. "Firm Says It Erred on Libya Consulting." *Boston.com*. Boston Globe Media Partners, 6 May 2011. Web. 6 May 2011.

Tye, Larry. *The Father of Spin: Edward L. Bernays and the Birth of Public Relations*. New York: Crown, 1998. Print.

Wiener, Jon. "Professors Paid by Qaddafi: Providing 'Positive Public Relations.'" *The Nation*. The Nation, 5 March 2011. Web. 5 May 2011.

JANE ADDAMS: A FOE OF
RHETORICS OF CONTROL

LANETTE GRATE

Writing resists.   —Sidney I. Dobrin, *Postcomposition*

Extensive scholarly work on propaganda by social scientists, historians, journalists, public relations professionals, and linguists emerged immediately after World War I. The study of postwar propaganda in the 1920s and 1930s was conducted by war journalists eager to expose propaganda techniques used to malign the enemy and bolster the fighting spirit; by public relations professionals who wanted to promote the profitable economic aspects of propaganda; by social scientists, sociologists, and psychologists interested in analyzing propaganda messages as a phenomenon related to behaviorism; and by progressive humanists alarmed that the use of propaganda to manipulate public opinion during the war might be continued in the postwar era by politicians to create a managed rather than a shared democracy. These scholars and professional writers published works that constitute the historical canon of propaganda studies. Conspicuously absent from the postwar canon are female writers like Jane Addams.

Although missing from the history of propaganda studies and not considered a propaganda analyst like her fellow progressive humanist John Dewey, Jane Addams, in her numerous speeches, essays, and books, not only examines propaganda techniques used by the powerful to coerce the powerless but also offers suggestions for resistance. Studied today, her insightful observations expose the danger to a shared democracy of a powerful political rhetoric aimed at the control and containment of information and people. To combat the damage war propaganda causes, Addams became an active rhetorical agent in the arena "where hegemony and democracy are contested" (Clifford 51). When scholars study Addams as a writer, they learn what radical writing is and what it can do. Addams's willingness—almost an ethical imperative—to challenge World War I propaganda makes her a model of a disruptive rhetor who uses critical inquiry to reveal the connection between language, power, and social control.

This essay will first introduce Jane Addams, a social activist, progressive reformer, critical pragmatist, cultural feminist, public intellectual, Nobel Peace Prize winner, writer, speaker, pacifist, and, to add one more description to the list, propaganda analyst. A review of the literature will show that Addams is missing from the literature of postwar and modern propaganda studies, although she was one of the earliest progressive humanist scholars to write about the connection between the use of propaganda and the maintenance of a managed democracy. This essay will focus on Addams's observations and critique of propaganda from 1898 to 1922 and conclude by affirming Addams's belief in the danger that modern propaganda poses to citizen participation in a shared democracy.

WAR, PEACE, AND PROPAGANDA

Jane Addams, the twentieth-century social activist and 1931 Nobel Peace Prize winner who cofounded and directed Hull-House in Chicago, is rightly identified as one of the most influential American women of all time. Before World War I, she was voted one of the three "greatest women in history," along with Susan B. Anthony and Madame Curie (Davis 200). In 1912, for example, the *American Magazine* called her "the foremost woman in America," stating, "She is known and loved by thousands and respected by millions" (qtd. in Addams, "Progressive's Dilemma" 13). According to biographer Allen Davis, "In the years before World War I, she was a symbol of the best [of] American Democracy, the best of American womanhood, and a semi-religious figure who explained all mysteries and assured everyone that despite poverty and tragedy everywhere, in the end, right would prevail" (211). Despite her public reputation suffering during and immediately after the war due to her pacifist stance, the writer of her obituary in the *New York Times* stated, "She was, perhaps, the world's best-known and best-loved woman" ("Jane Addams").

Born in 1860 in Cedarville, Illinois, Addams was raised by her father, John Huy Addams, a miller, property owner, and Illinois state senator. Addams attended Rockford Female Seminary, graduating in 1881, the year her father died. A trip to Europe in the 1880s introduced her to the settlement movement, and upon her return she cofounded Hull-House with her friend Ellen Gates Starr in 1889. Her books *Twenty Years at Hull-House* and *The Second Twenty Years at Hull-House* describe her work with her immigrant neighbors in the Nineteenth Ward in Chicago, where she was instrumental in addressing and ameliorating the abuses created by the industrial system by replacing philanthropic effort with political action.

Among her many political, social, and economic causes were improved factory safety codes, industrial insurance, old-age pensions, widows' pensions, establishment of a minimum wage, immigration protection, sanitation improvement, children and women labor laws, improved parks and recreations, antilynching laws, anti–white slavery laws, suffrage, and world peace. Before the war, Addams traveled extensively in Europe and was familiar with international cooperation, especially among women. In January 1915 Addams cofounded, with Carrie Chapman Catt, the Woman's Peace Party of the United States in response to the outbreak of European hostilities and was its first chairman. As Anna Garlin Spencer, speaking for the party, said, "We set ourselves to sympathetic understanding of those from whom we differ" (qtd. in Alonso 77). Addams chaired the International Congress of Women at The Hague in April 1915, attended by twelve hundred women from twelve different countries. The International Committee of Women for Permanent Peace later became the Women's International League for Peace and Freedom in 1919. Jane Addams was elected president, a position she held until her death in 1935.

Addams published ten books and collaborated on three. She also published over five hundred articles in magazines, newspapers, and journals. Today, Addams is studied as a cultural feminist, critical pragmatist, and political progressive. Her pacifism, as Terrance Macmullan points out in "On War as Waste: Jane Addams's Pragmatic Pacifism," is a "less studied matter" (87). Macmullan further states that "she pioneered positions on war and democracy later adopted by dominant figures in American philosophy, and . . . her work radically challenged dominant assumptions about the proper relationship between war and politics" (87). Addams scholar John Farrell believes that pacifism was Addams's intellectual legacy and focuses the last three chapters of his book on her pacifist work. Other scholars besides Farrell and Macmullan who have studied Addams's peace work include Harriet Hyman Alonso, Carrie Foster, Marilyn Fischer, and Judy D. Whipps. While more scholars are examining Addams's contributions to pacifism, further attention needs to be paid to the contributions she made to early propaganda critique and analysis. "War, peace, and propaganda," as psychologist and propaganda analyst Leonard Doob states, "are very intimately related. . . . To fail to mention this trio together is like trying to produce a three-legged stool that will stand erect on one or on two legs" (302). In questioning political rhetorical manipulation beginning with the Spanish-American War and continuing through World War I and into the postwar era, Addams was one of only a few public intellectuals[1] who refused to keep silent about mass persuasion techniques the Wilson administration used prior to and during the war to legitimize militarist aims, yet there is hardly any mention of her in the literature of propaganda studies.

REVIEWING LITERATURE IN PROPAGANDA STUDIES

In the literature of propaganda studies, Jane Addams is seldom, if ever, mentioned, despite the fact that she was actively analyzing and critiquing war propaganda, first in relation to labor disputes and later in relation to World War I, long before the acclaimed scholars in the field appeared. The following examples show how Addams is treated in the literature. Will Irwin mentions Addams only as an American pacifist negatively linked to Communism and blacklisted along with other "eminent and useful citizens" in the Red Scare following World War I (280). William Albig lists Addams in a selected references section of biographies and autobiographies of significant leaders (440–41). Leonard Doob makes no mention of Addams in any of his books. Michael Sproule identifies her as a "social-work reformer" who was a leader in the National Consumers' League (*Propaganda and Democracy* 112). *Propaganda and Mass Persuasion: A Historical Encyclopedia, 1500 to the Present* refers to Addams only as a pacifist (290) and prominent progressive reformer (413) but does not devote an entry to her as an individual connected in any way with the progressive humanist school of propaganda analysis.

One reason Addams is overlooked in propaganda studies is that she was overlooked in general in many studies. The *Stanford Encyclopedia of Philosophy*, which names Addams as the first female public philosopher in the history of the United States, says, "The dynamics of canon formation, however, resulted in her philosophical work being largely ignored until the 1990s" (Hamington). Canon formation dynamics were based on gender. As Addams scholar Katherine Joslin points out, "A woman's voice in time of war carried no serious intellectual or political weight" (xviii). This observation can be extended to the postwar era where the recognized propaganda criticism and analysis was written by men, some of whom had served as war correspondents at the front or worked for the Committee on Public Information. The public found it difficult to take seriously a female speaking about war propaganda, even one who had personally traveled to both neutral and belligerent nations in 1915, making observations and gathering information on the way propaganda was being used to control mass opinion; who had testified in Congress before the House Committee on Military Affairs as a representative of the Woman's Peace Party; and who had personally experienced propaganda attacks that not only damaged her reputation but also prevented her from publishing and speaking during the war years. Gesa Kirsch and Jacqueline Royster, feminist rhetorical scholars, point out that, for centuries, the history of rhetoric and writing was exclusively defined by Western patriarchal values (641). While the history of propaganda studies is a relatively new field, it was born within the same exclusive hierarchy that valued male over female voices.

Another reason for Addams's absence in the literature of propaganda studies is that her observations in regard to war propaganda were never compiled into one essay or one book devoted specifically to the study of propaganda. Instead, one finds her comments about war, peace, and propaganda woven into her essays, speeches, and books. Addams may also have been overlooked by history of propaganda scholars because of her research methods. She used her own personal experiences and observations to analyze and critique propaganda. Therefore, since her examinations were not conducted with statistics, surveys, or quantification, her methodology was considered "soft." For example, her personal observations on propaganda found in *Peace and Bread in Time of War* can be viewed on one level as a case study of propaganda techniques used to suppress pacifists who opposed the war. Case study approaches to propaganda critiques were often marginalized in favor of the growing trend in the 1930s toward quantitative science, which, because it was considered unbiased, could secure private foundation funding (Sproule, "Social Responses" 15). Thus, her observations may have been ignored due to her use of feminist methodologies in which she relied on her personal observations, lived experiences, self-reflection, and narrative rather than on a traditional, masculine, academic-research style. As Charlene Haddock Seigfried explains, Addams, as a writer, uses an "experimental method" that relies on narrative (xiii). Doob dismisses narrative, saying many writers have narrated their experiences with propaganda, but few have provided analysis (6). Further, Doob contends that narrations are only "valuable when they are placed within a social framework" (6), a framework that provides "the basis for a broad cultural interpretation" (7). Addams actually does both. She not only narrates her experience with numerous propaganda techniques that she had either directly encountered or observed, but she also analyzes those techniques by examining the relationship between government propaganda, the power of the press, and public suppression in American and European society.

Additionally, Addams may have been ignored due to her pacifism, an unpopular stance in any age when one's country is infected with war fever. Addams's unfaltering pacifist stance during World War I, one of only a few public intellectuals who openly opposed the war, caused a dark cloud of suspicion to follow her into the 1920s, when she was blacklisted during the Red Scare. This may have resulted in her contributions to the field of propaganda analysis being devalued or ignored, unlike John Dewey's; he supported the war and then was acknowledged as a propaganda analyst afterward with the 1927 publication of *The Public and Its Problems*. Sproule states that humanists and progressives such as Dewey and journalist Walter Lippmann were the first to offer a critique of propaganda after the war by raising the concern that the social control of public opinion prevented citizens from obtaining the information necessary to participate in democratic life ("Social Responses" 9–10). Although the humanist and progressive critique of propaganda as dangerous to a shared democracy dominated in the two decades after the war, according to Sproule, the humanist view declined because of a dependence by humanist scholars such as George Herbert Mead on abstract or grand theory, which could offer no "theory-praxis synthesis strong enough to compete with the growing measurement-management orientation in social science" (*Propaganda and Democracy* 78).

Interestingly, Addams was not only doing the work of propaganda analysis quite early, long before those considered to be leaders in the field, but her personal experience and observations of the social, cultural, historical, and even personal effects of propaganda on democratic participation shed light on the question Sproule says the leading propaganda analysts ignored in their search for a grand theory: "whether communication in a particular time and place improved or worsened democratic society" (*Propaganda and Democracy* 79). In other words, the acknowledged humanist theorists were "silent on the specific connections of propaganda to democracy" (78). In her observations regarding propaganda, whether during a labor strike or during a war, and concerning the way it excludes and assimilates, subjugates and coerces, Addams offers not an abstract attempt at a grand unified theory but what Lyotard calls "little narratives" (*Postmodern* xxiv), in which she "speaks as a listener, and not an author[ity]" (Lyotard and Thébaud 72). This position, not of authoritative theorist but of citizen-rhetor offering counternarratives to expose and combat hegemonic discourse, allows her to bear witness to a language of control that often remains invisible to the public it subjugates. Instead of presenting a truth claim in regard to propaganda, she offers something more crucial: a rhetoric of resistance.

Addams models in her resistance deviation from the norm—the crucial spark necessary to ignite and keep alive democratic discourse. In her writing, Addams is not only critiquing and analyzing but also deconstructing the rhetoric of mass control and replacing it with a democratic rhetoric of collaboration, inclusion, and cooperation. She urges an ideological shift away from an uncritical nationalistic allegiance and toward a more thoughtful expansive patriotism based on the principles of global citizenship and international cooperation (see *Newer Ideals of Peace*). In order to make this shift, Addams believes the one-way communication of any type of propaganda that obtains consent by coercion, misrepresentation, and suppression must be replaced with language that creates public consent through dialogue. The exposure to multiple perspectives will then lead to an informed public making decisions together as a democratic community—a community that has learned to use language constructively to solve domestic and international differences, rather than destructively to fulfill the militarist aims of a political party (*Peace and Bread* 138).

Those invested in a managed democracy, however, were eager to use new insights on propaganda not to enlighten and empower the public but to control it. Furthermore, Addams's views of a shared or participatory democracy were not shared by capitalist elites who lived by a much different definition of democracy; this, too, may be a reason why her insightful critique of propaganda failed to reach a wider audience. As Gloria McMillan points out, Addams had a difficult time getting "A Modern Lear"—her essay on the Pullman Strike—published due to the "ideological gulf" between Addams's conception of democracy and the conception of the capitalist elite (66). Her views of peaceful conflict resolution and an empowered, informed citizenry were problematic to those more interested in financial returns than in social equality. Addams insists that to maintain a shared democracy, political leaders must make it their aim "to replace coercion by the full consent of the governed, to educate and strengthen the free will of the people through the use of democratic institutions," and to realize that "this age-long process of obtaining the inner consent of the citizen to the outward acts of his government is of necessity violently interrupted and thrown back in war time" when political leaders use propaganda to twist and suppress information in order to coerce consent (*Peace and Bread* 65).

For whatever reason, Addams is absent from propaganda literature, a curious gap when one considers her early and extensive observations on war, peace, and propaganda.

PROPAGANDA ANALYSIS IN ADDAMS'S WRITING

Four of Addams's books specifically discuss war, peace, and propaganda: *Newer Ideals of Peace, Women at The Hague* (coauthored with Emily Greene Balch and Alice Hamilton), *The Long Road of Woman's Memory,* and *Peace and Bread in Time of War.* In these books Addams not only argues against war and advocates for pacifism but also observes, records, and analyzes propaganda techniques used to coerce public compliance. For example, in *Newer Ideals of Peace,* one of Addams's earliest observations about propaganda arises from a personal experience during the Spanish-American War. In 1898, seven murders occurred in her neighborhood. After investigating, she was able to "trace the murders back to the influence of the war" (143). This influence was so pervasive that even the children in the neighborhood were influenced and "played at war and at killing Spaniards" (144). Citing newspapers, theater posters, and casual conversations as the means of rhetorical circulation that focused the public's attention on the brutality of the war, Addams states, "Psychologists intimate that action is determined by the selection of the subject upon which the attention is habitually fixed" (143–44). As early as 1898, Addams made connections between the power of propaganda to negatively influence public opinion and behavior. "Simple people," she says, "who read of carnage and bloodshed easily receive suggestions" to perpetrate or condone violence themselves (143).

Social reformers such as Addams were well aware that publicity campaigns and the press could influence public opinion to stall or even dismantle needed social reforms. Before World War I, Addams analyzed the deceptive propaganda techniques both big business and trade unions relied on during labor strikes and discovered that the language used by both sides in the conflict bore a striking resemblance to propaganda methods employed during wartime. She states, "A tacit admission that a strike is war and that all the methods of warfare are permissible was made in Chicago during the teamsters' strike of 1905" (*Newer Ideals* 132). In fact, the unions were using "war phraseology" (130) and the "war element" (110) to create group loyalty. But even worse to Addams was the curious spell cast on the public that allowed the violence or "warfare" to take place. She asks, "How did the public become hypnotized into a passive endurance of a street warfare in which two associations were engaged, like feudal chiefs with their recalcitrant retainers?" (133). She answers her own question by stating that Chicago had grown accustomed "to warfare as a method of settling labor disputes" (135). In a chapter titled "Passing of the War Virtues," she suggests replacing militarism with industrialism or constructive action as opposed to destructive action as a solution to settling disputes without violence. In the literature of propaganda studies, the *Report on the Steel Strike of 1919* by the Commission of Inquiry, Interchurch World Movement, a study of the deceptive propaganda practices used by the steel industry to defeat striking workers, is mentioned as an example of anti-propaganda literature (Sproule, *Propaganda and Democracy* 20), but Addams's much earlier anti-propaganda observations found in *Newer Ideals of Peace* are not mentioned.

Addams coauthored with Emily Greene Balch and Alice Hamilton a collection of essays titled *Women at The Hague*. These essays explain the mediation efforts of pacifist women from both neutral and belligerent nations who met at the International Congress convened at The Hague in the Netherlands in April 1915. One aim of the book was to "correct the impression made upon the public by the contradictory accounts given through the press" (v). This statement indicates that the authors were aware that the press played an influential role in shaping public opinion about the war. In *The Long Road of Woman's Memory*, Addams critiques war as an outdated method to solve political problems. In the chapter titled "Challenging War," Addams speaks through the voice of a woman whose son has been killed in combat as she analyzes militarist propaganda that demonizes the enemy to appeal to the tribal instinct of self-preservation and loyalty to one's country. She suggests an alternative international perspective based not on national consciousness but on human consciousness as a substitute for war. In other words, she replaces allegiance to abstract ideals such as duty or loyalty to one's country with a real concern for human lives in every country.

In *Peace and Bread in Time of War*, her fourth book on the issue of war, peace, and propaganda, Addams writes about her own personal experience with propaganda suppression techniques used by the Wilson administration to silence pacifists, suppress dissent, and justify the war. Addams was well acquainted with what she terms the "opposition press" from her work at Hull-House and as a member of the Progressive Party. She says, "Hull-House had several times been the subject of sustained and inspired newspaper attacks, one, the indirect result of an exposure of the inefficient sanitary service in the Chicago Health Department [that] had lasted for many months; I had of course known what it was to serve unpopular causes" (77). Despite this acquaintance, Addams found the way the American press "systematically undertook to misrepresent and malign pacifists as a recognized part of propaganda and as a patriotic duty . . . rather overwhelming" and that "we came to regard this misrepresentation as part of the war technique and in fact an inevitable consequence of war itself" (77). In the chapter titled "Personal Reactions during War," Addams details how difficult it was for pacifists to go "against the impregnable weight of public opinion, the appalling imperviousness, the coagulation of motives, the universal confusion of a world at war" (86). These words indicate that Addams saw war propaganda as a complex hegemonic system, one that works by the promise of safety through assimilation for anyone who accepts the war agenda and by the threat of exclusion for anyone who questions or disagrees with that agenda.

Not only in her books but also in numerous speeches and essays, Addams identifies and critiques propaganda techniques used by the government and the government-controlled press to induce citizens to support war. For example, one propaganda technique she notes is the way political leaders justify their involvement in a conflict by saying they have no choice and by blaming each other for causing the war ("Is the Peace Movement a Failure?"). This propaganda is nothing more than "the old business of self-justification, of utilizing outgrown myths to explain the course of action which their governments have taken" ("What War Is Destroying" 64). She also notes the bait-and-switch technique of shifting war aims when the government tells the public that war is necessary for one reason, then changes the reason as the war progresses in order to continue the conflict ("Patriotism and Pacifists" 188). Another propaganda technique Addams observes is the use of emotional appeals such as "music, the march and the gold-bedecked uniform" to entice citizens to become soldiers (qtd. in *Proceedings* 106).

As a writer, Addams was particularly interested in the way political leaders manipulated language to coerce consent. She states:

> All through the centuries whether men were driven in tribes by the pangs of hunger to find land and food outside of their own territory, or whether they were impelled by the dynastic ambition of their rulers, by religious enthusiasm or by imperial vanity they have clothed warfare in high-sounding language and it has always had behind it noble emotions and fine endeavor at least on the part of the men actually engaged in it. (qtd. in *Proceedings* 106)

In other words, political rulers conceal their real motives of ambition, religion, vanity, or greed by using "fine phrases" (qtd. in *Proceedings* 214) or emotionally loaded words like "nationalism" and "patriotism" to move the people to support the war effort. One "fine phrase" Addams identifies is the oxymoron of "armed peace" used by government leaders to encourage a buildup of armaments. According to Addams, this buildup itself leads directly to war ("Is the Peace Movement a Failure?"). As to the war preparations she saw rapidly taking place in America in 1915, Addams, as chairman of the Woman's Peace Party, wrote to President Woodrow Wilson saying, "We believe in real defense against real dangers, but not in a preposterous 'preparedness' against hypothetical dangers" ("Protest against Preparedness"). Europe was exhausted, she notes, and America, an ocean away, was in no danger.

Accurately identifying the connection between a militarist government and a compliant rather than a questioning press, Addams analyzed the role "the armor-plated press" played in the "manufacturing of war sentiment" by creating "war scares," which also led directly to an unnecessary military and naval buildup in nations ("Peace on Earth").[2] Creating an imaginary enemy was one way the press helped the Wilson administration achieve its militarist objective. For example, the government and the government-controlled press, Addams contends, "portray the enemy as hideous or wicked or barbaric or 'weak'" (qtd. in *Proceedings* 214) in order to create hatred and fear, which leads to military conflict. The creation of a common enemy, Addams observes, exacerbates the fear of national danger, which perpetuates feelings of hatred and intolerance ("Patriotism and Pacifists" 188). The national media bolstered the idea of a common enemy by printing atrocity stories, which in turn fanned a united communal desire for revenge. For example, drawings printed in the press and government-approved posters of Germans killing babies and children inflamed national outrage. This enemy creation, Addams contends, is "an old method of welding people together" (189). Furthermore, she states, "we were absolutely unable to determine whether the hate produced the atrocities, or the atrocities the hate" ("Factors in Continuing the War" 83). Testifying before the U.S. House of Representatives Committee on Military Affairs in 1916, Addams argued that the "war contagion" had created a "war spirit" that caused men to clamor to defend America against an enemy that did not exist ("Statement" 5). In fact, since increased immigration in the late nineteenth and early twentieth centuries had caused a greater understanding of internationalism, the "enemy," Addams muses, is more than likely to be one's "next-door neighbors" (qtd. in *Proceedings* 214).

As a delegate to the Woman's International Peace Conference in 1915, Addams had already witnessed in both neutral and belligerent countries the European version of "war contagion" and "war spirit" she later identified in America in 1916. In Europe, she found the people of all nations "tremendously united" ("Address" 4) in their support of war. Whether in Germany or France, whether an "enemy" or an "ally," she discovered national unity absolute in each nation. Analyzing cause and effect, Addams notes that war propaganda created by the press activates the tribal instinct of solidarity, which leads to violence. The tribal appeal, Addams contends, "is universally used to induce men to go to war" (qtd. in Marshall 3). Identifying two of man's earliest instincts as "security from attack" and "security from starvation," Addams says, "Throughout the war the first instinct was utilized to its fullest possibility by every device of propaganda when one nation after another was mobilizing for a 'purely defensive war'" (*Peace and Bread* 116).

Familiar with the theory of the tribe, a concept that appeared often in her pre-war writing, Addams defines this tribal instinct of solidarity as a primitive nationalistic type of patriotism rather than a higher global concept based on loyalty to humanity. She writes, "Thousands of men marching to their death are under compulsion, not of this higher type of patriotism, but of a tribal conception, because of an irrational appeal which ought to have left the world long since. They march and fight because they have been told that they must thus save their homes from destruction" ("What War Is Destroying" 64). Addams concludes that the "mass psychology" used to convince humans to commit violence against other humans is largely based on a propaganda of fear. In other words, when threatened, whether the threat is real or created semantically, people of every nation respond by defending national ideals and their way of life in an automatic gesture of self-defense. Addams describes this solidarity phenomenon "as if the consciousness of one person overflowed into the consciousness of another" ("Address" 4). In each country, she found "much the same phrases in regard to the good qualities of the citizens within the country, and alas, very much the same phrases in regard to the enemy whom they were fighting" (4–5). What intrigued Addams was that this homogeneity of thought was replicated in nation after nation. She states, "It sounds incredible, does it not, to say these things in regard to all countries, but it is what we encountered in one country after another" (5). And the cause of this homogeneity, Addams believed, was the propaganda promulgated by the national press, the information technology of her day. Long before the war, in 1907, Addams realized the power of the press to create a "new common kingdom of the mind" (qtd. in *Proceedings* 214), which she hoped, unrealistically as it turned out, would lead to an international worldview and the end of war. Instead, Addams discovered, the press chose to use its power to incite hatred and violence and move nations to war rather than to create the conditions necessary for international cooperation. The press chose to use its power to help the government control a national community rather than to create a global one.

Press censorship is yet another propaganda technique that Addams studied. For example, in "The Revolt against War," the published speech she gave at Carnegie Hall on 9 July 1915 after her return from Europe, she expresses her belief that war propaganda is detrimental to democracy by calling attention to military censorship. In a shared democracy, citizens communicate through the press and depend on it to convey diverse views and opinions from which they are able to make a conscientious decision about the actions they wish to take as a nation; however, "in the warring countries nothing goes into the press except those things which the military censors deem fit and proper" (356). Thus, public opinion is conscripted to only one viewpoint—of those who advocate for the necessity of war. Addams again mentions government press censorship in a 1916 essay, "A Conference of Neutrals," in which she states, "With the military party in power in each country, taking the censorship of the press into their hands, the whole stream of communication which ordinarily makes for international public opinion in Europe has been stopped." By using writing as a conduit of distorted and misrepresented information, the real power of writing as "a complex system of interconnected relations" (Dobrin 145) is shut down. Noting that the same tendency to control public opinion by press censorship is true whether in England, France, or Germany, Addams asserts, "The general tendency of the press at present ... is to publish only the most inflaming statements issued by the extremists in the countries with which they are at war" ("Conference"). Addams believes that a shared democracy depends on the citizens' ability to freely communicate diverse opinions and that in time of war, that freedom disappears as a direct result of censorship.

Continuing her analysis of press censorship that was based on her personal observations and experiences in Europe in 1915 as a delegate to the Woman's International Peace Conference, she asks, "Does public opinion control the press or the reverse?" ("Factors" 84). Addams recognizes that the press on either side of a dispute controls public opinion by selecting and printing information it wishes to promote and by suppressing information it does not wish to promote ("Peace and the Press" 55): "The power of the press to determine these data gives it ultimate control over the minds of the multitude who read but one type of journal" (55). Astutely examining this propaganda technique of one-way communication, Addams observes, those advocating a different opinion such as peace are "denied all journalistic expression, while the war spirit is continually fed by the outrages of war" (56). In every European country she visited, whether Allied or Axis, the press controlled public opinion so completely that no citizen could "express any opinion contrary to that which the press had decided to foster as in the interest of patriotism and a speedy victory" (55). If a citizen were aware enough and brave enough to mount a counterhegemonic discourse, certain predictable preventive actions would be taken to silence or discredit that voice. For example, if a man in England suggested peace as an alternative to war, the press would attack him as "pro-German" and he "exposes himself to the most violent abuse" (55).

Addams focuses her critique of propaganda on the activities of both the regular and the scholarly press in promoting war. Even scholarly publications like the "Oxford Papers," Addams observes, succumbed to the war spirit: "From cover to cover one waits in vain for some indication of the calm and unprejudiced point of view indicating that the writers were able to rise above the turmoil of the moment and to speak the language of him who deals in eternal verities" ("What War Is Destroying" 64). The German university presses were no better in their failure to incorporate a dialogue rather than an official state monologue of fear and intolerance. Therefore, German citizens, like the American public, could not determine for themselves fact from fiction. Whether scholarly or popular, whether Allied or Axis, the press failed in its duty to inform the public, which would have allowed citizens to decide the best course of action they wished their elected representatives to take. Addams contends, "I think the newspapers are distinctly misleading; they are not interpreting public sentiment but are trying to make it for motives of their own" ("Statement" 8). In these comments, she calls attention to the power of the press in wartime to control public opinion rather than to convey the information necessary for citizens to form their own opinions and to determine their own actions.

Going even further in her critique of the press as the propagator of dangerous propaganda techniques, Addams believed that "the next revolution against tyranny would have to be a revolution against the unscrupulous power of the press" ("Peace and the Press" 56). In fact, the militarist press had become dogmatic like the medieval church, providing citizens "only such knowledge as it deemed fit for them to have" (56). Therefore, citizens, the ones sacrificing their lives and possessions, were not given the information they needed to make their own judgments about the necessity of war. The information the press fed the public ensured that the war would continue as long as the military and political leaders wanted it to continue. Addams observes that when the press is closed to the citizen with a different opinion, that citizen cannot exercise the pressure of public opinion upon elected officials. This ability to exert the pressure of public opinion is the foundation of a shared democracy.

Addams shows she was aware of the propaganda campaigns waged by both Allied and Axis powers. For example, she speculates that German propaganda was one of the reasons Russian soldiers were refusing to continue fighting, since German propaganda cast the war as the czar's war ("Tolstoy and the Russian Soldiers" 240). In the same essay, Addams also questions the British propaganda technique of dropping pro-democracy leaflets behind enemy lines to influence German soldiers and citizens to stop fighting: "If the Allies are seriously trying to treat with the German people as distinct from the government, the spoken word will certainly be found much more dependable as a vehicle of propaganda than the printed page, even if in our enthusiasm we attempt the naïve device of dropping democratic literature into the German trenches from aeroplanes" (241–42). It would be more efficacious, she maintains, to let deserting Russian soldiers revolting against autocracy convince the German citizenry to do the same and "free the land" (241). She finds the impersonal practice of Allied propaganda a naive attempt at democratic dialogue and contends that real democracy depends on "fraternal intercourse" (242). Addams clearly recognizes war propaganda as a rhetoric of control antithetical to democratic discourse.

To Addams, the term *propaganda* itself is neutral. She uses the term, which she equates with persuasion, often in regard to pacifist propaganda

("Patriotism and Pacifists") and industrial propaganda ("The Reaction of a Simple Women"). She had no qualms about using propaganda tactics herself to advance her social reform causes. For example, she says before the war, "We tried all sorts of new methods of propaganda" (*Peace and Bread* 9). These methods included poetry, songs, and plays. After the war she developed a peace strategy using emotive appeals and new technology to increase the communication of peace ideals and to influence public opinion to replace militarist with pacifist views (Farrell 195). Propaganda, then, could be used in positive ways to stimulate dialogue that would lead to social reform. However, when propaganda was used as a weapon to manipulate mass opinion and to silence opposition rather than as a means to activate public communication and civic participation through discussion and dialogue, Addams feared the danger to a democratic society such misuse would create. In her books, essays, and speeches, Addams observes the power of propaganda to create national unity in reaction to fear, a unity she believed led directly to war. Addams reveals a keen and critical ability to expose the relationship between propaganda and political suppression by analyzing the language and propaganda techniques government leaders and a complicit press used to create the public reaction they desired, which was unquestioning public support for militarist aims.

CONCLUSION

While Addams was acutely aware of the dangers to civil liberties of government-sanctioned mass manipulation by the press before and during the war, the majority of Americans would not recognize or admit the danger of propaganda until after World War I (Sproule, "Social Responses" 7).[3] Most Americans viewed propaganda during the war as a disreputable communication tactic used by their enemies. Few understood or acknowledged how propaganda was being used to control American public opinion. Jane Addams, however, had been consistently exposing the rhetorical tricks employed by governments, the press, industry, and labor unions, beginning with her observations of propaganda techniques used during the Spanish-American War and used against her own reform efforts in Chicago long before World War I. Whether it was because she was a woman or because she was a pacifist or because she was a radical rhetor, her prescient observations and warnings in regard to propaganda went unheeded before and during the war and unacknowledged afterward. While she may never be included in the pantheon of early twentieth-century propaganda analysts, Addams rises above such limiting labels and categories and shows herself to be a rhetorical agent who not only critically observed and reflected on her lived experience with propaganda but also challenged and confronted hegemonic discourse. Studying a writer like Addams moves us beyond composition studies into what Sidney Dobrin urges: a better understanding of writing, what it is, and what it does. As Victor Vitanza says, "Instead of liberating rhetoric, there can/should/ought to be rhetorics of resistance" (169).

If her ideas about war, peace, and propaganda could be distilled to a single statement, it might be that a ubiquitous political propaganda that preys on the public fear of a common national threat disseminated by an uncritical press with the intent to control, coerce, and subjugate the populace not only is antithetical to a participatory democracy but also destroys the possibility of international comity. Democratic debate and dialogue, Addams believed, must replace the one-way communication and fear-mongering in time of war. Dialogue will lead not only to a more informed citizenry but also to a shared democracy that benefits the many, rather than to a managed democracy that benefits only the elite few. Addams hoped that the people of every country would learn how to identify and how to resist a rhetoric of control and replace it with an alternative democratic rhetoric of cooperation and compassion. Her warnings about the destructive power of propaganda are clearly avant-garde and as relevant today as they were a century ago as we continue to examine and question political rhetoric backed by a complicit media that justifies America's presence and continued involvement in foreign wars.

Notes

1. Bourne wrote "Twilight of Idols" and "The War and the Intellectuals" in which he criticized the complicity of American intellectuals in the war spirit. Addams also blamed elites such as intellectuals, editors, professors, and religious leaders for "energetically pushing forward the war against the hesitation and dim perception of the mass of people" (*Peace and Bread* 37).

2. In 1913 the American press was still balanced between an antiwar press that published antiwar sentiment and antiwar cartoons and what Addams identified as the "armor-plated press" that advocated for war. By 1915 the balance had disappeared.

3. While World War I popularized American interest in propaganda analysis, it was actually the muckrakers at the beginning of the century who sounded the first alarm of the destructive use of propaganda to control mass opinion (Sproule, *Propaganda and Democracy* 22). Addams would have

been familiar with Ray Stannard Baker, a muckraker, who exposed in his article "How Railroads Make Public Opinion" the way railroad corporations used the press to influence public opinion to defeat railroad regulation legislation. Addams intervened as an arbitrator for Pullman workers in the Pullman Strike of 1894. She gave a speech in 1896 titled "A Modern Lear" on the strike and its ethical lessons.

Works Cited

The abbreviation *JAPP* is used throughout the Works Cited as shorthand for Mary Lynn McCree Bryan, ed., *The Jane Addams Papers Project*, Microfilming Corporation of American and University Microfilms International, 82 reels (Western Michigan University: Waldo Library, 1984–85).

Addams, Jane. "Address by Jane Addams, Chicago Auditorium, July 24, 1915." Stenographic transcription, annotation. 22 pp. *JAPP* 47:1224–45.
———. "A Conference of Neutrals." *Survey* 35 (22 January 1916): 495. Print.
———. "Factors in Continuing the War." *Women at The Hague*. New York: Macmillan, 1915. 82–98. Print.
———. "Is the Peace Movement a Failure?" *Ladies' Home Journal* 31 (November 1914): 5. *JAPP* 47:1083.
———. *The Long Road of Woman's Memory*. 1916. Intro. Charlene Haddock Seigfried. Urbana: U of Illinois P, 2002. Print.
———. "A Modern Lear." *Survey* 29.5 (2 November 1912): 131–37. Print.
———. *Newer Ideals of Peace*. New York: Macmillan, 1907. Print.
———. "Patriotism and Pacifists in War Time." *City Club [of Chicago] Bulletin* 10 (16 June 1917): 184–90. *JAPP* 47:1543–49.
———. *Peace and Bread in Time of War*. 1922. Ed. Katherine Joslin. Urbana: U of Illinois P, 2002. Print.
———. "Peace and the Press." *Independent* 84 (11 October 1915): 55–56. *JAPP* 47:1262–63.
———. "Peace on Earth." *Ladies' Home Journal* 30 (December 1913): 27. Print.
———. "The Progressive's Dilemma: The New Party." *American Magazine* 75 (1912): 12–14. *JAPP* 47:608–10.
———. "A Protest against Preparedness: A Letter to President Wilson." *The Commoner* 15 (1915): 6. Print.
———. "The Reaction of a Simple Woman to Trade Union Propaganda." *Survey* 36 (1 July 1916): 364–66. *JAPP* 47:1362–64.

———. "The Revolt against War." *Survey* 34.16 (17 July 1915): 355–59. *JAPP* 47:1218–22.

———. *The Second Twenty Years at Hull-House.* New York: Macmillan, 1930. Print.

———. "Statement [on preparedness] of Miss Jane Addams, of Chicago, Ill., Representing the Woman's Peace Party." *To Increase the Efficiency of the Military Establishment of the United States.* U.S. Congress, House Committee on Military Affairs, Hearing before the Committee on Military Affairs, January 13, 1916, pp. 3–15. 64th Cong., 1st sess., 1916. Washington, D.C.: GPO, 1916. *JAPP* 47:1299–311.

———."Tolstoy and the Russian Soldiers." *New Republic* 12 (29 September 1917): 240–42. *JAPP* 47:1564–66.

———. *Twenty Years at Hull-House.* New York: Macmillan, 1910. Print.

———. "What War Is Destroying." *Advocate of Peace* 77 (1915): 64–65. Print.

Addams, Jane, Emily Greene Balch, and Alice Hamilton. *Women at The Hague.* New York: Macmillan, 1915. Print.

Albig, William. *Public Opinion.* New York: McGraw-Hill, 1939. Print.

Alonso, Harriet Hyman. *Peace as a Woman's Issue: A History of the U.S. Movement for World Peace and Women's Rights.* New York: Syracuse UP, 1993. Print.

Baker, Ray Stannard. "How Railroads Make Public Opinion." *McClure's Magazine* 26.5 (1906): 535–49. Print.

The Commission of Inquiry, the Interchurch World Movement. *Report on the Steel Strike of 1919.* New York: Harcourt, Brace and Howe, 1920. Print.

Bourne, Randolph. "Twilight of Idols." 1917. *The World of Randolph Bourne.* Ed. L. Schlissel. New York: Dutton, 1965. 191–203. Print.

———. "The War and the Intellectuals." June 1917. *War and the Intellectuals: Essays, 1915–1919.* Ed. Carl Resek. New York: Harper and Row, 1964. 3–14. Print.

Bryan, Mary Lynn McCree, ed. *The Jane Addams Papers Project* [*JAPP*]. Microfilming Corporation of American and University Microfilms International, 82 reels. Western Michigan University: Waldo Library, 1984–85.

Clifford, John. "The Subject in Discourse." *Contending with Words: Composition and Rhetoric in a Postmodern Age.* Ed. Patricia Harkin and John Schilb. New York: MLA, 1991. 38–51. Print.

Davis, Allen F. *American Heroine: The Life and Legend of Jane Addams.* New York: Oxford UP, 1973. Print.

Dewey, John. *The Public and Its Problems.* 1927. Chicago: Swallow, 1954. Print.

Dobrin, Sidney I. *Postcomposition*. Carbondale: Southern Illinois UP, 2011. Print.

Doob, Leonard W. *Propaganda: Its Psychology and Technique*. New York: Henry Holt, 1935. Print.

Farrell, John. *Beloved Lady: A History of Jane Addams' Ideas on Reform and Peace*. Baltimore: Johns Hopkins UP, 1967. Print.

Fischer, Marilyn, and Judy D. Whipps, eds. *Writings on Peace: Jane Addams*. London: Continuum Intl., 2005. Print.

Foster, Carrie A. *The Women and the Warriors: The U.S. Section of the Women's International League for Peace and Freedom, 1915–1946*. New York: Syracuse UP, 1995. Print.

Hamington, Maurice. "Jane Addams." *The Stanford Encyclopedia of Philosophy*. Ed. Edward N. Zalta. Summer 2010 ed. Web. 15 August 2011.

Irwin, Will. *Propaganda and the News or What Makes You Think So?* New York: Whittlesey, 1936. Print.

"Jane Addams: A Foe of War and Need." *New York Times*. New York Times, 22 May 1935. Web. 15 August 2011.

Joslin, Katherine, ed. Introduction. *Peace and Bread in Time of War*. By Jane Addams. Urbana: U of Illinois P, 2002. ix–xxxiv. Print.

Kirsch, Gesa E., and Jacqueline J. Royster. "Feminist Rhetorical Practices: In Search of Excellence." *College Composition and Communication* 61.4 (2010): 640–72. Print.

Lyotard, Jean-François. *The Postmodern Condition: A Report on Knowledge*. Trans. Geoff Bennington and Brian Massumi. Minneapolis: U of Minnesota P, 1984. Print.

Lyotard, Jean-François, and Jean-Loup Thébaud. *Just Gaming*. Trans. Wlad Godzich. Minneapolis: U of Minnesota P, 1985. Print. Vol. 20 of *Theory and History of Literature*. Wlad Godzich and Jochen Schulte-Sasse, series eds. 66 vols. 1981–98.

Macmullan, Terrance. "On War as Waste: Jane Addams's Pragmatic Pacifism." *Journal of Speculative Philosophy* 15.2 (2001): 86–104. Print.

Marshall, Edward. "War's Debasement of Women." *New York Times* 2 May 1915, sec. 5: 3–4. *JAPP* 47:1164–66.

McMillan, Gloria. "Keeping the Conversation Going: Jane Addams' Rhetorical Strategies in 'A Modern Lear.'" *Rhetoric Society Quarterly* 32.3 (2002): 61–75. Print.

Proceedings of the National Arbitration and Peace Congress, New York, April 14th–17th, 1907. Ed. Charles H. Levermore. New York: American Peace Congress, 1907. 106–10, 213–16. Print.

Propaganda and Mass Persuasion: A Historical Encyclopedia, 1500 to the Present. Ed. Nicholas J. Cull, David Culbert, and David Welch. Santa Barbara: ABC-CLIO, 2003. Print.

Seigfried, Charlene Haddock, ed. Introduction. *Democracy and Social Ethics.* By Jane Addams. Urbana: U of Illinois P, 2002. ix–xxxviii. Print.

Sproule, Michael J. *Propaganda and Democracy: The American Experience of Media and Mass Persuasion.* Cambridge: Cambridge UP, 1997. Print.

———. "Social Responses to Twentieth-Century Propaganda." *Propaganda: A Pluralistic Perspective.* Ed. Ted J. Smith. New York: Praeger, 1989. 5–22. Print.

Vitanza, Victor J. "Three Countertheses: Or, a Critical In(ter)vention into Composition Theories and Pedagogies." *Contending with Words: Composition and Rhetoric in a Postmodern Age.* Ed. Patricia Harkin and John Schilb. New York: MLA, 1991. 139–72. Print.

THE PSYCHOLOGICAL POWER OF PROPAGANDA: FROM PSYCHOANALYSIS TO KENNETH BURKE

GAE LYN HENDERSON

> Recently the newspapers in this country have carried stories that make it appear that a large segment of the scientific world is in a disagreement with the government's nuclear testing program in regard to the harmful effect of fallout resulting from atomic explosives.... The President has questioned these reports . . . as he has said, it is not impossible to suppose that some of the "scare" stories are Communist inspired. —Senator George Malone (R-Nev.), 12 September 1957, in Richard L. Miller, *Under the Cloud*

War propaganda became a staple of the American economy during the twentieth century. One brilliant rhetorician, philosopher, and literary critic, Kenneth Burke, observed during his lifespan (1897–1993) the propaganda battle that justified both world wars and its evolution during the Cold War with resultant tragic nuclear testing. During the Great Depression, with other artists, writers, and activists concerned they were experiencing the failure of capitalism, Burke suggested that the propaganda battle might well be taken up by progressives to propose alternatives to capitalism—new social orders that might mitigate human suffering. But war propaganda trumped experimental, socialist, and revolutionary attempts at change. The United States recovered from the Depression and continued to sustain itself economically through military/defense industries; thus, government and capitalist interests became tightly interwoven in the production and dissemination of capitalist/war propaganda. As a witness to this history, Burke offers an intriguing contribution to propaganda theory because, although he makes a complex nuanced case for using propaganda, he also, repeatedly, shows how and why propaganda can be dangerous and, most important, how it can be resisted. For Burke, language always is symbolic action; his writings therefore intervene, protest, and fight against obfuscating, oversimplifying discourse motivated by capitalism and warmongering.

At the same time, Burke's formalist analyses locate him as a New Critic. Yet against notions of a "pure" art that exists for its own (transcendent) sake, Burke sees art and literature as sociologically functional, even, at times, propagandistic. Questions that motivate Burke may also trouble his readers: Can art effect social change without being propaganda? When (if ever) should art be deployed as propaganda? And if propaganda is widely persuasive, how can it be resisted? Burke ultimately shows that propaganda works because of the way the "symbol-using animal" processes stimuli (*Language* 3). He both responds to Sigmund Freud's psychoanalytic theory and anticipates contemporary neuroscience, analyzing various interpretive strategies we use to make sense of information. He also explains the human tendencies to identify and divide, to develop psychological allegiances and make preconceived judgments.

By closely reading excerpts from Burke's work, such as "Literature as Equipment for Living," "The Nature of Art under Capitalism," "The Rhetoric of Hitler's 'Battle,'" and *A Rhetoric of Motives*, we learn about the psychological power of structure/form in creating expectations, the hortatory functions of art in a capitalist system, the powerful techniques that Adolf Hitler used to scapegoat Jews, and Burke's imperative that citizens examine propaganda closely and particularly question government war and weapons policy. Burke's heuristics can help us directly counter and question policies shored up by deceptive propaganda, such as the decisions surrounding Cold War nuclear proliferation and testing that exposed millions to deadly radiation.

BURKE'S PSYCHOANALYTIC PRECURSORS: LE BON AND FREUD ON FOLLOWING

Burke's insights about the relationship between psychology and rhetoric emerge from the challenge psychoanalysis presented at the beginning of the twentieth century to previous notions of a unitary Cartesian self. Brent Robbins finds it telling that Freud's work emerged simultaneously with Edmund Husserl's concept of "life world" and Ludwig Wittgenstein's "everyday language games" (par. 20). Robbins argues, "Like phenomenology and the linguistic tradition, psychoanalysis can be understood as a movement toward returning the human being to the world and to language, which . . . are deeply intertwined" (par. 20). In 1895, French psychologist Gustave Le Bon's *La Psychologie des Foules* (*The Crowd: A Study of the Popular Mind*) warned that civilization was being dangerously transformed by the power of the masses. Le Bon not only anticipated how twentieth-century mass movements would instigate revolution and world wars but also provided a propaganda manual later studied by both Benito Mussolini and Hitler. Le Bon's work prompted Freud's 1921 *Massenpsychologie und Ich-Analyse* (*Group Psychology and the Analysis of the Ego*). Freud provocatively labeled Le Bon's text as "deservedly famous" while finding fault with its lack of depth (6). Le Bon did not present data or substantiate his theories about group behavior beyond reference to historical examples. Playing the role of anthropologist, Le Bon surveyed crowd behavior and observed its irrational and hypnotically motivated character, particularly the group tendency to rely on prestigious and charismatic leaders. Freud went a step further in explicating the psychic roots of followership and posing its unconscious and libidinal origins.

Le Bon specifies that he refers not only to a literal crowd but to a psychological one. While he does not clearly define the unconscious, he nonetheless attributes the crowd's behavior to its function—the unconscious simply exists as unintelligent mind. Group situations release instincts, normally held in check, and thus the sense of individual responsibility disappears (30). Further, Le Bon notes that ideas and emotions spread quickly, with contagious enthusiasm (30): "As soon as a few individuals are gathered together they constitute a crowd, and, though, they should be distinguished men of learning . . . the faculty of observation and the critical spirit possessed by each of them individually at once disappears" (43). Individual identity seems lost as the members of the group become subject to hypnotic suggestion (31). In his critique, Freud points out that although Le Bon relies heavily on the notion of group hypnosis, he fails to mention "the hypnotist" (12). Freud explains, "When a hypnotist gives the command to sleep, which is often done at the beginning of hypnosis, he is putting himself in the place of the subject's parents" (75). The leader of the crowd represents the "dreaded primal father" (76). Freud argues that "the group still wishes to be governed by unrestricted force; it has an extreme passion for authority; in Le Bon's phrase, it has a thirst for obedience" (76).

Even though Le Bon does not use the word "hypnotist," *The Crowd* explicates the skill of effective crowd control. Leaders employ three primary influential techniques: "affirmation, repetition, and contagion" (124). Leaders must affirm, repeat, and disseminate catchphrases and images because "a crowd thinks in images, and the image itself immediately calls up a series of other images, having no logical connection with the first" (41). Thus, the crowd is subject to mass hallucination. Thirty-eight years later, in *Mein Kampf*, Hitler echoes these principles: "The receptivity of the great masses is very limited, their intelligence is small, but their power of forgetting is enormous. . . . All effective propaganda must be limited to a very few points and must harp on these in slogans until the last member of the public understands" (180–81).

Although Hitler is viewed as an ingenious autodidact, Le Bon makes the intriguing point that a successful leader may be better off without remarkable intelligence: "By showing how complex things are, by allowing of explanation and promoting comprehension, intelligence always . . . blunts . . . that intensity and violence of conviction needful for apostles. The great leaders of crowds of all ages . . . have been of lamentably narrow intellect" (194). Perhaps Le Bon's analysis helped educate Hitler about the advantage of gross oversimplification. According to Hitler,

> The function of propaganda is . . . not to weigh and ponder the rights of different people . . . not to make an objective study of the truth . . . and then set it before the masses with academic fairness. . . . As soon as our own propaganda admits so much as a glimmer of right on the other side, the foundation for doubt in our own right has been laid. (182–83)

Hitler's authoritarian demand here brings to mind Le Bon's analysis of why followers follow. Le Bon believes the leader's prestige overwhelms the crowd: prestige is a "domination [that] entirely paralyses our critical faculty, and fills our soul with astonishment and respect" (130).

Freud, however, probes deeper into the issue of a leader's charismatic attraction. His theory (now common knowledge) is that originary identification results from the child's "special interest" in the parental figure, for example the wish to become the father. At the same time, this wish is complicated by the desire for union with the mother. Freud proffers the example of a young girl who identifies with, or adopts, a symptom of her mother's, such as a cough. This represents psychically the guilty "realization . . . 'You wanted to be your mother, and now you *are*—anyhow so far as your sufferings'" (48).

Freud lists three steps of identification: the subject becomes emotion-ally attached to an object, the object becomes a surrogate for a libidinal attachment, and, finally, identification transfers to other people who seem to share a quality in common with the object (50). In this third instance, "the identification leaves entirely out of account any object-relation to the person who is being copied" (49). Freud's subsequent example makes his abstractions more concrete. He imagines a girl in a boarding school who receives a letter that provokes her into a jealous, hysterical rage: "Then some of her friends who know about it will catch the fit. . . . The other girls would like to have a secret love affair too, and under the influence of a sense of guilt they also accept the suffering involved in it" (49). Freud does not discuss the inherent textuality of this example.[1] Tellingly, the very source of the secret love, the jealousy, the hysterical reaction, and the object-relations identification is the letter.

The fact that identification occurs through the letter, be it word, lan-guage, or symbol system, is the key realization with which Burke, and others such as Jacques Lacan, complicates Freud's definition. For Burke, identification is rhetorical, a property of language. The human being, in terrible realization of its separateness, tries to connect with one or more others through communication. Burkean identification, a concept elabo-rated in his *Rhetoric of Motives*, becomes, in James Comas's view, "argu-ably, the most profound reconceptualization of rhetoric since the classical tradition" (518).[2] Language's inherent rhetoricity always encourages us either to identify with another (person/interlocutor/group) or to discover points of difference. Burke acknowledges the psychoanalytic realization that identification occurs because of unconscious forces beyond our con-trol, but, in addition, through what he names the rhetorical "Wrangle," we continually and consciously analyze, argue about, and rewrite the pa-rameters of our persuasion: "*Rhetoric* must lead us through the Scramble, the Wrangle of the Market Place, the flurries and flare-ups of the Human Barnyard, the Give and Take, the wavering line of pressure and counter-pressure, the Logomachy, the onus of ownership, the Wars of Nerves, the War" (*Rhetoric* 23). By reconceiving rhetoric (and propaganda) through the lens of identification, Burke (1) shows the socialization process through which persuasion occurs, (2) reveals the possibility of multilayered, de-ceptive, and "cunning" strategies that characterize motivated rhetorical performance, and (3) disrupts what otherwise might be an unconscious, inevitable identification/division process and theorizes the possibility of change (36).

PROPAGANDA IN A CAPITALIST SYSTEM:
DESIRING "TINNY THINGS"

The term *propaganda* shows up in Burke's work repeatedly,[3] but his broad examination of language, philosophy, art, and the complicated revisioning of rhetoric that Comas describes locates the notion of propaganda in a large context. Burke is historically viewed as one of the founders of New Criticism. As such, his obituary in the *New York Times* in 1993 reported that Burke "wrote that art and the artist must take priority over politics" and yet followed immediately with "[he wrote] that art should have a 'hortatory function' that issues a call to action" (Lyons). Surely even a casual reader might see a direct conflict between the two clauses: if art has a responsibility to change the world and elicit action, then clearly such action politicizes art. We can locate Burke's ultimate critique of propaganda, as discourse that oversimplifies and obfuscates, in this apparent conflict and as a creative and evolving response to the twentieth century's politically sponsored death of millions of human beings and the undeniable suffering of many more.[4]

European nationalism, imperialism, and militarism in the early twentieth century put America into large-scale conflict in World War I. The war was marketed to "Make the World Safe for Democracy" by the U.S. Committee on Public Information. A member of that committee, Edward Bernays, authored in 1928 a how-to manual, *Propaganda*, derived from Freudian theory. Bernays, nephew of Sigmund Freud and considered the founder of the public relations industry in the United States, asks, "If we understand the mechanism and motives of the group mind, is it not possible to control and regiment the masses according to our will without their knowing about it?" (71). His answer is a resounding yes. Bernays draws on both Le Bon and Freud to show how people act based on unconscious desires: "Man's thoughts and actions are compensatory substitutes for desires . . . [he feels] obliged to suppress" (75).

Not all audiences appreciated Bernays's unabashed capitalist apologetics. Burke satirizes Bernays's "How to Restore Public Confidence in Business and Finance" in an unpublished manuscript, "Principles of Wise Spending."[5] Burke's speaker, J. Krock Uphander, flatters his audience, a convention of "America's leading financiers and industrialists," as "princes . . . the true rulers of the modern State . . . risen to their position of eminence because of the law of the *survival of the fittest*. America's elite" (1). Uphander explains that the "Bernays man," or public relations counsel, takes a role historically relegated to clergy, teaching illiterate "serfs" their place in society to retain power for the nobility (6). But today a problem exists: "with the spread of education, our present illiterates can read," resulting in the necessity for "symbol specialists" who use print to influence the public (6). Uphander cites Bernays's advice that business should follow the "great political dictators" who "manipulate the minds of their citizenry" (8). Although the Depression has turned public opinion against business, the Bernays man can orchestrate an "epic" pro-business campaign utilizing (in Bernays's own words) "publicists, economists, leaders in research, the heads of great educational institutions" (qtd. in Burke, "Principles" 9). Uphander further advises executives to donate to colleges, noting that educators will be well served by the "genius of the financial endowments," not thereby bribed, of course, but simply "enlisted" by "*loyalty,*—for no loyal man would bite the hand that feeds him" (10). Uphander notes that, fortunately, even the Supreme Court is "sympathetic"—again, not because they have been bought but because of "the solidarity between your interests and their interests . . . as lawyers of your corporations" (11). Although the public cannot all become "happy corporation lawyers," Uphander promises to "systematize the educative process, making it work day and night for you" (11). The public relations counsel will help people understand that economic recovery has already been achieved: "The clear fact of recovery is hidden from their blunt discernment by the mere cultural lag of eleven or twelve million unemployed" (11). Burke's parody seems even more applicable today given corporate influence on government and economic policy. Burke's biting sarcasm toward Bernays's ingratiating posture, proposal to influence education/justice systems, and uncritical reliance on dictators' propaganda techniques provides just one example of his larger critique of American capitalism.

If propaganda were an instrumental tool that could be used equally well to sell both war and cigarettes (as Bernays's after-the-war mass marketing achieved), and if the "masses" were an unconscious "herd" virtually ignorant of the engineering of their enlistment in and/or purchase of these various means of hastening quick or slow death, then propaganda perhaps should also be used as a tool by those whose education or experience allow them to see through nefarious manipulations and who want to fight repressive power. Such was the sentiment of Burke's contemporary W. E. B. Du Bois, African American writer and activist who pronounced in 1926, "All Art is propaganda" (573). Du Bois insisted, in a pre–civil rights era, that when the descendants of slaves continue to be repressed and discriminated against in a country that asserts its citizens' equality and freedom, art must stand for change if it is to justify its own existence.

In *Kenneth Burke in the 1930s*, Ann George and Jack Selzer explain how Burke negotiated his way between artistic communities with opposing views. Similarly to Du Bois, a number of intellectuals during the Depression adopted socialist or communist identities as they urgently tried to remediate the suffering of their world. They felt a moral duty to help those who were losing everything they had, even starving. These revolutionaries believed that art must be focused on specific proletarian values—art must expose the suffering of the working class and actively recruit people toward change, if not revolution. Other thinkers held to long-established notions that art existed in a realm removed from societal struggle. During this period, various New Critics like John Crowe Ransom and I. A. Richards wrote about art for its own sake, as universal, as respite away from societal trouble, as transcending time. New Critics focused their study on the multiple meanings, ambiguities, and yet unity of a work of literature or art (George and Selzer 16–45). In his 1935 speech to the American Writers' Congress, Kenneth Burke complicates the issue:

> The complete propagandist, it seems to me, would take an interest in as many imaginative, aesthetic, and speculative fields as he can handle.... The writer's best contribution to the revolutionary cause is implicit. If he shows a keen interest in every manifestation of our cultural development, and at the same time gives a clear indication as to where his sympathies lie, this seems to be the most effective long-pull contribution to propaganda he can make. (qtd. in George and Selzer 18)

Here Burke voices a New Critical aesthetic, arguing for implicit rather than explicit critique, while at the same time offering instruction on propaganda. He further offers his famous advice that Americans would not respond to Marxist labels: call them "the people," he argued, rather than "workers" if you want to enlist their allegiance. Reactions to the speech were mixed because many expected more straightforward Marxist oratory rather than lessons in rhetoric. According to Gregory Clark, "Burke was doing more than lecturing in rhetorical tactics. He was attempting to educate this secessionist element of the American public in their need to collaborate with the many very different others who were engaged in the project of maintaining a shareable concept of national community" (80). In essence, he was addressing a larger audience than those in the room. George and Selzer detail the inherent rhetoricity of his motives: "Burke is often depicted as some sort of inspired genius set apart from society, the brilliant but eccentric hermit of remote Andover farm. . . . The evidence indicates a very different Burke, a highly social Burke who conceived his ideas while in conversation and congress with any number of interesting intellectual circles" (29). Thus George and Selzer mirror Burke's typifying move of undercutting binary oppositions, problematizing attempts to define Burke as either Marxist or New Critic, as well as attempts to resolve the implied opposition between art for social change and art as aesthetics. "Burke proposed to recapture and reassert an aesthetic attitude, separate from the practical frame, separate from the Marxist economic critique. . . . The ultimate goal, he suggests, is not to create a system in which everyone has access to unlimited commodities but rather to create a system in which people do not so crave 'tinny things'" (83). Burke's critique of capitalism, then, is not only that it prevents "the people" from fair access to material goods but also that it constantly reinforces and stimulates their desires for those objects. While some voices in several communities saw him as a traitor to their cause, Burke embraced the complexity of conflicting positions, his continuing committed critique of materialism, and his value for the aesthetic. As Clayton Lewis puts it, in "all of Burke's pairs, each term shares identities with, and is divided from, its opposite" (371). Burke tolerated ambiguities, saw contraries as productive, found meaning in the tension of the opposites, and negotiated ways in which one theory showed evidence for the other.

Burke's definition of propaganda is not simple, nor is it isolated from his understanding of other rhetorical strategies. His assessment and critique of propaganda evolves over time and is complicated by the values and context in which it is deployed. To better see that evolution, it is helpful to examine some of his major arguments.

LITERARY FORM: CREATING APPETITES FOR "SUCCESS"

Perhaps a beginning question to consider is how Burke's theory of literary form, articulated in *Counter-Statement* and later developed in *The Philosophy of Literary Form*, may add to our understanding of propaganda. *Counter-Statement*, Jack Selzer explains, represents Burke's critical engagement with modernist views on art and with the Greenwich Village literary milieu of the World War I years that preceded the Great Depression (19). Selzer describes "Psychology and Form," one of the book's key essays: Burke "reconceives form such that it is far less a static textual feature and far more a dynamic act of cooperation among writer, reader, and text" (26) and asserts his oft-quoted prescription "Form is the creation of an appetite in the mind of the auditor, and the adequate satisfying of that appetite" (*Counter-Statement* 31). In other words, the structural elements of a literary text, or any text, predispose readers to at least unconsciously predict or anticipate a particular resolution. Readers' expectations are psychologically aroused for the purpose of, to use a Burkean/Pascalian phrase, "directing the intention" (*Language* 43).[6]

A clear example of this process shows up in Burke's later essay "Literature as Equipment for Living." Here the New Critic argues implicitly *against* a purely art-for-art's-sake aesthetic by arguing explicitly *for* art's inherent sociological import: "I am simply proposing, in the social sphere, a method of classification with reference to *strategies*" (261). He shows that writing across genres, from the clichéd proverb to Shakespearean tragedy, shares sociological, strategic functions. To illustrate, Burke challenges the "easy consolation" of "inspirational literature," a genre popular not only in the 1920s but also today (258). He suggests that people dealing with the "confusion" of modern life are primed for reassurance and comfort: "People are only too willing to 'meet a man halfway' who will *play down* the realistic naming of our situation and *play up* such strategies as make solace cheap" (258). Faced with modern realities of uncertainty, fear, pain, and poverty, people understandably gravitate toward formulas for faith, optimism, health, and success. They want to believe. When Burke cites the title "How to Buy Friends and Bamboozle Oneself and Other People," he of course aims at Dale Carnegie's best-selling 1937 guide for successful sales techniques and public speaking (258).

Burke analyzes what we might label (in New Age parlance) as inspirational literature's "laws of attraction," its compelling magnetism that preys upon our human need for hope. In a Marxist vein, he suggests that the text itself, the material object, structures the encounter with "solace." Solace becomes the desire elicited by and embedded in the text, desire for the possibility of relief, for illusion that transcends what is:

I'll wager that, in by far the great majority of cases, such readers make no serious attempt to apply the book's recipes. The lure of the book resides in the fact that the reader, while reading it, is then living in the aura of success. What he wants is *easy* success; and he gets it in symbolic form by the mere reading itself. To attempt applying such stuff in real life would be very difficult, full of many disillusioning problems. (258)

The success book's literary form, its structure, creates its own reality, or perhaps more accurately its own *illusion*, of expected bliss. The widespread appeal of the promised solutions for humanity's ills makes for an "adequate satisfying of that appetite" in its readers, for at least as long as the extravagant reading experience lasts. In the self-help manual (or in capitalist-inspired propaganda), the literary form itself, irrespective of content, may provoke the appetite for financial success and promise its ultimate satisfaction.

Burke repeatedly reminds us that American mass-mediated capitalism is reinforced and reproduced in both commercial and literary texts: "For what is our advertising, what is our 'success' fiction in the average commercial magazine, what are our cinematic representations of the 'good life,' but a vast method of determining the criteria of a nation, and thus its conduct, by the assistance of art?" (*Counter-Statement* 90). Advertising, movies, and "success fiction" repeatedly create and reinforce desires for wealth. They further inculcate the belief that our highly competitive system provides a means to satisfy those desires. Later, in "The Nature of Art under Capitalism," Burke makes the case for an artistic counterargument: "It seems that under conditions of competitive capitalism there must necessarily be a large *corrective* or *propaganda* element in art" (276). Art should embody a "hortatory function, an educational element of suasion or inducement; it must be partially *forensic*. Such a quality we consider to be the essential work of propaganda. Hence we feel that the moral breach arising from [capitalist] vitiation of the work-patterns calls for a propaganda art" (277). In the same essay, though, Burke acknowledges the comforting function that certain genres have for people demoralized by inequities and who struggle to avoid despair. He comments that "the literature of sentimentality," while "annoying and self-deceptive" to the "hardened 'intellectual'" (277), yet can be functionally helpful. While intellectuals critique the capitalist system, the fact remains that change is slow: "Along with our efforts to alter it [capitalism], must go the demand for an imaginative equipment that helps to make it tolerable. . . . For this reason the great popular comedians or handsome movie stars are rightly the idols of the people" (277). Such sentimental art makes life endurable and may therefore be tolerated as long as at the same time we work to change social injustice. But he further advocates that a more thoughtful nuanced art could better serve the same purpose: "One might wish more of our pretentious authors were attempting to do the same thing more pretentiously" (277). Finally, furthering his theme of seeing sociological and strategic value even in the sentimental text, he concludes the essay with a sound spanking of "proletariat" or Marxist literature. It fails as (good) propaganda because it "shows us so little of the qualities in mankind worth saving" (277–78). Such "harsh" literature, in its "sheer dismalness," also fails aesthetically: "Too often, alas, it serves as a mere device whereby the neuroses of the decaying bourgeois structure are simply transferred to the symbols of workingmen. Perhaps more of Dickens is needed, even at the risk of excessive tearfulness" (278). Burke recognizes that if the goal of art is to improve the human condition, perhaps some positive messages may be *required*. Purporting a general attitude of "sheer dismalness" may not contribute to desperately needed social change.

It is crucial to understand that Burke in defining art in terms of propaganda is not devaluing art; rather, he is contextualizing it as a purposeful, rhetorical, social action.[7] As much as some critics and readers may want to keep art locked in an ivory tower, removed from life's battles, Burke insists that as we attempt to keep it so removed, we merely wall ourselves up to support the status quo, to resist change: "Since pure art makes for acceptance, it tends to become a social menace in so far as it assists us in tolerating the intolerable" (276). Art for art's sake prefers to see power remain unchallenged, but perhaps more urgent, those who want to change the world may want to take advantage of the rhetorical power of art. Art is rhetorical (and potentially propagandistic) because it ultimately serves either a conservative or a progressive function. But this functional definition of the rhetorical and persuasive power of art does not preclude the critic from evaluating some rhetorics as preferable to others. Indeed, the critic's unremitting responsibility is to examine and respond to the value-ridden nature of not only art but all texts. The critical reader determines whether any propaganda, artistic or instrumental, remains unexamined and therefore dangerous.

PROPAGANDA ANALYSIS: FEARING
AND DESTROYING THE DEVIL

In 1939, Burke demonstrated this careful analysis in "The Rhetoric of Hitler's 'Battle,'" his response to *Mein Kampf*. He addresses looming anxieties of the World War II era: Who is this Adolf Hitler? What is the source of his raw power? Is he a sincere fanatic or a seasoned manipulator? Are Americans at risk of being similarly persuaded, controlled, even duped? These questions necessitate a careful examination of Hitler's text. Burke points out that the popular response of naming the author a monster is sure to win popular agreement but does little else: "If the reviewer but knocks off a few adverse attitudinizings and calls it a day, with a guaranty in advance that his article will have a favorable reception among the decent members of our population, he is contributing more to our gratification than to our enlightenment" (164). The questions for Burke then become psychological: What can we learn from *Mein Kampf*? What desires are elicited? "Let us try also to discover what kind of 'medicine' this medicine-man has concocted, that we may know, with greater accuracy, exactly what to guard against, if we are to forestall the concocting of similar medicine in America" (164). Hitler-as-medicine-man offers to cure cultural ills. He painfully exposes deep injuries, gaping wounds, but at the same time claims the secret of remedy. Thus, Burke shows the Freudian underpinnings and implications of Hitler's prison narrative/political manifesto. Pain and desire intermingle in the text; Hitler's propaganda becomes the vehicle for educing desire and promising its fulfillment.

Burke explores how oversimplification strategically constructs a false unity. Hitler carefully paints an enemy, a "single enemy" (qtd. in Burke, "Rhetoric" 166). "It is part of the genius of a great leader," Hitler professes, "to make adversaries of different fields appear as always belonging to one category only, because to weak and unstable characters the knowledge that there are various enemies will lead only too easily to incipient doubts as to their own cause" (166). Hitler argues that various antagonists with multiple reasons for opposition create complications that might weaken "the fighting will" and dangerously promote "objectivity" or the complicating "question . . . whether actually all the others are wrong and their own nation or their own movement alone is right" (166). Burke, in his "Prologue in Heaven," does exactly the opposite as the Lord repeatedly reminds Satan, "It's more complicated than that" (277).

For Hitler, the unifying figure that summons up fear and loathing, his devil, is the "international Jew" (qtd. in Burke, "Rhetoric" 166). Burke explains that the *idea* of the enemy, the constructed-devil, becomes material, literal: "So, we have, as unifying step No. 1, the international devil materialized, in the visible, point-to-able form of people with a certain kind of 'blood,' a burlesque of contemporary neo-positivism's ideal of meaning, which insists upon a *material* reference" (167). Burke points out here that the epistemology of neopositivism, which relies on material evidence, becomes parody, a joke, as illogical and unfounded arguments solicit credibility by pointing to proof of some real-life example. Hitler, by constructing an "essentialized ... enemy," suggests not only "the cunning with which the 'Jewish plot' is being engineered" but also the danger of seduction (167). While the good leader, Hitler, provides the German people with the protection of "a dominating male" who "woos" and then "commands them," the Jew "poisons their blood by intermingling with them" (167). The sexual imagery is deliberate, Burke contends, as Hitler repeatedly associates the danger of intermarriage with Jews to societal ills of "syphilis, prostitution, incest" (167). The blatant racism works because conveniently the Aryan noble race in search of the good life is presented a Jewish scapegoat for society's dysfunctions, problems, injustice. Hitler's *Struggle* becomes the Aryan struggle.

Hitler's unifying vision of a common enemy is so powerful that it raises the question of intent: "Was his selection of the Jew, as his unifying devil-function, a purely calculating act?" (168). Burke argues that although the notion of the Jewish devil may appear to be the deliberate creation of a genius manipulator, it is in reality the likely result of visceral hatred Hitler developed from life experience: "It seems that, when Hitler went to Vienna, in a state close to total poverty, he genuinely suffered. He lived among the impoverished; and he describes his misery at the spectacle" (168). But perhaps even more revelatory, Burke sees that intellectual uncertainty became intolerable for Hitler and suggests he solved his bouts of cognitive dissonance with "rage" (168): "During this time he began his attempts at political theorizing; and his disturbance was considerably increased by the skill with which Marxists tied him into knots" (168). The notion of the patriarchal intellectual fencing match between master and student becomes nightmarish when the bested student's anger projects his own inadequacies outward. Hitler admits, "One did not know what to admire more: their glibness of tongue or their skill in lying. I gradually began to hate them" (169).

Burke notes that Hitler textually justified that hatred as grandiose religious duty: "I am acting in the sense of the Almighty Creator: *By warding off Jews I am fighting for the Lord's work*" (170, emphasis Hitler's). Rather than seeing his hatred of Jews as emotional lapse, Hitler rewrote it as the logical conclusion of his rational self. Burke is astonished that Hitler believed himself in a fight between reason and emotion, and "it was 'reason' that won! Which prompts us to note that those who attack Hitlerism as cult of the irrational should emend their statements to this extent: irrational it is, but it is carried on under the *slogan* of 'Reason'" (170–71).

In sum, Burke demonstrates "the substance of Nazi propaganda" as "endless repetition," "spectacle," a revised "world view," and at its core a "bastardization of fundamentally religious patterns of thought" (186–88). Burke shows clearly that propaganda requires critical reception or its audience may fall victim to "sheer deception" (188).

Propaganda analysis is one essential critical move, but how can individuals learn to think more critically, examine group allegiances, and apprehend complexity? Many of Burke's essays and books tackle these questions, but this chapter will take up one additional example. As previously mentioned, in *A Rhetoric of Motives*, Burke examines both the possibility of rhetorical (and social) unity and the inescapability of division. Both unity and division inhere in language and, to a large extent, structure human interaction. Barbara Biesecker comments on Burke's complex analysis of social identifications:

> In defining the social as a unity that both is and is not, Burke . . . draws the reader's attention to the fact that the social is a catachresis, a "mystery." It is a thing to which there belongs no proper referent, a "communion of estranged entities" [Burke, *Rhetoric*]. The social, which is to say the "we," is what might be called in contemporary parlance a textual chain, a "reality" woven of discontinuities and constitutive differences. (48)

Within Burke's "communion of estranged entities," humans employ rhetoric and fabricate various textual chains as they struggle with social problems, political decisions, and moral questions.

BURKE'S CITIZEN-BASED MORALITY:
CHALLENGING COLD WAR PROPAGANDA

In *A Rhetoric of Motives*, Burke explains how moral distinctions are dispersed in late capitalism. Burke notes that a "technical expert," working on weapons of destruction, for example, may believe he has no moral responsibility: "The extreme division of labor . . . [has] made dispersion the norm" (30–31). The expert is concerned only to perform his special task well; ensuing consequences are far removed from consideration. Burke finds troubling this separation of work from consequences: "The true liberal must view almost as an affront . . . [the way in which] the principles of a specialty cannot be taken on their face, simply as the motives proper to that specialty" (31). Burke further warns, "One's morality as a specialist cannot be allowed to do duty for one's morality as a citizen" (31). It is perhaps inherent in what Burke calls "symbolic action," or in the nature of language itself, that human beings cannot escape engaging in political and moral questions. According to James Kastely, this realization also marks Plato's work: "The Socratic practice of refutation argues that it is the nature of language as a formal system to implicate creatures who participate in symbolic action in political concerns, and most immediately to entangle them with problems of injustice and inadvertent injury" (6). If humans as symbol-using animals are required to confront injustice and injury, then a salient question is how to do so ethically.

Burke published the text in 1950; it reflects his keen observations of Cold War propaganda that eventually justified sustained nuclear testing. Today, Downwinders continue to lobby Congress to provide financial compensation for Cold War propaganda victims: those people who contracted cancers, suffered illness, and lost family members (and for perhaps millions who suffered such consequences unknowingly) as a result of the U.S. government deploying "over a hundred aboveground atomic tests" and, in total, over nine hundred bombs at the Nevada Test Site (Miller 8; Dickson). Burke predicted such disastrous consequences by illustrating how language inherently sets up binary oppositions that oversimplify complex realities. He identifies the theological categories built into language—good and evil—that discourage careful examination of how *facets* of evil and good can be intertwined and enmeshed. Because binary categories pervade language, often this leads to end-justifies-the-means thinking and decision making. Burke protests: "Some means are relatively purer than others. Their nature makes them better able than other means to serve the given purpose. Thus, even a blow with a fist might be considered closer to the nature of peace than a blast from a shotgun. (In general, though not in all cases)" (*Rhetoric* 155). Note how carefully Burke qualifies his generalization: "though not in all cases." He shows that choices have nuanced implications, implications that deserve serious and sustained analysis. For Burke, the act of attention becomes a moral responsibility:

> A tongue-lashing might be closer to peace than a blow; an argument closer than a tongue-lashing; a plea closer than an argument; a compliment closer than a plea, etc. This being the case, a scrupulous man will never abandon a purpose which he considers absolutely good. But he will choose the purest means available in the given situation. As with the ideal rhetoric in Aristotle, he will consider the entire range of means, and then choose the best that this particular set of circumstances permits. (155)

The arsenal built by the Soviet Union superpower created the ostensible necessity for the United States to test nuclear bombs. What was the true danger? In his comprehensive history of the nuclear disarmament movement, Lawrence Wittner cites the testimony of Anatoly Chernyaev, who during the nuclear buildup of the Cold War served as "an official in the International Department of the Central Committee of the Communist Party" (5): "The Soviet Union was not 'planning to organize or begin a nuclear war. Among our elders, there was not a single person . . . seriously preparing for a nuclear war with the United States'" (4–5). Of course, Wittner explains that the Soviets indeed did build up tremendous weaponry, legitimately concerned about matching U.S. proliferation. Power became centralized in a Soviet military-industrial complex in the same way that it did in the United States (5).

However, Downwinders, such as Mary Dickson (who lost her sister to lupus and is herself a survivor of thyroid cancer), remind us that during the Cold War we killed our own people: testing exposed thousands to radiation who died of cancer and other illness.[8] Their deaths were somehow justified as a necessary cost of deterring the enemy: "They will still say it was worth the risk, worth the price, because we won the Cold War." The devastation of nuclear testing is perfectly encapsulated in Burke's sarcastic denunciation:

> The doctrine that "the end justifies the means" becomes a mockery (as it always is when not corrected by a methodical concern with a *hierarchy* of means, and an exacting effort to choose the very best means possible to the given situation). For it can be made to justify *any* means, hence can become a mere "eulogistic covering" for means so alien to the nature of the avowed end, and so far below other means actually available, that it amounts to nothing but a blunt perverting of that end. (*Rhetoric* 155–56)

The "avowed end," protecting the American people, became horribly perverted as innocents were harmed by fallout. Richard Miller, in *Under the Cloud: The Decades of Nuclear Testing*, explains that "nuclear clouds . . . passed not only over Utah, Nevada, and Arizona, but over the entire continent. . . . Like the soldiers maneuvering in the desert, every person alive during the 1950s and early 1960s lived under the atomic cloud" (8–9).

Dickson recalled her visit in 1990 to the Soviet Union. With Russian political scientists she traveled over muddy dirt roads, in a car without working windshield wipers, to visit a major research institute; at the institute she was surprised to find they still used card catalogs rather than computers. The fearsome enemy of the Cold War appeared much less frightening than she had been led to believe growing up in the 1950s and 1960s:

> I left there crying, thinking, oh my god, this was the big threat? This country that can't pave its roads, this country that doesn't even have computers in a major research institute, where cars don't have working windshield wipers, this is what it was all about, this is why so many Americans died and got sick? It really struck me how ridiculous. . . . [We were] a large industrial-military complex out of control. It was self-perpetuating. What were they looking for that they had to test 928 bombs?[9] What more could they possibly have learned? Once something with the military gets going . . . it feeds on itself.

Dickson's assessment echoes Burke's sentiment. He is deeply concerned with the "cult of 'cold war': . . . old men are given to talk of a cold war, which younger men are potently prone to translate into talk of a 'shooting war'" (*Rhetoric* 154). Fear of war feeds development of weapons that feed the likelihood of war. On the nuclear level this has continued, Wittner reminds us, "for more than half a century," with rhetoric and action clearly juxtaposed: "Again and again, government officials have told us how fortunate we have been to have benefited from their wise leadership, a leadership devoted to fostering national security through the amassing of overwhelming military power" (ix). In reality something quite different occurred. Wittner explains that nuclear weapons policy became a campaign—for weapons buildup, for enthusiastic readiness, and for war itself: "This is not because they were particularly evil people, but because they were locked into a traditional system of national defense in a world of competing nation-states" (ix–x). It is this deadly traditional system, and its inherent rhetoricity, that Burke urges must be challenged: "Return to this suicidal association (or 'identification') if you must. But at least put it to the dissociative test . . . not imposed upon you by a dismal rhetoric of warmongering" (*Rhetoric* 154). For Burke, democracy and the freedom of humanity are threatened, not by foreign enemies, but by the way patriotism is *identified* with military buildup: "No one in the world is free so long as large sections of our population, however inattentively, are being bound by the identifying of patriotism with military boastfulness" (154). Moral citizenship, then, demands a rhetorical dismantling of the symbols that endanger freedom—Burke's "dissociative test." Rhetoric is a "spellbinder" but also offers the inherent possibility of resymbolization, reidentification, resistance, change, and choice: "Persuasion involves choice, will; it is directed to a man only insofar as he is *free*. This is good to remember, in these days of dictatorship and near-dictatorship. Only insofar as men are potentially free, must the spellbinder seek to persuade them" (50).

Many of Burke's numerous analyses, beyond the scope of this chapter, offer insight into how and why propaganda persuades, the values that may impel or constrain its use, and its definition as communication that oversimplifies and obfuscates. The larger issue for students of Burke becomes understanding not just the mechanisms of literary form, religious heuristics, or military identifications but how we, to paraphrase Burke, use terminology (language and other symbols) to reflect, select, and deflect our constructed story of reality (*Language* 45). A fascinating possibility for future research may be comparing Burke's multiple heuristics, such as notions of literary form, the dramatistic pentad, psychological identification, logology, and the terministic screen, with research on the brain. For example, Vladimir Alexandrov, in his 2007 "Literature, Literariness, and the Brain," concludes from his review of neuroscience studies that while the left hemisphere of the brain processes grammar and syntax, the right hemisphere interprets metaphor, emotion, irony, humor, and inferences and makes sentences cohere into larger paragraph-level meaning: "It is possible to hypothesize a connection between the right hemisphere's involvement in processing figurative language and its role in building non-syntactical types of global coherence" (109). Studies thus are beginning to map how the brain may be activated by slogans and other forms of propaganda into consequent states of emotion and meaning making. In a 2008 study, Vasily Klucharev, Ale Smidts, and Guillén Fernández used magnetic resonance imaging to document "left-lateralized brain activity in prefrontal and temporal cortices" and memory formation in the medial temporal lobe, showing that subjects' brains responded favorably to a product when an expert testified as to its value (par. 1). While neuroscience accumulates evidence to experimentally document the effects of persuasion in general and propaganda in particular, we may continue to rely on Burke's challenge to "bring ourselves to realize . . . just how overwhelmingly much of what we mean by 'reality' has been built up for us through nothing but our symbol systems" (*Language* 5). Burke expects that such realizations will inform our choices as citizens in a democracy and help us see through the oversimplifications that make propaganda so dangerous.

Notes

1. Neither does Freud mention the gendered implications of the incident; this omission could serve as an example of Burke's "terministic screen": people in patriarchal culture name female behavior hysterical without seemingly a realization of the significantly limited access to power that may be a viable factor in eliciting such behavior (*Language* 5).

2. Comas argues that Burkean identification radically rethinks traditional rhetoric's assumption of intentionality. "Instead, Burke argues, rhetoric should be understood in terms of 'identification,' allowing examinations of not only an audience's nonconscious identification with certain interests, but also the complexities of the rhetor's identification with the audience, including the sense of audience that the rhetor has internalized through the life-long process of socialization" (518). Comas finds this a new moralized ontology for rhetoric.

3. See two examples in *A Grammar of Motives*: Burke's discussion of how Japanese propagandists utilized "active-passive *grammar*" ("The Japanese were told they were not to think of the Japanese forces as passively suffering attack, but as actively drawing the enemy closer, so that the eventual counterblow might be more effective" [264]), and his explication of how the pentad in literature normalizes propaganda:

> The propagandistic ingredient in works like *Pilgrim's Progress* and *Robinson Crusoe* (and in general, the novel of middle class *sentiment*) could be dropped [in capitalist culture]. For the development of business had so circumscribed the concepts of practical or moral utility within monetary limits, that the original religious and moralistic vocabulary of bourgeois apologetics became more and more like a sheer Rhetorical evasion of the Grammatical realities. (267–68)

4. The definition I attribute to Burke here is based on my interpretation of his discussions of propaganda. His sense of the term as it develops in his work aligns with other major theorists: Jacques Ellul shows in his 1965 *Propaganda: The Formation of Men's Attitudes* that democracy takes on the character of totalitarian societies when propaganda becomes the means to democratic ends: "A man who lives in a democratic society and who is subjected to propaganda is being drained of the democratic content itself—of the style of democratic life, understanding of others, respect for

minorities, re-examination of his own opinions, absence of dogmatism" (256). For Ellul, propaganda is a sociological phenomenon, one rooted in the relationship between the individual and society, and must be examined and countered on that basis. In an instructive 2002 addition to propaganda discourse, *The Idea of Propaganda: A Reconstruction*, Stanley Cunningham provides a general definition of propaganda: "a cluster of properties and conditions, one of which is an uncaring attitude or disregard for genuinely informative and truthful speech acts. What most comprehensively situates propaganda, then, is not intentional or deliberate falsehoods although often enough these too are part of propaganda, but rather a mental posture or habitude of careless disregard of truth-conditions, and of choosing to ignore them" (52).

5. Drafts of this essay are located in the Kenneth Burke Archive at Pennsylvania State University. Page numbers refer to the most complete draft of the essay.

6. Blaise Pascal's critique of the Jesuit practice of "directing the intention" shows how the priests created a rationale for dueling to occur accidentally; potential participants claimed only the intention of taking a walk: "For it was perfectly proper to go for a walk; and in case one encountered an enemy bent on murder, it was perfectly proper to protect oneself by shooting in self-defense" (Burke, *Language* 45). Burke explains that the terministic screen similarly directs the "*at*tention" but unconsciously (45). The beginnings of the terministic screen appear in the notion of literary form as the reader/audience has been socialized to expect the encultured outcome of various plots or structuring devices.

7. In "Burke on Propaganda in Art," Hedengren explains that Burke favors a propaganda art if it "treats its audience as people, not pawns" (par. 2). In "Burke in/on Public and Private: Rhetoric, Propaganda, and the 'End(s)' of Humanism," Pruchnic analyzes various rhetorical "registers" Burke employs in both public and private genres that demonstrate his commitment to humanism.

8. Estimates of American lives lost during the Cold War era due to military operations and/or detainment by the Soviet Union vary from 33 to 389 ("Cold War Casualties"; "Soviets Held"). American deaths from nuclear testing are estimated at 11,000–15,000 (Edwards; Epstein). Samuel Epstein, professor emeritus of public health, reported in 2010 that the "CDC estimate of fifteen thousand deaths is too low."

9. This is the number of atomic bomb tests carried out at the Nevada Test Site during the testing years.

Works Cited

Alexandrov, Vladimir E. "Literature, Literariness, and the Brain." *Comparative Literature* 59.2 (2007): 97–118. Print.

Bernays, Edward. "How to Restore Public Confidence in Business and Finance." *Economic Forum*, Winter 1936, 273–83. Cited in *Public Relations, Edward L. Bernays and the American Scene: Annotated Bibliography of and Reference Guide to Writings by and about Edward L. Bernays from 1917–1951.* Boston: F. W. Faxon Company, 1951. Archive.org. Web. 15 May 2016.

———. *Propaganda.* 1928. New York: Ig, 2005. Print.

Biesecker, Barbara. *Addressing Postmodernity: Kenneth Burke, Rhetoric, and a Theory of Social Change.* Tuscaloosa: U of Alabama P, 1997. Print.

Burke, Kenneth. *Counter-Statement.* 1931. Berkeley: U of California P, 1968. Print.

———. *A Grammar of Motives.* 1945. Berkeley: U of California P, 1969. Print.

———. *Language as Symbolic Action: Essays on Life, Literature, and Method.* Berkeley: U of California P, 1966. Print.

———. "Literature as Equipment for Living." *The Philosophy of Literary Form: Studies in Symbolic Action.* 1941. New York: Vintage, 1957. 253–62. Print.

———. "The Nature of Art under Capitalism." *The Philosophy of Literary Form: Studies in Symbolic Action.* 1941. New York: Vintage, 1957. 271–78. Print.

———. *The Philosophy of Literary Form: Studies in Symbolic Action.* 1941. 3rd ed. Berkeley: U of California P, 1973. Print.

———. "Principles of Wise Spending." Microfilm Reel 20 (P 15), Kenneth Burke Papers (Burke-3), Special Collections Library, University Libraries, Pennsylvania State University.

———. "Prologue in Heaven." *The Rhetoric of Religion: Studies in Logology.* 1961. Berkeley: U of California P, 1970. 273–316. Print.

———. "The Rhetoric of Hitler's 'Battle.'" *The Philosophy of Literary Form: Studies in Symbolic Action.* 1941. New York: Vintage, 1957. 164–89. Print.

———. *A Rhetoric of Motives.* 1950. Berkeley: U of California P, 1969. Print.

Clark, Gregory. *Rhetorical Landscapes in America: Variations on a Theme from Kenneth Burke.* Columbia: U of South Carolina P, 2004. Print.

"Cold War Casualties." AmericanColdWarVets.org. Web. 12 May 2016.

Comas, James. "Philosophy of Rhetoric." *Encyclopedia of Rhetoric and Composition: Communication from Ancient Times to the Information Age.* Ed. Theresa Enos. New York: Garland, 1996. 515–18. Print.

Cunningham, Stanley B. *The Idea of Propaganda: A Reconstruction*. Westport, Conn.: Praeger, 2002. Print.

Dickson, Mary. Personal interview. 15 April 2007.

Du Bois, W. E. B. "Criteria of Negro Art." *The Critical Tradition: Classic Texts and Contemporary Trends*. 3rd ed. Ed. David H. Richter. Boston: Bedford/St. Martin's, 2007. 569–74. Print.

Edwards, Rob. "Nuclear Test Fall-Out Killed Thousands in US." NewScientist.com. 1 March 2002. Web. 1 July 2014.

Ellul, Jacques. *Propaganda: The Formation of Men's Attitudes*. Trans. Konrad Kellen and Jean Lerner. New York: Knopf, 1965. New York: Vintage, 1973. Print.

Epstein, Samuel. "Did the Atom Bomb Test Fallout Cause Cancer?" Huffington Post.com. 23 December 2010. Web. 11 May 2016.

Freud, Sigmund. *Group Psychology and the Analysis of the Ego*. Trans. and ed. James Strachey. New York: W. W. Norton, 1989. Print.

George, Ann, and Jack Selzer. *Kenneth Burke in the 1930s*. Columbia: U of South Carolina P, 2007. Print.

Hedengren, Mary. "Scholar's Note: Burke on Propaganda in Art." *KB Journal* 7.2 (2011). Web. 15 May 2014.

Hitler, Adolf. *Mein Kampf*. Trans. Ralph Manheim. 1962. Boston: Houghton Mifflin, 1999. Print.

Kastely, James L. *Rethinking the Rhetorical Tradition: From Plato to Postmodernism*. New Haven: Yale UP, 1997. Print.

Klucharev, Vasily, Ale Smidts, and Guillén Fernández. "Brain Mechanisms of Persuasion: How 'Expert Power' Modulates Memory and Attitudes." *Social Cognitive and Affective Neuroscience* 3.4 (2008): 353–66. Web. 15 May 2014.

Le Bon, Gustave. *The Crowd: A Study of the Popular Mind*. New York: Viking, 1960. Print.

Lewis, Clayton W. "Burke's Act in *A Rhetoric of Motives*." *College English* 46.4 (1984): 368–76. Print.

Lyons, Richard D. "Kenneth Burke, Philosopher, 96, and New Criticism Founder, Dies." *New York Times* 21 November 1993, Obituaries sec. Web. 15 May 2014.

Miller, Richard L. *Under the Cloud: The Decades of Nuclear Testing*. The Woodlands, Tex.: Two-Sixty Press, 1991. Print.

Pruchnic, Jeff. "Burke in/on Public and Private: Rhetoric, Propaganda, and the 'End(s)' of Humanism." *Burke in the Archives: Using the Past to Transform the Future of Burkean Studies*. Ed. Dana Anderson and Jessica Enoch. Columbia: U of South Carolina P, 2013. 120–42. Print.

Robbins, Brent Dean. "The Psychology-Rhetoric Relationship: A Brief Historical Sketch." MythosandLogos.com. 27 April 2010. Web. 22 July 2014.

Selzer, Jack. "Kenneth Burke among the Moderns: *Counter-Statement* as Counter Statement." *Rhetoric Society Quarterly* 26.2 (1996): 19–49. Print.

"Soviets Held U.S. POWs." *Baltimore Sun* 12 November 1992. Web. 1 July 2014.

Wittner, Lawrence S. *Toward Nuclear Abolition: A History of the World Nuclear Disarmament Movement, 1971 to the Present.* Stanford: Stanford UP, 2003. Print.

ELIZABETH BOWEN'S WAVERING ATTITUDE TOWARD WORLD WAR II PROPAGANDA

STEFANIA PORCELLI

From the moment this war began, there was, for this state, only one policy possible, neutrality.
—Eamon de Valera, 1941 speech on Irish neutrality

Neutrality is at times a graver sin than belligerence.
—Louis D. Brandeis, *Chosen People/Neutrality*

Propaganda is an all-pervasive linguistic and visual phenomenon, ubiquitous in everyday life and exploited widely in communication, political discourse, and advertisement. Over time, art also has been involved in propaganda. In a 1941 radio address, George Orwell famously affirmed that "propaganda in some form or other lurks in every book, that every work of art has a meaning and a purpose—a political, social and religious purpose—that our aesthetic judgments are always colored by our prejudices and beliefs" (126). *The Frontiers of Art and Propaganda* (from which this quotation is taken) was broadcast during the Second World War,[1] when propaganda had already acquired the status of a crucial weapon in modern warfare and when governments invested much of their effort in the "war of words."[2] This chapter investigates Anglo-Irish writer Elizabeth Bowen's insight into and involvement with propaganda through examples of her fiction and nonfiction writings focused on Ireland:[3] the espionage reports she wrote to Winston Churchill between 1940 and 1942,[4] a selection of three short stories written in the 1940s, and "Ireland," an undated, twenty-page typescript archived at the Harry Ransom Center at the University of Texas at Austin, which is an essay or probably the script for a documentary film. Bowen's ambiguity toward British propaganda and Irish neutrality in these writings may be traced to her rich dual identity. Her commitment on one hand and criticism on the other are the keys to understanding propaganda—a phenomenon that has several implications on different levels, ranging from linguistic to political to moral. Bowen's literary production and political reports show precisely the tension between the claim of independence and the necessity to commit, both on the personal and the collective level, which the dichotomized language of wartime cannot untangle.

In her World War II writings, Bowen effectively depicts war as a discursive practice as well as a material activity. However, while she barely refers to the physical activity of war, she poignantly conveys the idea that "conversations are the leading thing in this war" (*Heat of the Day* 63) and constantly refers to the propaganda campaigns carried out during the conflict, ironically demystifying their slogans. A case in point is her 1949 novel, *The Heat of the Day*, in which characters are confronted with their obligations toward the state at war—that is, with their duties as citizens, emphasized by massive rhetoric campaigns extolling comradeship and commitment. The protagonist, Stella, meets all demands of wartime propaganda, including her involvement in home-front activities. Yet, she cannot comply with the rhetoric of the ideal citizen, with the myth of comradeship, and above all with the image of the mother who is proud that her son has joined the army. The uniform he wears triggers the image of a corpse:

> Each time, at the first glance, her eyes cried out: "What are *they* doing to you?" She saw how exposed, naïve, and comically childishly slender his neck looked rearing out of the bulky battledress collar; she saw the grain of his skin harshening over face-bones not so much less fine than hers. Through his hair now stiff to the roots from cropping she perceived the bony planes of his skull. His eyes, like hers, were set in their sockets in a striking rather than lifelike way. (51, emphasis in original)

The pronoun "they" is particularly significant with respect to the language used for propaganda purposes, which usually hides an ideological conflict between "us" and "them" (van Dijk 18–19). Yet, as I will point out with regard to the short story "Unwelcome Idea," Bowen often blurs the linguistic barrier between "us" (the heroes) and "them" (the enemy). "They" refers to the propaganda producers, that is, to the governmental departments in charge of it, or to the papers that spread information and instructions to the population. Stella does not feel the sense of unity advocated by the propaganda machine: "Your 'we' is my 'they'" (*Heat of the Day* 40). Identification in a common "we" would lead only to the dissolution of her own individuality in a mass society easily manipulated.

What makes a text propaganda? One answer may be that it directly or indirectly influences human choice in current political and ideological conflicts. The meaning of the message in propaganda is clear and exists a priori, rather than being created in the text. Although propaganda may be engrafted in a variety of social and political contexts, it thrives particularly in war. War is linguistically constructed as the "just" fight for freedom by the governments that wage it or fight it, to the point that subjects are manipulated into surrendering their rights, accepting the suspension of democracy demanded by the state of exception produced by the conflict. Human lives are shaped by political propaganda, which entails the demonization of the enemy on one hand and narratives of heroism on the other. In this way, through a rhetorical twist, the "military disaster" of Dunkirk became Britons' "finest hour" in Churchill's speech of 18 June 1940 (314). Being a powerful communicative process, literature can help perpetuate narratives of heroism or, alternatively, deconstruct ongoing political discourse. In his pioneer introduction to the relations between literature and propaganda, A. P. Foulkes argues that literature has worked both as "integration propaganda" (a term borrowed from Jacques Ellul's influential study *Propaganda*), meaning a practice aimed at producing inertia or conformity, and as demystification (that is, in a subversive and questioning way), in particular during the twentieth century (Foulkes 11, 44, 56).

Writers have often offered their services as propagandists in wartime. Peter Buitenhuis's book *The Great War of Words* specifically deals with the efforts of several authors in support of the Allied cause during the First World War. In 1914, for the first time, a group of British authors met in London in order to discuss how they could contribute to the Allied effort (xv). Together they created the myth of an innocent and just Britain versus a violent, inhuman Germany. The practice was so effective that those in the rising Nazi movement, and Joseph Goebbels especially, took it as a model to imitate for their propaganda machine (Knightley 79–112, 217–41).[5]

The cases of George Orwell, Dylan Thomas, and many others clearly show that propaganda activity was a fully established practice among writers during World War II. As Heather Bryant Jordan explains, "Very soon the ministry became a magnet for those who wrote for their living" (98). The ministry she refers to is the Ministry of Information (MoI), responsible for the propaganda machine. Among the writers she mentions, however—Graham Greene, Cecil Day-Lewis, Laurie Lee, Elizabeth Bowen, John Betjeman, John Lehman—Elizabeth Bowen stands out as the only person with an Anglo-Irish background, as well as the only woman.

BETWEEN ENGLISH COMMITMENT AND IRISH NEUTRALITY

Bowen cannot be considered a propaganda writer sensu stricto, although a memorandum for a contract with Strand Film proves that she was supposed to write a script for that company,[6] which produced propaganda films for the MoI (the same company also commissioned Dylan Thomas to write a number of scripts for propaganda documentary films). The subject of the film was supposed to be the Norwegian resistance to the Nazis. Although there is no evidence in her subsequent correspondence and papers that she actually wrote the screenplay, it is certain that her work for the MoI led to the writing of a number of reports, in which Bowen compiled her impressions on Irish attitudes toward the war and commented on the language and media of British World War II propaganda.

Bowen was born in 1899 in Dublin and owned a country house in County Cork, which was one of the so-called Big Houses belonging to the Protestant Ascendancy. Married to an English educational administrator who subsequently worked for the BBC, she spent the World War II years in London, where she served as an Air Raid Precaution warden. In 1940 she volunteered her services to the MoI. Her assigned task was to assess how Irish public opinion would react if Britain were to take over Irish ports. Her literary and political production of the time offers the perspective of a writer who had a special relationship with both sides involved and can shed light on the way British propaganda and Irish censorship widened the gap between Ireland and Britain, preventing fruitful communication and fostering division instead of cooperation in the war for democracy against Hitler. Whether Bowen should be considered a spy (British) or a traitor (Irish) is a question that ignores Bowen's specific position, her hyphenated identity, and her ambiguous sense of belonging: "I am not placed: I do not qualify," she wrote toward the end of her life (*Pictures and Conversations* 35), a statement absolutely relevant to the evaluation of her work in the field of war propaganda.

British home-front propaganda had the task to sustain civilian morale by means of the press and other media, including films, radio broadcasts, pamphlets, and "weapons on the wall," as posters were sometimes called.[7]

External propaganda was instead aimed at enemy, neutral, allied, and empire countries. Bowen's political reports, as well as her short stories and novels, show that she was not only aware of the relation between information and media but also highly involved in the new environment produced by technologies of mass communication—that is, in the "media ecology"[8] of the time— constantly stressing the connection between the message and the medium. According to her, the lack of technologically advanced means of communication prevented factual information and British propaganda from spreading in Ireland: "The reduction or slowing of trains has, inevitably, affected the postal service"; "daily papers make such small printings, that, in many cases, readers arrange to 'share'"; "the supply of new films has been greatly reduced" (*"Notes on Eire"* [hereafter *NE*] 30, 31). The British government could not rely on any official Mass Observation[9] in Ireland and had mostly to resort to confidential reports written by individuals, which is why Bowen was appointed the difficult task to assess the effect of war propaganda in that neutral nation.

In the early months of the war, British propaganda was not very successful in America either. In fact, the outbreak of the war prompted a "propaganda phobia" in the United States, and isolationists vigorously defended neutrality in the media (Cull 34–38). British propaganda was met with distrust, at least until the United States decided to enter the war after being directly attacked. The new state of Ireland, however, remained neutral throughout the conflict for fear of becoming the target of German aerial and naval warfare. Ireland became, then, strategically crucial to the British war effort, but no attempt was made at understanding the rationale behind Irish neutrality. As Bowen argued in a 1941 book review, "The psychological geography should be recognised now that wartime geography puts Ireland so vitally on the map" (Walshe 76). Yet, Irish psychological distance from Britain was not without consequences, as she was to admit later on:

> As a whole, Ireland forms, willy nilly, a key point to Europe's Atlantic front: the ports, the accommodation for troops withheld by the (then) Irish Free State[10] were provided by Ulster. Alone among the Dominions (of which she was then one) the Irish Free State chose to remain neutral. Her neutrality was, throughout, respected—one has yet to compute at how great a cost. (Bowen, "Ireland Today" 119)

Allied propaganda—the "war of words" over Irish neutrality—aimed at convincing Ireland to keep Britain's "back door" closed, whereas Irish censorship aimed at squelching such propaganda (Cole ix). In fact, Irish neutrality indirectly allowed German action against Allied convoys. By November 1940, British shipping losses in the Atlantic had become so severe that in a speech delivered on 5 November 1940, Churchill declared, "The fact that we cannot use the South and West coasts of Ireland to refuel our flotillas and aircraft and thus protect the trade by which Ireland as well as Great Britain lives, is a most heavy and grievous burden and one which should never have been placed on our shoulders, broad though they may be" (411). Being in Ireland when the speech was reported in the Irish press, Bowen registered the effects it had on the population in a note dated 9 November:

> The flare-up of resentment and suspicion on this side (since November 6th, when Mr. Churchill's speech appeared in the morning papers) is all the more to be regretted because, since August, pro-British feeling and sympathy for the British cause had been steadily on the increase here. I was struck by this, and impressed by the change of atmosphere, when I arrived in Eire in the middle of last month. (I think I mentioned this, or suggested this, in my notes). Perhaps I only realise now, by contrast, how propitious things here, till November 6th, had been. (*NE* 11)

In her opinion, British campaigns exacerbated Irish response: "When I arrived over here last July I found this country in a state of alarm and anger caused by an unfortunate British press campaign" (11–12). The same note makes an important point about the production of art for propaganda in Ireland: "The writer as propagandist in any sense seems to be ineffective in this country" (15).

ENDLESS TALK

Since Bowen kept no diary, it is difficult to assess when she decided to work in Ireland for the MoI. Only when her travel plans were fixed did she inform Virginia Woolf, expressing her contrasting feelings about leaving London, in a letter dated 1 July 1940:

> I think I told you I had asked the Ministry of Information if I could do any work, which I feel *was wanted*, in Ireland. On Saturday morning I had a letter *from them* saying yes, *they did want* me to go. Now it has come to the point I have rather *a feeling of dismay* and of *not wanting to leave this country.* . . . I shall be at Bowen's Court just, but I expect *they will also want me* to move about the places. I don't know much till I've seen Harold Nicolson [at that time parliamentary secretary and member

of the MoI in Churchill's 1940 wartime government of national unity].
I hope I shall be some good: I do feel it's important. As far as my feeling
goes *I feel low at going away,* so can only hope *to be some good* when I
am there. (*Mulberry Tree* 215–16, emphasis added)

The passage proves that she volunteered her service, but the language seems
to deny her own agency, since she is never the subject of the repeated verb
"want." What she considers her moral duty is conveyed through the use
of impersonal expressions ("was wanted," "they did want," "they will also
want") and words with a positive connotation ("important," "some good"),
whereas her personal inclination is expressed through the use of negative
constructions ("not wanting to leave" and, later in the letter, "I shall wish I'd
never left") and active verbal forms. A first contrast thus emerges between
individual needs and war demands, conveyed by an impersonal "they."

In her letter she does not clarify what her task was but seems eager to
witness any turning points in the ongoing war:

> *It will all mean endless talk*, but sorting out talk into shape might be
> *interesting*. I suppose I shall also finish my book. . . . If there's to be an
> invasion of Ireland, I hope it may be while I am there . . . but if anything
> happens to England while I am in Ireland *I shall wish I'd never left*, even
> for this short time. I suppose the Ministry will give me a come-and-go
> travel permit. (216, emphasis added)

In her reports she constantly stressed the discursive quality of the war.
"Talk (I mean talk in ordinary conversation) in this country cuts more ice
than anything else. My object has been to see the widest possible number
of people of different kinds" (report of 13 July 1940, *More of Her Espionage
Reports* [hereafter *ME*] 6). Collecting information and opinions was indeed
her primary task.

As she saw it, "speech, and speech with a bias, is the nation's delight"
("Ireland Today" 120). In the 9 November report, she wrote that "the
childishness and obtuseness of this country cannot fail to be irritating
to the English mind" (*NE* 12). Irish people appeared to be very isolated,
either "apathetic or nonchalant" toward the war. Only "older and thinking people" felt "great uneasiness as to the safety of Eire" (report of 13
July 1940, *ME* 7). Later, in February 1942, when she testified to "a renewed
wave of bomb-nervousness," she hypothesized that this could be "deliberately stimulated, at this juncture, by the de Valera government for its
own purpose. Also being stimulated through plugged talk by German

agents in Eire" (*NE* 20). Thus, rumors—either spread by the government or by the enemy—seemed to function as a tool for manipulating public opinion. Bowen also complained that in Ireland there was no anti-gossip campaign (*ME* 6)—a top priority issue on the agenda of the MoI in Britain, which famously adopted the motto "Careless Talk Costs Lives." She also titled one of her short stories "Careless Talk," which is a brilliant literary interpretation of the official slogan and hinges upon the idea that even everyday talk can pass information on to the enemy spies.[11]

Apart from the occasional apprehension about a possible German or British invasion or the fear of a blitz, the atmosphere Bowen reported from Ireland was one of stagnation and apathy. Most of her Irish detractors have focused on her depiction of Irish people as sentimental, pro-German religious fanatics, and sometimes anti-Semitic. This is true in part, especially when she refers to James Dillon, leader of the Fine Gael party, or to Eamon de Valera, who is never a positive figure in her reports. Nonetheless, these detractors completely overlook Bowen's attempt at understanding Irish citizens' attitudes, their fear of air raids, and their sense of independence from Britain enhanced by neutrality.[12] Lingering on the idea that such a choice was "Eire's first *free* self assertion" (*NE* 12, emphasis in original) and "first autonomous gesture" (37), Bowen finds a positive side of Irish neutrality after all. Most important, those critics fail to consider that Bowen not only reported on Ireland but also commented on British attitudes toward the young, and presumably immature, state of Ireland.

The interest of her reports lies in the emphasis she put on communicative approaches, which are precisely the focus of propaganda studies. She seemed to envision a new kind of information strategy in Ireland, different from the propaganda Britain had been using: "While propaganda is suspect and, I understand, forbidden, very much could be done by unofficial diplomacy, and should be done <u>soon</u>" (*ME* 6, emphasis in original). Her advice was that Britain should take into account that Irish mentality was conditioned by fear, lack of information, and religion (*NE* 16). Moreover, the MoI had to "mitigate the tactlessness, with regard to this country, of the British press" and use broadcasting instead (12). As for the language to be used, the word "revolutionary" had to be avoided, given the associations it brought to the Irish mind, namely "chaos, red flags and barricades." "Reconstructive" seemed a better word, one that she decided to use instead (16).

Because during the war many Irish people worked in England and went back with the most defeatist news, Bowen suggested that "any propaganda directed to Irish workers in England would reach, and have an effect on, the Irish in Eire" (*NE* 27). Therefore, British propaganda should tactfully broadcast messages apparently addressed to England but in fact intended for Eire (12). This happened, indeed, in 1941 when the BBC started a program called *Irish Half Hour*, ostensibly aimed at Irish people serving in the forces but actually targeting the Irish audience at home (Wills 199). It might be seen as, and to some extent was, manipulative, but Bowen was also a "realist" (Cole 48) and knew that a wrong campaign would in fact help the enemy. Her intent—the results of which are unknown—was to influence Irish public opinion: "I have emphasized since I have been here (I hope rightly) that England has no wish that Eire should enter the war" (*NE* 12). Maybe she hadn't been instructed to do so, but it seemed to her extremely important to advertise the "English goodwill and sympathy to this country" (*ME* 6). Moreover, "everything must be done to counteract the Irish idea that England is going to lose the war" (6–7). She strongly advocated for a clear statement that England had no intention to send troops to Ireland (7).

Bowen's awareness of propaganda techniques as it appears from these passages recalls the remarks made by Harold Lasswell, who, in a chapter called "Conditions and Methods of Propaganda," suggests that "a propagandist can alter the organization of his activities . . . and substitute one device of communication with another, but he must adjust himself to traditional prejudices, to certain objective facts of international life, and to the general tension level of the community" (185). Similarly, Bowen advocated that British propaganda should be adjusted according to the tensions already at work in Ireland, especially between Irish and Anglo-Irish: "The Anglo-Irish would be doing much better service to both England and Eire if they would not so zealously represent themselves as England's stronghold here" (*NE* 17). These words stress Bowen's interest in the matter of self-representation as a tool of political mediation. Her desire for mediation is fully expressed in the following passage: "I could wish some factions in England showed less anti-Irish feeling. . . . The charge of 'disloyalty' against the Irish has always, given the plain facts of history, irritated me. I could wish that the English kept history in mind more, that the Irish kept it in mind less" (13). Bowen's collaboration with the MoI was a skeptical one in the end. She knew that a population's acceptance of militaristic actions entailed a great (above all linguistic) effort by politicians and media. As Orwell asserts, "All propaganda is lies, even when one is telling the truth" (411). One of the positive sides of the inefficacy of British propaganda in

Ireland was therefore that "the stereotyped, or completely conditioned, mind seemed to me rarer in Dublin than in London. . . . Public opinion in Dublin is almost dangerously fluid. It is, at the same time, less homogeneous than in any English city I have known" (*NE* 14). As a matter of fact, propaganda was affecting British freedom of thought as much as censorship was fostering Eire's isolationism.

Censorship, which kept the Irish in a state of apathy, was in a way the unavoidable counterpart of British propaganda. "The insufficiency of all news produced uneasiness," Bowen noted ("Ireland Today" 120). She wished the Irish were better informed and blamed this insufficiency on both sides—Irish censorship and inadequate British propaganda. News from England did not filter in: "British news reels are not allowed in cinemas here, as nothing connected with war news may be shown. All 'amusement' films whose plots relate to either the present or the 1914 war were banned last autumn" (*ME* 17). The same was true of American films: *The Great Dictator* was not shown in Ireland. Bowen believed the country's press to be free only in name (21). And of course the Emergency regulation did not allow the media to mention the thousands of Irish citizens who were serving in the British Armed Forces or moved to Britain to support the wartime effort as civilians, although Ireland never restricted its citizens from joining other armies. There was even a ban on wearing the uniform of a foreign army, a regulation introduced especially against the British uniform (Wills 418). In this way censorship kept Ireland isolated and fostered its attitude to keep clear of commitment and action. In Bowen's view, neutrality had great costs, not only for the Allies but also for Ireland itself.

Although Bowen considered her reports on Ireland of absolute importance, and the War Cabinet also took them into consideration, they have neither attracted much critical attention as historical documents nor been related to her fictional writings.[13] In fact, the reports depict the evolution of public opinion in Ireland and also provide details about the personality of public figures. In particular, there has been no acknowledgment that Bowen, while reporting on Irish "childishness," was also commenting about British "rudeness" in conducting the war of words over its neutrality. Only recently (in 2011) have some of her reports been reprinted in the collection *Elizabeth Bowen's Selected Irish Writings*, edited by Eibhear Walshe.[14]

Walshe's collection includes another interesting text for propaganda studies, because it highlights the role of censorship in the rhetoric of neutrality. The text is an undated typescript with the generic mark "Ireland" in pencil on it, held at the Harry Ransom Center. It has a curious story, and its scope is unclear. "Ireland 1950" was the title assigned to it by Walshe; Allan Hepburn, who first published it in a 2010 collection of Bowen's previously unpublished broadcasts and interviews (*Listening In*), titles it "Ireland Today."[15] According to Hepburn, it might be the script for a documentary film, probably written in 1960 (Bowen, *Listening In* 355).[16] The correspondence between Bowen and her agent, Spencer Curtis Brown, shows that she was commissioned to write a script on "Ireland today" by CBS.[17] A two-episode documentary film was indeed broadcast in 1961 by CBS, titled *Ireland: The Tear and the Smile*.

While in the reports she tries to understand the reasons behind Irish neutrality and to mediate between the two countries, in the text "Ireland" (to which I will refer as "Ireland Today," following Hepburn), Bowen is strongly critical of the country's neutrality:

> With a certain grimness, the Irish faced out their isolation. The isola-tion, however, was in itself *impairing*—it made for neutrality's *negative*, *losing* side. Travel between Ireland and England was *suspended*: con-tacts, communication suffered accordingly. Censorship, of a cautiously *nulling* kind, inhibited Irish newspapers. Postal censorship (which had to operate at the British as well as the Irish end) clamped down on personal stories of war experience—Dublin, for instance, knew of the London blitz only by *bloated*, *uncertain* and *ghastly* rumour. Gratitude for exemption from the horrors mingled, in certain Irish people, with a sensation of being *side-tracked*, of being *out of step* with their genera-tion. The insufficiency of all news produced uneasiness: what might next be brewing? *Worst*, there was the taboo on judgement—for if one is neutral one must not take sides—fostered a listless irresponsibility. It became first *discouraging*, later *unnecessary*, to think. ("Ireland Today" 120, emphasis added)

Here, a series of adjectives and verbs with negative connotations pile up, leading to the final, relentless statement. Even conceding that neutrality "represented Ireland's first independent decision," no positive aspect of it could be envisioned, at least in this passage (119). Written after the war, with the knowledge of Nazi crimes and of all the shipping losses in the Atlantic, the text seems to be even harsher than Bowen's wartime reports about neutrality. After all, the reports were addressed to a cabinet that could decide to invade the country. And Bowen did not wish it to happen.

Hepburn assumes that "Ireland" is the script she submitted to CBS, but he had no opportunity to see the documentary (Bowen, *Listening In* 356).

A copy of both episodes of *Ireland: The Tear and the Smile* is available, however, at the Irish Film Institute in Dublin.[18] Although the narration does not match Bowen's text, the content of the documentary touches upon the topics she had tackled as typical features of a war of words: partition, religion, censorship, economy, emigration, bilingualism.

The film is rather different from the script—that is, from "Ireland Today." It is less radical in its political assessments. It is uncertain whether "Ireland Today" was the text Bowen sent to CBS, but if it was, CBS changed it during production and still credited its narrative parts to Bowen, a revision she was very upset about: "I didn't write that, I didn't write that" (qtd. in Glendenning 363). However, Bowen's text is much more relevant for an analysis of her view on Ireland. It is, indeed, more passionate, to some extent unyielding in its remarks about Irish illusion and escapism, inaction, and useless "parley" (Bowen, "Ireland Today" 120).

THE COUNTERNARRATIVE OF THE SHORT STORIES

During the war, Bowen wrote a great amount of literary criticism and two memoirs: *Bowen's Court*, the history of her family in County Cork, and *Seven Winters*, focused on her childhood in Dublin; both appeared in 1942. But she published no novels, and her literary production consisted almost exclusively of short stories. She was, indeed, a great "short story-ist"—to use a common expression of hers—throughout her career, and the story seemed to her "the ideal *prose* medium for wartime creative writing" (*People* 314, emphasis in original). Wartime was no time for lyrical vision or contemplation; neither was it time for lengthy narratives. The fragmented landscape, material and psychological, found in the modernist refashioning of the nineteenth-century short story a more congenial analogue. Literature had become an experimental battlefield, as it were, a war territory in which the reassuring, comfortable body of tradition was torn to fragments.

Among Bowen's many short stories, only ten "have identifiable Irish settings," and "six of these were written during the Second World War at the same time of her two Irish memoirs" (Walshe 3–4). Her reports on Ireland are worth mentioning along with her memoirs. Even allowing for the difference between official, political notes and literature, Bowen's fiction provides another site of investigation into both issues of neutrality and propaganda, although interpretation of the fiction appears to be more challenging. Unlike propaganda, literature is not a one-way communication system; in fact, it can produce "a counter-vision which in turn creates the sense of ideological distance which renders propaganda visible" (Foulkes 6). To better elucidate Bowen's attitude toward the political situation ensuing from the conflict and her understanding of the language of politics and propaganda, it is worth examining three short stories, included in the 1941 collection *Look at All Those Roses* and in the volume *The Demon Lover and Other Stories*, which was published in 1945 and later reprinted in *The Collected Stories of Elizabeth Bowen* (hereafter *CS*).

Some of the stories were no doubt inspired by her several trips to Ireland between 1940 and 1942. Her notes on Irish public opinion and life might have prompted insights she could not include in her reports; they found their way, this time by no means instrumentally, into her fiction. The fiction she wrote during the war expresses an even stronger ambivalence than her reports and dramatizes her ambiguity toward British war propaganda. On the one hand, she felt the moral obligation to engage herself in the war effort; on the other, she questioned the way war propaganda was conducted and how it manipulated individual freedom.

In her report dated 19 July 1942, Bowen accounted for the way war affected Ireland despite neutrality, for instance in terms of fuel, clothes, and paper shortage. Since her previous visits, doubts about neutrality had begun to thicken. "We'd be better off if we were in the war" was a remark Bowen often heard during her stay (*NE* 29). To sustain its neutral position, the Irish government had to resort to internal propaganda, and since "it is not easy to 'sell' Austerity in the name of anything so negative as Neutrality" (29), as it happens, the government had to give it another name, "Emergency." Once again, language clearly played a crucial role in wartime, both in belligerent and neutral countries. While the British newspapers attacked Irish neutrality and Churchill insisted on its being a menace to British security, the Irish government used a rhetoric of survival, self-sufficiency, autonomy, and patriotism, which occasionally linked with religious pacifism. De Valera was a key actor in constructing this moral neutralism, yet this was above all a pragmatic choice for self-preservation (see, for example, O'Driscoll).

The outcome of such opposite propagandas resulted in what seems a great linguistic and material confusion. The short story "Unwelcome Idea" (*CS* 573–77) especially stresses the discursive dimension of the conflict by means of a dialogue between two women. Miss Kevin and Mrs. Kearny meet by chance on a tram. The first is laden with parcels, because "they all say, buy now. You never know" (574). The second has just said goodbye to her sister, who is evacuating with her whole family, although citizens have been told not to move: "'But the latest thing I hear they say now in the paper is that we'll be shot if we don't stay where we are. *They say* now we're all to keep off the roads—and there is my sister this morning with her car at the door. Do you think they'll halt her, Miss Kevin?'" (575, emphasis added). Particularly pervasive is the anaphoric use of the phrase "they say" throughout the text. The deictic "they" (which needs a specific context or a previous mention in order to be understood), however, has no precise referent and might alternatively refer to common sense and opinion, to the press, or to the government. It is true that the character refers to "the latest thing I hear they say now in the paper." Ironically, she happens to carry a "month-old magazine" with her, which stresses the gap between up-to-date information and rumors, and questions official news through humor. The Irish government, while exploiting the fear of invasion (first by Britain, later by Germans), did not invest much effort in preparing the population for such a dreadful event (see the note dated 21 July 1940, *ME* 12), as clearly emerges from Miss Kevin's answer:

> "They might," says Miss Kevin. "I hear they are very suspicious. I declare, with the instruction changing so quickly it's better to take no notice. You'd be upside down if you tried to follow them all. It's of the first importance to keep calm, *they say*, and however would we keep calm doing this, then that? Still, we don't get half the instructions they get in England. I should think they'd really pity themselves . . ." (*CS* 575, emphasis added)

As she feels the moral obligation to participate in the war effort, Miss Kevin is the literary representation of the people whom Bowen described as feeling "side-tracked" and "uneasy" with the lack of information in the script "Ireland Today" (120). And Bowen explicitly complains about the scarce availability of newspapers, for example, in the already mentioned report of 19 July 1942 (*NE* 31) and in the note dated 31 July 1942 (33). In the latter, she also observes that women were not, especially in the country, keen readers of newspapers. "Unwelcome Idea," therefore, juxtaposes the thorough information system of England with the confused instructions from the Irish government and press, which in Bowen's opinion created apathy or discord. Yet, the short story also adds another interpretative layer to this discourse, namely the tension between the sexes. Women do not often feature in the official notes, whereas they are protagonists in most of her short stories. As the conversation between the two characters unfolds, the title "Unwelcome Idea" loses its connection to the danger of invasion, either by Britain or by Germany, and acquires a new meaning. It refers to the opinion held by Miss Kevin's father, who acts as if his wife and daughter had "originated the war to spite him: he doesn't seem to blame Hitler at all" (*CS* 576). In wartime, women were singled out as dangerous actors everywhere: even the "Careless Talk" campaign in Britain, although addressed to both men and women, had a special target in women as the "leaking vessels of gossip" (Rau 35), testified by the poster series "Keep Mum, She's Not So Dumb." So the story questions both Irish propaganda and wartime discourse as a whole, while at the same time exposing a gender issue.

"Summer Night" (*CS* 583–608) is also located in Ireland. It has been read as a demystification of the myth of the Battle of Britain by Angus Calder in his book *The Myth of the Blitz* and is rightly considered as one of Bowen's "three masterworks," together with "The Disinherited" and "The Happy Autumn Fields" (Lassner 97), the latter also written during the war and in part set in a (probably Irish) countryside. "Summer Night" is a subtle text. No violent act is portrayed, yet the war haunts every scene: "Each moment is everywhere, it holds the war in its crystal" (*CS* 599). The atmosphere is so charged that one of the characters wonders whether a battle is being fought (599). The story is made up of three segments. The car ride of the protagonist, Emma, who is going to meet her lover, Robinson, connects two places. The first place is her home, where she leaves her family and her pro-war husband; the second is Robinson's house, where a drama takes place between him and "the neutral man," Justin Cavey, witnessed by the latter's deaf sister, Queenie. The adulterous Emma—an echo of Madame Bovary—embodies a romantic vision of idealized love as well as the excesses of modern technology and speed: as she drives, her car becomes an extension of her body. Robinson, on the other hand, remains a cold master of technology throughout the narration. For these reasons, Angus Calder reads this imagery and implications in the light of the myth of the Blitz: "Bowen, it seems to me, subtly works on a paradox implicit in the Myth of the Battle of Britain: that the manic abandon of Knights of the Air depends on the skills of engineer, manager and mechanic: wartime mythologisers found ways . . . of presenting technical men as heroic" (256). But this "fairytale," at first boosted by technology, must die in the "childish part of her mind" (*CS* 605). Heroism turns out to be phony and heroism narratives deceptive.

The story also depicts "self-deceived and self-enclosed characters wishing for connection and regeneration" (Lassner 101). It is the "neutral Irishman,"

Justin Cavey, who affirms that "there's been a stop in our senses and in our faculties that's made everything round us so much dead matter" (*CS* 588). As William J. McCormack points out, "We recognize the opinion as a familiar Bowen one" (233). However, despite his being the most talkative character in the story, Justin fails to communicate, thus becoming the symbol of an Ireland whose neutrality stands for alienation. On the contrary, his sister, Queenie—whose deafness embodies the highest degree of seclusion and estrangement from the external world—turns out to be the symbol of another Ireland that can connect "the prose and the poetry" through an act of imagination and empathy. The questions arise, then, whether action (that is, taking sides) is necessary and whether, as Bowen sometimes seems to suggest, it always entails fighting: "Talk, parley, had ended in what?—nothing. There must be action. Action involved the gun" ("Ireland Today" 118). "Summer Night" in the character of Justin confirms the uselessness of uncommitted discourse. Yet the story does not directly contrast war and neutrality; it rather challenges Ireland's incapacity to grow up. In this way, by representing her split identity, Bowen's stories foreground her wavering and questioning attitude to propaganda, British or Irish.

Coming back to Ireland in 1942, Bowen encountered the general feeling that Ireland was suffering "the effects of war without reaping any of war's benefits" (*NE* 20), meaning that while in England the war increased employment, in Ireland unemployment was fostered by neutrality. "The number of people who say (or at least imply) that Eire would have done better to enter the war in 1939 seems to have markedly increased" (20–21): this idea is dramatized in "Sunday Afternoon" (*CS* 616–22), where sixteen-year-old Maria decides to go to London and give up Irish escapism for action with a view to enter "history." She refuses a country "secluded behind glass," where people are eager to know about London, provided that the news is not "dreadful" (616). The news is carried by someone who seems a counterpart of Bowen. Like the writer, Henry is visiting Ireland but has a "ministry" job in London. Lack of newspapers, as we have seen, was sometimes compensated for by news brought by people traveling from England, namely commuting workers. But there were also other travelers between the two countries, those who had joined the British army or contributed in the civil service, as Maria wishes to do, according to her own moral obligations.

Henry feels the urge to be back in London soon, although his flat has been recently bombed (just as Bowen's was in 1940). "One cannot stay away for too long" (*CS* 618), as Bowen also wrote to Virginia Woolf upon acceptance of her engagement with the MoI. Yet, the story ends forecasting Maria's future: "You will no longer be Maria, as a matter of fact. . . . You may think action is better—but who will care for you when you only act? You will have an identity number, but no identity" (622). What has become here of Bowen's criticism of Irish slackness and smugness, inactivity and isolation? "Summer Night" and "Sunday Afternoon" portray an Ireland that refuses war and modernization for the sake of individuality. In the war, Maria will become a number; she will lose her name, her own self: Henry calls her Miranda, who gives up her innocence by entering the "brave new world" of history.

MORAL TENSION AND POLITICAL ACTION

These short stories tackle the issue of involvement and neutrality in a multifaceted way, which is typical of Bowen's writings, especially of her fiction. Yet ambiguity lingers in her nonfiction as well, as the result of a dramatic double bind. Although very critical of Irish neutrality, she was never in favor of a British invasion of Ireland. In her opinion, Britain would commit a great mistake in invading Ireland in order to use Irish ports, or even in threatening invasion. The Cabinet was to be discouraged from taking action. And she succeeded, as even Jack Lane admits: "Churchill wanted to know how Irish people would respond to a British invasion and take-over of Irish ports. As it happened, Ms. Bowen was able to warn that it would be a disastrous mistake, and militarily counter-productive" (*NE* 7). It is possible that Churchill really followed Bowen's advice. As Brian Girvin comments, reviewing Clair Wills's *That Neutral Island*, "Valera was fortunate that Winston Churchill read some of these reports because they were even-handed and detailed." While Robert Tobin has recently raised doubt as to whether those reports had any effect on Whitehall's policy toward Ireland (73), a file by the secretary of state for foreign affairs Lord Cranborne, reproduced in *"Notes on Eire,"* reads:

> I think you may like to glance at this in spite of its length. Mrs. Cameron is by profession a novelist—Elizabeth Bowen—who resides in Ireland and travels there, and previous reports by her to the Ministry of Information have struck us as very sensible and well balanced. The present report also strikes one as a shrewd appreciation of the position. (*NE* 10, 11)

Dated 25 November 1940, the file is attached to the report of 9 November. It accounts for the suspicion stirred up by Churchill's broadcast about the Irish ports, on the "unfortunate British campaign," and on the value of neutrality as an independent act, while suggesting the use of a tactful broadcast instead of the press (11–12). Bowen's allegiances, unlike what Lane states, lay on both sides, or rather on neither side. She had two countries, or, like women in Virginia Woolf's *Three Guineas*, no country. While questioning the role of British propaganda, Bowen was also calling for an act of moral responsibility on the part of Ireland, exactly because of her bond with that country. At times she was the mouthpiece of Ireland's neutrality, which she perceived as an act of independence. Then, as the number of Allied soldiers who drowned in the Atlantic following German U-boat attacks increased, she receded. Irish neutrality became a "set-back" in the country's growing process, making it "harder to become adult in Ireland" ("Ireland Today" 120). Her problematic attitude toward propaganda enacts a tension between innocence and commitment, romantic vision and responsibility, the same tension that connotes the characters of her short fiction. After all, Bowen's volunteering to work as an Air Raid Precaution warden and to "spy" on Ireland for the Ministry of Information was her only strong, unambiguous political act.

Notes

1. Initially broadcast over BBC Overseas Service, *The Frontiers of Art and Propaganda* was printed in *The Listener* on 29 May 1941 and later reprinted in *Collected Essays*.

2. An expression commonly used with regard to propaganda, and probably crystallized after the publication of Asa Briggs's influential book *The War of Words*.

3. The present essay is the outcome of the research I carried out at the Harry Ransom Center at the University of Texas at Austin with support from an Alfred A. and Blanche W. Knopf Fellowship in 2010. Materials collected in the archive were of fundamental importance for my project on Elizabeth Bowen and the discourse of propaganda.

4. Most of the notes Bowen wrote on Ireland were destroyed after the war was over (Jordan 100). Of the original two hundred or more reports, only a few survived and were partially published in 1999 in *"Notes on Eire"* by Jack Lane and Brendon Clifford, who intended to demonstrate that Bowen had spied on Ireland, betraying the faith of the people who had had intimate conversations with her during the war. They also aimed at excluding Bowen from the canon of Irish literature, arguing that she was an English writer who had just happened to be born in a part of the empire. A second

collection, *More of Her Espionage Reports from Ireland to Winston Churchill*, was issued, edited by Jack Lane alone, in 2009, after a fierce and not very insightful debate had raged in the *Irish Examiner* (2008) over Bowen's political allegiances (see *Elizabeth Bowen: A Debate in the "Irish Examiner"*).

5. Paradoxically, Goebbels's ministry, in its turn, functioned as an example for the English Ministry of Information, which had been closed down in 1919 and reestablished in 1939 (MacLaine 12).

6. The memorandum is also archived at the Harry Ransom Center at Austin (HRC 13.2).

7. See, for example, the website devised by Paul Vyšný.

8. Media ecology has been defined as

> the study of media environments, the idea that technology and techniques, modes of information, and codes of communication play a leading role in human affairs. Media ecology is the Toronto School, and the New York School. It is technological determinism, hard and soft, and technological evolution. It is media logic, medium theory, mediology. It is McLuhan Studies, orality-literacy studies, American cultural studies. It is grammar and rhetoric, semiotics and systems theory, the history and the philosophy of technology. It is the postindustrial and the postmodern, and the preliterate and prehistoric. Media ecology is all of these things, and quite a bit more. (Strate)

9. The Mass Observation project was started in 1937 by a group of anthropologists and continued throughout the war, giving indication as to whether propaganda campaigns were being successful or needed to be adjusted.

10. Here Bowen is imprecise: under the 1937 constitution, the term "Free State" was dropped, and the country was called simply "Ireland" (in Irish, "Eire").

11. I have dealt with this topic in a paper titled "'Careless Talk Costs Lives': War Propaganda and Wartime Fiction in Elizabeth Bowen's *The Heat of the Day.*"

12. Pacifism, in the reports, is never seen as underlying Eire's choice for neutrality.

13. With the exception of Cole and Wills.

14. Some of the extant reports are interspersed in a volume of critical writings by Bowen—lectures, essays, and reviews all focusing on Ireland—now made available to the general public. The volume does not contain any fictional texts, but the accurate introduction provides interesting connections with Bowen's novels and short stories.

15. My quotations from "Ireland" refer to this edition (which I therefore cite as "Ireland Today") throughout this chapter.

16. He also concedes that internal evidence shows that the text might have been written between 1952 and 1954. According to J'nan Sellery and William O. Harris, the typescript "Ireland," held at the Harry Ransom Center, was published in *House and Garden* in 1954. Hepburn had included another essay, titled "Ireland," in *People, Places, Things: Essays by Elizabeth Bowen* (164–69), stating that it was published in *House and Garden* in 1954. This second text—to my knowledge—is not held at the Harry Ransom Center, unlike what Sellery and Harris write in their bibliography.

17. See the correspondence file 11.6 in the Bowen Collection at the Harry Ransom Center.

18. I am grateful to Karen Wall, access officer at the institute, for providing me with a DVD copy of the film. The title of the documentary might have been inspired by a sentence in Bowen's available text, which reads "In the climate, as in the temperament of the people, for all the smiles, there is a melancholy, an underlying sombreness" ("Ireland Today" 117).

Works Cited

Bowen, Elizabeth. *Bowen's Court*. London: Longmans, Green, 1942. Print.

———. *The Collected Stories of Elizabeth Bowen*. Introd. Angus Wilson. 1980. London: Vintage, 1999. Print.

———. *The Demon Lover and Other Stories*. London: Jonathan Cape, 1945. Print.

———. *The Heat of the Day*. 1949. London: Vintage, 1998. Print.

———. "Ireland." Elizabeth Bowen Collection, Harry Ransom Humanities Research Center, University of Texas, Austin, HRC 6.5. TS.

———. "Ireland Today." *Listening In: Broadcasts, Speeches, and Interviews*. Ed. Allan Hepburn. Edinburgh, Scot.: Edinburgh UP, 2010. 116–29. Print.

———. *Look at All Those Roses*. London: Gollancz, 1941. Print.

———. *More of Her Espionage Reports from Ireland to Winston Churchill*. Ed. Jack Lane. Aubane, Ire.: Aubane Historical Soc., 2009. Print.

———. *The Mulberry Tree: Writings of Elizabeth Bowen*. Ed. Hermione Lee. 1986. London: Vintage, 1999. Print.

———. *"Notes on Eire": Espionage Reports to Winston Churchill, 1940–2, with a Review of Irish Neutrality in World War 2*. Ed. Jack Lane and Brendon Clifford. Aubane, Ire.: Aubane Historical Soc., 1999. Print.

———. *People, Places, Things: Essays by Elizabeth Bowen*. Ed. Allan Hepburn. Edinburgh, Scot.: Edinburgh UP, 2008. Print.

——. *Pictures and Conversations*. New York: Knopf, 1975. Print.

——. *Seven Winters*. Dublin: Cuala, 1942. Print.

Briggs, Asa. *The War of Words*. Vol. 3 of *The History of Broadcasting in the United Kingdom*. Oxford: Oxford UP, 1970. Print.

Buitenhuis, Peter. *The Great War of Words: Literature as Propaganda 1914–18 and After*. London: BT Batsford, 1989. Print.

Calder, Angus. *The Myth of the Blitz*. 1991. London: Pimlico, 1992. Print.

Churchill, Winston Spencer. *Blood, Sweat and Tears*. 1941. Whitefish, Mont.: Kessinger, 2005. Print.

Cole, Robert. *Propaganda, Censorship and Irish Neutrality in the Second World War*. Edinburgh, Scot.: Edinburgh UP, 2006. Print.

Cull, Nicholas John. *Selling War: The British Propaganda Campaign against American "Neutrality" in World War II*. New York: Oxford UP, 1995. Print.

Elizabeth Bowen: A Debate in the "Irish Examiner." Aubane, Ire.: Aubane Historical Soc., 2008. Print.

Ellul, Jacques. *Propaganda: The Formation of Men's Attitudes*. Trans. Konrad Kellen and Jean Lerner. New York: Knopf, 1965. Print.

Foulkes, A. P. *Literature and Propaganda*. London: Methuen, 1983. Print.

Girvin, Brian. "That Neutral Island." *Times Higher Education* 23 March 2007. Web. 1 June 2012.

Glendenning, Victoria. *Love's Civil War: Elizabeth Bowen and Charles Ritchie; Letters and Diaries 1941–1973*. Ed. Judith Robertson. London: Pocket, 2010. Print.

Ireland: The Tear and the Smile. Dir. Willard Van Dyke. Script by Elizabeth Bowen. CBS, 1961. DVD.

Jordan, Heather Bryant. *How Will the Heart Endure: Elizabeth Bowen and the Landscape of War*. Ann Arbor: U of Michigan P, 1992. Print.

Knightley, Philip. *The First Casualty: From Cinema to Vietnam; The War Correspondent as Hero, Propagandist, and Myth Maker*. New York: Harcourt, 1975. Print.

Lassner, Phyllis. *Elizabeth Bowen: A Study of the Short Fiction*. New York: Twayne, 1991. Print.

Lasswell, Harold D. *Propaganda Technique in World War I*. Cambridge: MIT P, 1971. Print.

MacLaine, Ian. *Ministry of Morale: Home Front Morale and the Ministry of Information in World War II*. London: George Allen and Unwin, 1979. Print.

McCormack, William J. *Dissolute Characters: Irish Literary History through Balzac, Sheridan Le Fanu, Yeats and Bowen*. Manchester, U.K.: Manchester UP, 1993. Print.

O'Driskoll, Mervyn. "Keeping Britain Sweet: Irish Neutrality, Political Identity and Collective Memory." *Collective Memory in Ireland and Russia.* Ed. N. Keogh and A. Sorokin. Moscow: Rospen, 2006. 98–119. Print.

Orwell, George. *The Collected Essays, Journalism and Letters of George Orwell.* Vol. 2, *My Country Right or Left: 1940–1943.* Ed. Sonia Orwell and Ian Angus. London: Secker and Warburg, 1968. Print.

Porcelli, Stefania. "'Careless Talk Costs Lives': War Propaganda and Wartime Fiction in Elizabeth Bowen's *The Heat of the Day.*" *Challenges for the 21st Century: Dilemmas, Ambiguities, Directions.* Ed. Richard Ambrosini et al. Rome: Edizioni Q, 2011. 107–13. Print.

Rau, Petra. "The Common Frontier: Fictions of Alterity in Elizabeth Bowen's *The Heat of the Day* and Graham Greene's *The Ministry of Fear.*" *Literature and History* 14.1 (2005): 31–55. Print.

Sellery, J'nan, and William O. Harris. *Elizabeth Bowen: A Bibliography.* Austin: Humanities Research Center, U of Texas at Austin, 1981. Print.

Strate, Lance. "Understanding MEA." *In Medias Res* 1.1 (1999). Web. 15 June 2009.

Tobin, Robert. *The Minority Voice: Hubert Butler and Southern Irish Protestantism, 1900–1991.* New York: Oxford UP, 2012. Print.

Van Dijk, T. A. "Discourse Analysis as Ideology Analysis." *Language and Peace.* Ed. Christina Schäffner and Anita L. Wenden. Aldershot, Eng.: Dartmouth, 1995. 17–33. Print.

Vyšný, Paul. "Weapons on the Wall: British Propaganda Posters of the Second World War." *British Propaganda Posters of the Second World War.* N.p., 2003. Web. 15 January 2012.

Walshe, Eibhear, ed. *Elizabeth Bowen's Selected Irish Writings.* Cork, Ire.: Cork UP, 2011. Print.

Wills, Clair. *That Neutral Island: A Cultural History of Ireland during the Second World War.* Boston: Harvard UP, 2007. Print.

Woolf, Virginia. *A Room of One's Own and Three Guineas.* Oxford: Oxford UP, 1992. Print.

PROPAGANDA DEFINED

THOMAS HUCKIN

> Don't believe everything you think.
> —Anonymous, bumper sticker

Anyone undertaking the study of propaganda should have a clear idea of exactly what the object of study is, beginning with a definition of the term. By specifying certain features, a proper definition serves to focus attention on those aspects of the topic that merit it. Furthermore, the term *propaganda* is almost four hundred years old, and during that time its meaning has undergone significant change. Because the chapters in this volume range over different periods of modern history, an awareness of this semantic evolution is essential in understanding these different studies and in linking them together into a coherent narrative.

The main purpose of this chapter is to provide a definition of propaganda as it is currently understood in American English. I do so by compiling the findings of a quasi-random survey of dictionary and expert definitions, from which I offer a composite definition. Embedded in that definition is the sense of propaganda being a *manipulative* practice, which invites discussion about whether such manipulation is intentional or not. I argue that it is, but not necessarily consciously so. This leads to a more theoretical discussion of how propaganda is indeed most effective when it is disseminated unconsciously by the broad public, which ironically is also its most impacted victim. The chapter concludes by asserting that the study of contemporary propaganda must take into account this unconscious form of self-persuasion and the role it plays in what has been described as "inverted totalitarianism" (Wolin 44).

I begin, though, with a brief history of the term and some examples of its current usage.

HISTORY

The term *propaganda* was first used by the Catholic church in the late sixteenth century, in internal Vatican discussions about combating the growing spread of Protestantism (Marlin 15). As a nominalization of the verb *propagate*, the term referred simply to written and spoken efforts to spread church doctrine, thereby increasing the church's membership, and thus had an entirely neutral connotation. In 1622, Pope Gregory XV convened a committee of cardinals under the rubric *Congregatio de Propaganda Fide*, literally "Congregation for the Propagation of the Faith," and this date is generally credited as the first time the term was used publicly. For approximately three centuries thereafter, the term continued to have mainly this sectarian meaning and was seldom used outside that context, though church opponents would occasionally employ it with a pejorative connotation (Miller 10). In his 1856 book *English Traits*, Ralph Waldo Emerson used the term *propagandist* to favorably describe British imperial policy (Miller 10). In Skeat's *Etymological Dictionary of the English Language*, there is no entry at all for *propaganda*, even though there is one for *propagate*.

In the early twentieth century, however, use of the term *propaganda* accelerated. In some cases it was used with a favorable connotation. In a 1907 article titled "Anti-militarist Propaganda and Socialist Workers' Leagues," for example, V. I. Lenin urged the use of propaganda to instill the proper attitude among young Communists, noting that "everywhere anti-militarist propaganda among young workers has yielded excellent results. That is of tremendous importance. The worker who goes into the army a class-conscious Social-Democrat is a poor support for the powers that be" (204). During World War I, the British government made extensive use of propaganda, targeting allies and neutral nations in an effort to gain their support for the war effort. In their internal documents, British officials at the Ministry of Information and elsewhere freely used the term *propaganda* to describe their various publications (pamphlets, news reports, postcards, films, and the like), seemingly not attaching much if any opprobrium to the word. Indeed, the Minister of Information at that time, Brendan Bracken, wrote that

> propaganda . . . is a perfectly respectable name, attached to one of the most profoundly religious institutions in the world. It is really too respectable a veneer to put upon a thing like the Ministry of Information. I do not mind the use of the word "propaganda." In fact, I welcome it. There is nothing wrong with the name except that it connotes to certain minds something that they do not really understand. (Bracken 926; qtd. in Marlin 21)

The journalist Walter Lippmann, in his analysis of World War I, used the term with a similarly positive connotation to describe how the French high command used propaganda to elevate the spirits of the citizenry. The following example comes from Lippmann's 1922 seminal work, *Public Opinion*:

> Within the life of the generation now in control of affairs, persuasion has become a self-conscious art and a regular organ of popular government. None of us begins to understand the consequences, but it is no daring prophecy to say that the knowledge of how to create consent will alter every political calculation and modify every political premise. Under the impact of *propaganda*, not necessarily in the sinister meaning of the word alone, the old constants of our thinking have become variables. (158, italics mine)

In general, however, World War I was the time when the term *propaganda* began to take on a markedly pejorative connotation, due mainly to heavy use of the technique by both sides in that conflict. According to George Creel, head of the U.S. Office of War Information, Germany's relentless deployment of propaganda during the war caused American officials to downplay their own, equally heavy use: "We did not call [our own efforts] propaganda, for that word, in German hands, had come to be associated with deceit and corruption" (3). Meanwhile, the Russian Revolution gave rise to Leninist agitational propaganda (*agitprop*), which also was referred to pejoratively, in contrast to American *information*. When Adolf Hitler and Joseph Goebbels later emulated these early German and Soviet examples in producing their Nazi propaganda, the term *propaganda* took on an even more negative sense in the English-speaking world. Subsequently, the use of propaganda by Soviet Russia and Communist China during the Cold War consolidated this pejorative meaning.

The powerful role that propaganda played during World War I was not lost on the American business community of that time. Drawing inspiration from Lippmann's 1922 book, Edward Bernays, the American nephew of Sigmund Freud, used some of his uncle's ideas about psychoanalysis to promote commercial products and services, thereby founding the public relations industry. Conscious of the stigma attached to the word *propaganda*, however, Bernays took care to instead call his messages *education*. In his 1923 book, *Crystallizing Public Opinion*, he defined propaganda as follows: "Education is valuable, commendable, enlightening, instructive. Propaganda is insidious, dishonest, underhanded, misleading. Each of these nouns carries with it social and moral implications. . . . The only difference between 'propaganda' and 'education,' really, is in the point of view. The advocacy of what we believe in is education. The advocacy of what we don't believe in is propaganda" (212).

Bernays subsequently had something of a change of heart and tried to resurrect a more neutral meaning for the term. In his 1928 book, *Propaganda*, he notes that "I am aware that the word *propaganda* carries to many minds an unpleasant connotation. Yet whether, in any instance, propaganda is good or bad depends upon the merit of the cause urged, and the correctness of the information published" (48). Elsewhere in the book he argues that propaganda is an important part of a democratic society because the masses need guidance from a tiny group of natural leaders, or "invisible governors" (37). This more neutral sense of the word was adopted decades later by Anthony R. DiMaggio in his 2008 book-length analysis of propaganda use during the war on terror. Citing Bernays, DiMaggio states that "propaganda . . . is not necessarily inherently 'good' or 'bad' . . . [and] it does not, at its core, require deliberate deception" (23).

But Bernays was swimming against the tide. Since the 1920s, the term *propaganda* has had a decidedly negative connotation. One good example can be found in this 1966 definition from communication scholar Leonard Doob: "Propaganda can be called the attempt to affect the personalities and to control the behavior of individuals toward ends considered unscientific or of doubtful value in a society at a given time" (240). Another is in this 1982 definition from the *Encyclopedia Britannica*:

> Propaganda is the more or less systematic effort to manipulate other people's beliefs, attitudes, or actions by means of symbols (words, gestures, banners, monuments, music, clothing, insignia, hairstyles, designs on coins and postage stamps, and so forth). Deliberateness and a relatively heavy emphasis on manipulation distinguish propaganda from casual conversation or the free and easy exchange of ideas. The propagandist has a specified goal or set of goals. To achieve these he

deliberately selects facts, arguments, and displays of symbols and presents them in ways he thinks will have the most effect. To maximize effect, he may omit pertinent facts, and he may try to divert the attention of the reactors (the people whom he is trying to sway) from everything but his own propaganda. (36)

CONTEMPORARY USAGE

The term *propaganda* continues to have a strongly pejorative connotation in contemporary usage. This can be demonstrated empirically through a search of modern computerized databases containing a large number of diverse samples of contemporary speech and writing. A particularly good resource in this regard is Mark Davies's *Corpus of Contemporary American English*, a 425-million-word computerized compendium of attested samples of published American English writing and speech equally divided across a range of genres (academic journal articles, fiction writing, spoken news commentary, news writing, and magazine stories) from 1990 to the present. As of October 2010, the database contained 3,988 instances of the word *propaganda*. The 100 most recent of these included typical examples such as the following:

- "It gives him a huge platform to promulgate his, his particular brand of **propaganda** around the world. I think he ought to be at Guantanamo . . ." (spoken news commentary, ABC *This Week*, 2010)
- "We showed the Taliban's **propaganda** video of the attack to some of the men who fought there." (spoken news commentary, NBC *Dateline*, 2010)
- "The first of those mistakes is haste. The publicity release for Al Gore's **propaganda** film, *An Inconvenient Truth*, began thus: 'Humanity is sitting on a . . .'" (magazine story, *American Spectator*, 2010)
- "Finally, Stalin's soldiers were poorly motivated and badly trained. Soviet **propaganda** proclaiming that the Finns would welcome them as liberators . . ." (magazine story, *Military History*, 2010)
- ". . . evidence the group has a connection to al-Qaida. However, the group's **propaganda** clearly shows that they have been inspired and motivated by bin-Laden . . ." (written news report, Associated Press, 2010)
- "Bateson's interest was in Nazi **propaganda** films and their relationship to German fantasies of family life." (academic writing, *Anthropology Quarterly*, 2010)

- "... government, economics, and history curriculae, essentially replacing textbooks with right-wing political **propaganda**." (academic writing, *The Humanist*, 2010)
- "... a Hauser fellow at Harvard Law School, suggests that such education smacks of **propaganda** or religious proselytizing." (academic writing, *Middle East Quarterly*, 2009)

In almost every one of the 100 examples examined, the word *propaganda* is associated with some sort of negativity, ranging from extreme cases, like Soviet Communism, Al Qaeda terrorism, or Nazi Germany, to more subtle ones, such as religious proselytizing and insurance industry promotional literature; conversely, the term never occurs in conjunction with referents deemed to be positive by most Americans, such as *American* or *Christian* or *democratic*. And this random sampling covers a broad range of public genres. Thus, objective evidence from a large sampling of contemporary public writing and speech shows that the term *propaganda* today has a wholly pejorative connotation in American public (and presumably private) discourse.

TOWARD A CONTEMPORARY DEFINITION

Beyond this common understanding, though, there are significant differences in how people understand and use the term *propaganda*. For example, is propaganda necessarily untruthful or misleading? Is it harmful? Is it necessarily intentional, or can it be the unconscious byproduct of some other form of communication? Since computerized databases such as the *Corpus of Contemporary American English* referred to above cannot answer such questions, we need to turn to lexicographers, propaganda theorists, discourse analysts, and other experts. And here we find some significant differences regarding answers to these questions.

The *American Heritage College Dictionary*, for example, defines *propaganda* merely as "the systematic propagation of a doctrine or cause or of information reflecting the views and interests of its propagators" (1096). The *Cambridge Advanced Learner's Dictionary* goes further, suggesting that propaganda is deliberately and purposefully misleading: "information or ideas, which are often false, that an organization prints or broadcasts to make people agree with what it is saying." Similar in kind is this definition from the *Oxford Dictionaries* stating that propaganda is "information, especially of a biased or misleading nature, used to promote a political cause or point of view." The *Macmillan Dictionary* follows suit but is even stronger in its intimation that propaganda is false: "information, especially false information, that a government or organization spreads in order to influence people's opinions and beliefs." *Webster's Dictionary* goes further still, stating that propaganda is meant to do harm: "the spreading of ideas, information, or rumor for the purpose of injuring an institution, a cause, or a person; ideas, facts, or allegations spread deliberately to further one's cause or to damage an opposing cause; *also*: a public action having such an effect."

A number of contemporary scholars have weighed in with their own definitions. Nancy Snow, in *Propaganda, Inc.*, cites this definition from Everett M. Rogers's *History of Communication Study*:

> Three important characteristics of propaganda are that (1) it is inten-
> tional communication, designed to change the attitudes of the targeted
> audience; (2) it is advantageous to the persuader in order to further the
> persuader's cause vis-à-vis an audience (which explains why advertising,
> public relations, and political campaigns are a form of propaganda); and
> (3) it is usually one-way information (i.e., a mass media campaign) as
> opposed to education which is two-way and interactive. (214)

Anthony Pratkanis and Elliot Aronson, in *Age of Propaganda*, define it as follows: "[Propaganda is] mass 'suggestion' or influence through the ma-nipulation of symbols and the psychology of the individual. Propaganda is the communication of a point of view with the ultimate goal of having the recipient of the appeal come to 'voluntarily' accept this position as if it were his or her own" (11). James Shanahan, in *Propaganda without Propa-gandists*, gives this definition: "[Propaganda is] a form of communication in which specific interests achieve aims through covert and perhaps un-conscious manipulation of social structure and communication systems." Randal Marlin, in *Propaganda and the Ethics of Persuasion*, defines it as follows: "[Propaganda is] the organized attempt through communication to affect belief or action or inculcate attitudes in a large audience in ways that circumvent or suppress an individual's adequately informed, rational, reflective judgment" (22). Garth S. Jowett and Victoria O'Donnell, in *Pro-paganda and Persuasion*, offer this definition: "Propaganda is the deliber-ate, systematic attempt to shape perceptions, manipulate cognitions, and direct behavior to achieve a response that furthers the desired intent of the propagandist" (7). Jacques Ellul, the subject's foremost theorist, offered this partial definition in 1965: "Propaganda is a set of methods employed by an organized group that wants to bring about the active or passive participation in its actions of a mass of individuals, psychologically unified through psychological manipulations and incorporated in an organization" (61).

A COMPOSITE DEFINITION

It is to be expected that these various lexicographical and theoretical sources will vary somewhat in their definitions, erring on the side of caution. That is, they are more likely, out of scholarly prudence, to omit some feature of a word meaning than to include an inappropriate one. One approach to defining a term, then, would be to include only those features that are agreed upon by all authoritative sources. But that approach tends to drain all the blood out of a term and leave it undistinguished from its lexical neighbors. This methodological problem is best resolved by creating a composite definition that incorporates all the lexical features endorsed by a significant number of authorities.

The definition of *propaganda* I offer below is such a composite. None of the definitions of the term given above is entirely complete: each contains certain defining features of propaganda, but none contains all of them. Because each of these features is attested to by its inclusion in some authoritative definitions and because none of these features is incompatible with the others, I claim that my definition, which comprises *all* such features, is richer and more useful than any other.

What *are* the features of propaganda included in these various definitions? This list contains the features mentioned by at least two of the above sources:

1. Propaganda generally contains *false or misleading* information. This is noted explicitly in both the *Oxford* and *Macmillan* dictionaries but is only hinted at in the others. Of course, the truth value of information can be contested according to context, belief systems, and perspective: what is propaganda to one person may be truth to another, a difference resolvable only by the weight of argument and supporting evidence.

2. Propaganda is *manipulative* in the sense that it attempts to persuade people by devious or unfair means. Jowett and O'Donnell; Shanahan; Ellul; and Pratkanis and Aronson all specifically mention this feature. Others (*Webster's*; *Cambridge*; *Macmillan*; Snow/Rogers; Marlin) imply it in their choice of words like "rumor," "allegations," and "one-way information."

3. Propaganda is addressed to a *mass audience*, thus distinguishing it, for example, from mere gossip circulated among a small group of acquaintances. This feature is implied in the *Cambridge* and *Macmillan* dictionary definitions and is made explicit by Snow/Rogers; Pratkanis and Aronson; Ellul; and Marlin.

4. Propaganda is *advantageous* to the propagandist or to the party he or she represents. It must serve the propagandist's interests (*Webster's*; Snow/Rogers; Shanahan; Jowett and O'Donnell; implied by Ellul) and/or damage opposing interests (*Webster's*).

5. Propaganda must be crafted and disseminated *systematically*, in some kind of "organized" fashion (Marlin; Ellul); see *American Heritage* and Jowett and O'Donnell.

6. Propaganda is typically very *one-sided*, concealing information that would enable its audience to assess its truth value through critical examination (Snow/Rogers; Marlin; Pratkanis and Aronson; see also Ellul).

There may be some redundancy in this list, in that the characteristic manipulativeness (feature 2) of propaganda is strongly implied by the combined effect of at least two other features, namely 1 and 4. According to the *American Heritage College Dictionary*, to manipulate means "1. To operate or control by skilled use of the hands; handle, 2. To influence or manage shrewdly or deviously, 3. To tamper with or falsify for personal gain." Commenting on the synonymy of *manipulate, exploit*, and *maneuver*, it notes that "the central meaning shared by these verbs is 'to influence, manage, use, or control to one's advantage by artful or indirect means'" (825). The terms *deviously* and *falsify* clearly point to the "false or misleading" aspect of feature 1; and the phrases "for personal gain" and "to one's advantage" clearly echo the "advantageous" aspect of feature 4. Thus, by subsuming feature 2 under features 1 and 4, we can use Occam's razor to eliminate it.[1]

Putting these features together yields the following composite definition:

Propaganda is *false or misleading* information or ideas addressed to a *mass audience* by parties who thereby gain *advantage*. Propaganda is created and disseminated *systematically* and *does not invite critical analysis or response*.

In my view, all five of the features (italicized) in this definition are both necessary and sufficient for a proper definition of *propaganda*. If the information is truthful, it is not propaganda. If the information is addressed only to an individual or small group, it is not propaganda. If the communication is not in the source's interest, it is not propaganda. If the information is created and disseminated only in random or accidental fashion, it is not propaganda. If the information is conveyed in a way designed to stimulate the audience's rational, critical judgment, it is not propaganda.

None of the dictionary or expert definitions cited above capture all five of these defining features. The *American Heritage College Dictionary*'s definition, "The systematic propagation of a doctrine or cause or of information reflecting the views and interests of its propagators," for example, does not include the idea of the information being false or misleading or the idea of the audience's critical judgment being intentionally impeded. The *Macmillan Dictionary*'s definition ("information, especially false information, that a government or organization spreads in order to influence people's opinions and beliefs") omits the idea that such spreading of information is done systematically and the idea that it is designed to block the audience's critical judgment. Similar shortcomings can be found in all the other dictionary and expert definitions presented above.

METHODOLOGICAL RAMIFICATIONS

Let me now comment on each of the five key features, noting in particular how they should be included in any propaganda analysis.

False or misleading information: A great deal of discursive manipulation, or propagandizing, occurs not through false information per se but through the withholding of adequate information. For example, the propaganda campaign carried out by the Bush administration in the run-up to the U.S. invasion of Iraq in 2003 featured not so much blatant lies as an unending number of insinuations, half-truths, omissions, and other "textual silences" (Huckin, "Textual Silences" and "On Textual Silences"). Although such silences are a staple of propaganda campaigns, they tend to be overlooked in propaganda analysis. Hence, when talking about propaganda containing misleading information, analysts should take care to point out that such information is often misleading precisely because it hides important countervailing information through simple omission.

Mass audience: Propaganda is meant to effect political or commercial change, which can occur only through large numbers of people choosing to vote or purchase in certain ways. As Ellul says, "If the action obtained by propaganda is to be appropriate, it cannot be individual; it must be collective. Propaganda has meaning only when it obtains convergence, coexistence of a multiplicity of individual action-reflexes whose coordination can be achieved only through the intermediary of an organization" (28). A proper propaganda analysis should attempt to identify the target audience and rhetorically assess, even with an otherwise highly variegated group, whatever common characteristics the propagandist may be trying to exploit.

Advantage: Propaganda is always purposeful, its main purpose being to benefit the propagandist at the expense of the target audience. This overriding purpose accounts for the use of false or misleading information and for the circumvention of the audience's rational judgment, both of which advantage the propagandist. The propaganda analyst should attempt to identify the likely benefits accruing to the propagandist.

Systematically: This refers to whatever larger systems are in play regarding the creation and dissemination of propaganda. Some such systems have to do with logistics, business channels, and the technical capabilities of the media being used. Others are more abstract, including for example ideological and political systems. As much of the value in doing propaganda analysis resides in noting how a given piece of propaganda fits into the larger sociopolitical context, it is imperative that the analyst take these considerations into account.

Does not invite critical analysis or response: In some definitions of propaganda (not given here), the idea of circumventing critical judgment is characterized as simply making emotional appeals. Certainly, appeals to emotion can qualify under this heading, but there are many other ways a propagandist might not invite a critical response, for example through the use of logical fallacies or omissions of key information. The propaganda analyst needs to look for such elements in the propaganda message's content.

INTENTIONALITY AND CONSCIOUSNESS

According to the traditional view as depicted in the "History" section of this chapter, propaganda is the deliberate product of calculating minds, be they high officials of the Catholic church in the seventeenth through nineteenth centuries, a Russian political theorist like Lenin, or a public relations expert like Edward Bernays. Does this mean that propaganda is always intentionally created? Jowett and O'Donnell claim it is: "Propaganda is the *deliberate, systematic* attempt to shape perceptions." So does Rogers (qtd. in Snow): "[Propaganda] is intentional communication, designed to change the attitudes of the targeted audience." So also does *Webster's* (sense 3): "ideas, facts, or allegations spread *deliberately*." Indeed, the composite definition created above strongly implies agents who intentionally *design* and *create* information that they then *disseminate* to a certain audience so as to gain *advantage*. So I think the answer is clearly yes: propaganda is always created intentionally, not accidentally.

However, this is not to say that propaganda is always created and disseminated *consciously*. Nor does it have to be the product of some individual mind, after the fashion of Bernays or Goebbels. As Ellul notes in *Propaganda*,

> A common view of propaganda is that it is the work of a few evil men, seducers of the people, cheats and authoritarian rulers who want to dominate a population; that it is the handmaiden of more or less illegitimate powers. . . . According to this view, the public is just an object, a passive crowd that one can manipulate, influence, and use. . . . This view seems to me completely wrong. . . . Nowadays propaganda pervades all aspects of public life. (118–19)

In so doing, it "must express the fundamental currents of society" (38, 43). Such a view of propaganda as being ubiquitous and all-pervasive clearly conceives of the general public as being not merely victims of propaganda but also unwitting accomplices. Ellul calls this modern form of propaganda *sociological propaganda* and notes that it is "a phenomenon much more difficult to grasp than political propaganda, and is rarely discussed" (63). In contrast to traditional political propaganda, which, like Nazi or Soviet propaganda, works in top-down fashion, sociological propaganda "produces a progressive adaptation to a certain order of things, a certain concept of human relations, which unconsciously molds individuals and makes them conform to society" (64); elsewhere Ellul refers to it as *horizontal propaganda* (79). (A similar concept is espoused by James Shanahan under the heading of "the new propaganda"; note the title of his 2001 anthology, *Propaganda without Propagandists*, and the reference to "unconscious manipulation" in his definition of propaganda given earlier.)

Ellul elaborates on this idea of unconscious manipulation as follows:

Sociological propaganda springs up spontaneously; it is not the result of deliberate propaganda action. No propagandists deliberately use this method, though many practice it unwittingly, and tend in this direction without realizing it. For example, when an American producer makes a film, he has certain definite ideas he wants to express, which are not intended to be propaganda. Rather, the propaganda element is in the American way of life with which he is permeated and which he expresses in his film without realizing it. We see here the force of expansion of a vigorous society, which is totalitarian in the sense of the integration of the individual, and which leads to involuntary behavior. (64)

As I have argued elsewhere ("Textual Silences"), intentionality can be "dispersed" throughout a discourse community, arising not from the ingenuity of a single agent but from the collective presuppositions, so to speak, of the entire community. In the hands of an individual member, these community intentions can be manifested without conscious thought. Likewise, John Searle, in a discussion of what he labels "collective intentionality," asserts that intentionality is not necessarily conscious: a collectivity can have intentions of its own without being consciously aware of them (7). Ludwig Fleck's discussion of scientific thought illuminates this point. Fleck noted that scientific knowledge advances not so much individually as communally, through "a community of persons exchanging ideas or maintaining intellectual interaction" or *thought collective*. He claimed that "the individual within the collective is never, or hardly ever, conscious of the prevailing thought style, which almost always exerts an absolutely compulsive force upon his thinking and [with] which it is not possible to be at variance" (41).

I submit that this social construction of knowledge in science is similar to what happens in a system of "inverted totalitarianism" such as that described by Sheldon Wolin: "In coining the term 'inverted totalitarianism' I tried to find a name for a new type of political system, seemingly one driven by abstract totalizing powers, not by personal rule, one that succeeds by encouraging political disengagement rather than mass mobilization, that relies more on 'private' media than on public agencies to disseminate propaganda reinforcing the official version of events" (44). Wolin goes on to note that "inverted totalitarianism has emerged imperceptibly, *unpremeditatedly*, and in seeming unbroken continuity with the nation's political traditions" (46, emphasis mine). Thus we have a system that, like others, relies on propaganda to establish and expand its power but, unlike some others, does so via an incremental process that allays awareness and hence resistance. As an example, Wolin describes the monolithic reaction of the U.S. mass media to the 9/11 attacks:

> In a society where freedom of speech, media, and religion are guaranteed, where quirkiness is celebrated, why was the result unison? How is it that a society that makes a fetish of freedom of choice can produce a unanimity eerily comparable to that of a more openly coercive system? Is it a process like the "hidden hand" of Adam Smith's free market where, unprompted by any central directorate, the uncoordinated actions of individuals, each concerned to advance his self-interest, nonetheless produce an overall effect that is good for all? (6)

By acknowledging that propaganda can be and, I would argue, *is* most typically disseminated collectively and unconsciously, we can arrive at a deeper understanding of how exactly it works. In particular, instead of restricting our attention to the prototypical examples of propaganda—advertisements, political campaign messages, blog postings, and the like—we should take a broader view and look for the more subtle and actually more widespread cases, the "pre-propaganda" that prepares the ground for active propaganda or, in Ellul's words, "the creation of feelings or stereotypes useful when the time comes" (31). For it is these inobvious cases that offer more penetrating insight into the cultural and ideological frameworks of a society, as illustrated by Wolin's example and commentary above. What is the unspoken "common sense" that produced the "monolithic reaction" to 9/11 of which Wolin speaks? More generally, what are the collective presuppositions of our society? Why do we citizens routinely recycle various myths (for example, about the "superiority" of laissez-faire capitalism, about our armed forces "protecting our various freedoms" by fighting endless wars overseas, about the United States having "the best health care in the world") when such beliefs are demonstrably wrong?

CONCLUSION

Marlin notes that "the study of propaganda is a complex undertaking. It is not always easy, for example, to determine the extent to which propaganda activity is directed from above as distinct from spontaneously generated by individuals or groups below" (62). Studies of contemporary propaganda must take into account this integration of vertical and horizontal propaganda that leads to the kind of "political disengagement" that Wolin speaks of—a condition that is especially striking, and alarming, at a time when the country is going through one economic crisis after another, is dealing with high levels of unemployment and home foreclosures, is bogged down in multiple wars overseas, is facing an imminent shredding of the safety net, is sacrificing environmental protection to the profiteering of multinational corporations, and has effectively given over political sovereignty to the monied interests who can now make unlimited campaign donations to their favorite politicians.

These problems are due, in large part, to the successful propagandizing of the citizenry, which has continually been outmaneuvered by corporate America and its political vassals in the federal and state governments. To some degree this can be attributed to specific forms of propaganda on specific issues, for example news stories about Saddam Hussein's so-called weapons of mass destruction or glossy advertisements about the desirability of subprime, adjustable-rate mortgages. But these cases of "vertical" propaganda are usually quite obvious, easy to detect, and easy to analyze; and they may not even be the most potent instances of propaganda. More important, I think, are the "horizontal" cases, the ones that involve the sort of sociological propaganda that Ellul speaks of. Study after study (for example, Frank; Leopold; Westen) has documented how we the American people ourselves have been complicit in the ongoing de facto neofeudalism in this country, often voting against our own best economic interests (or not voting at all) and failing to stand up to the corporate takeover of our sovereignty.

Trying to understand this "horizontal" phenomenon is where propaganda analysis today, in my view, can be most useful. Two pathways for investigation in particular hold promise—that of distraction and that of fear. Distraction in the form of mass entertainment has of course long been a standard technique used by oppressive political regimes to divert people's attention away from their oppression, going back to the gladiatorial combats and circuses of the Roman Empire and beyond. A more recent example is found in Aldous Huxley's 1932 dystopian novel *Brave New World* with its feelies, soma, and orgy-porgy entertainment. In a later (1965) essay titled "Propaganda in a Democratic Society," Huxley wrote this:

> In their propaganda today's dictators rely for the most part on repetition, suppression and rationalization—the repetition of catchwords which they wish to be accepted as true, the suppression of facts which they wish to be ignored, the arousal and rationalization of passions which

may be used in the interests of the Party or the State. *As the art and science of manipulation come to be better understood, the dictators of the future will doubtless learn to combine these techniques with the non-stop distractions which, in the West, are now threatening to drown in a sea of irrelevance the rational propaganda essential to the maintenance of individual liberty and the survival of democratic institutions.* (29–30, emphasis mine)

Neil Postman's classic 1985 book, *Amusing Ourselves to Death*, is a full-length exposition of Huxley's observation. Postman notes that "the Founding Fathers did not foresee that tyranny by government might be superseded by another sort of problem altogether, namely, the corporate state, which through television now controls the flow of public discourse in America" (139). He continues, "Tyrants of all varieties have always known about the value of providing the masses with amusements as a means of pacifying discontent. But most of them could not have even hoped for a situation in which the masses would ignore that which does not amuse" (141). Writing before the age of the Internet, Postman's indictment singles out television as the main source of political disengagement; if he were writing today, one can easily imagine him aiming his criticism at Facebook and Twitter instead.

The second likely source of political disengagement, in my view, is the climate of fear that has been cultivated by various political administrations and the corporate-owned mass media, especially since the attacks of 9/11. Wolin's book, published in 2008, is the best exposition I know of on this topic. Wolin writes,

Inverted totalitarianism thrives on a politically demobilized society, that is, a society in which the citizens, far from being whipped into a continuous frenzy by the regime's operatives, are politically lethargic, reminiscent of Tocqueville's privatized citizenry. Roughly between one-half and two-thirds of America's qualified voters fail to vote, thus making the management of the "active" electorate far easier. Every apathetic citizen is a silent enlistee in the cause of inverted totalitarianism. Yet apathy is not simply the result of a TV culture. It is, in its own way, a political response. Ordinary citizens have been the victims of a counterrevolution that has brought "rollbacks" of numerous social services which were established only after hard-fought political struggles, and which the earlier Republican administrations of Eisenhower and Nixon had accepted as major elements in a national consensus.

> Rollbacks don't simply reverse previous social gains; they also teach political futility to the Many. And along the way they mock the ideal and practice of consensus.
>
> Where classic totalitarianism—whether of the German, Italian, or Soviet type—aimed at fashioning followers rather than citizens, inverted totalitarianism can achieve the same end by furnishing substitutes such as "consumer sovereignty" and "shareholder democracy" that give a "sense of participation" without demands or responsibilities. An inverted regime prefers a citizenry that is uncritically complicit rather than involved. President Bush's first words to the citizenry after 9/11 were not an appeal for sacrifice in a common cause but "unite, consume, fly."
>
> Yet elements of inverted totalitarianism could not crystallize in the absence of a stimulus that would rouse the apathetic just enough to gain their support and obedience. The threat of terrorism supplied that element. It could evoke fear and obedience on demand . . . without causing paralysis or skepticism. (64–65)

The threat of terrorism, as of this writing, persists. However, in the midst of yet another economic recession, other fears have taken even greater hold—fear of joblessness, fear of losing one's home or one's life savings, fear of going without medical care. But although according to public opinion polls such fears are on the minds of most Americans, they are manifested not in any citizen uprisings against the political establishment but only in private conversations with family, friends, neighbors, even strangers—that is, in horizontal propaganda.

In any case, whether or not distraction or fear (or both, perhaps working together) is the main source of the political disengagement we are witnessing in America today, the definition I have proposed in this chapter will direct the analyst's attention to those aspects of propaganda that are most characteristic of all propaganda while also being applicable to the newer and more powerful sociological propaganda theorized by Ellul—propaganda that works horizontally as much as it does vertically. Both traditional propaganda and the newer sociological propaganda comprise "false or misleading information or ideas addressed to a mass audience by parties who thereby gain advantage"; both types are "created and disseminated systematically and do not invite critical analysis or response." The definition I have proposed here is thus to be preferred over all the others reviewed, for two main reasons. First, it is the most complete definition, representing as it does a composite of features from all the others.

And second, it is more in keeping with the more sophisticated nature of propaganda today and our more sophisticated understanding of it. In particular, it takes into account the often uncertain agency involved in the creation and dissemination of propaganda in this Information Age (compare Marlin: "It is not always easy . . . to determine the extent to which propaganda activity is directed from above as distinct from spontaneously generated by individuals or groups below"). My definition is deliberately worded in such a way as to capture this uncertainty.

Note

1. See van Dijk for extended discussion of the concept of discursive manipulation.

Works Cited

Bernays, Edward. *Crystallizing Public Opinion.* New York: Boni and Liveright, 1923. Print.

———. *Propaganda.* Brooklyn: Ig, 1928. Print.

Bracken, Brendan. *Parliamentary Debates: 5th Series—Volume 401.* London: HMSO, 1980. Print.

Cambridge Advanced Learner's Dictionary. Cambridge University Press. 2016. Web. 6 May 2016.

Creel, George. *How We Advertised America.* New York: Harper, 1920. Print.

Davies, Mark. *The Corpus of Contemporary American English: 450 Million Words, 1990–Present.* Provo: Brigham Young University, 2008. Web.

DiMaggio, Anthony R. *Mass Media, Mass Propaganda.* Lanham, Md.: Lexington, 2008. Print.

Doob, Leonard. *Public Opinion and Propaganda.* 2nd ed. Hamden: Archon, 1966. Print.

Ellul, Jacques. *Propaganda: The Formation of Men's Attitudes.* New York: Vintage, 1965. Print.

Fleck, Ludwig. *Genesis and Development of a Scientific Fact.* Chicago: U of Chicago P, 1977. Print.

Frank, Thomas. *What's the Matter with Kansas? How Conservatives Won the Heart of America.* New York: Henry Holt, 2004. Print.

Huckin, Thomas. "On Textual Silences, Large and Small." *Traditions of Writing Research.* Ed. Charles Bazerman et al. New York: Routledge, 2010. 419–31. Print.

———. "Textual Silences and the Discourse of Homelessness." *Discourse and Society* 13.3 (2002): 347–72. Print.

Huxley, Aldous. *Brave New World.* New York: Harper and Row, 1932. Print.

Huxley, Aldous. *Brave New World Revisited.* New York: Harper and Row, 1965. Print.

Jowett, Garth S., and Victoria O'Donnell. *Propaganda and Persuasion.* 5th ed. Los Angeles: Sage, 2012. Print.

Lenin, Vladimir I. *Selected Works of V. I. Lenin.* Moscow: Progress, 1977. Print.

Leopold, Les. *The Looting of America: How Wall Street's Game of Fantasy Finance Destroyed Our Jobs, Pensions, and Prosperity.* White River Junction, Vt.: Chelsea Green, 2009. Print.

Lippmann, Walter. *Public Opinion.* New York: Free, 1922. Print.

Macmillan Dictionary. Macmillan Publishers Limited. 2009–16. Web. 6 May 2016.

Marlin, Randal. *Propaganda and the Ethics of Persuasion.* Peterborough, Ont.: Broadview, 2002. Print.

Miller, Mark Crispin. Introduction. *Propaganda.* By Edward Bernays. Brooklyn: Ig, 1928. 9–33. Print.

Oxford Dictionaries. Oxford University Press. 2016. Web. 6 May 2016.

Postman, Neil. *Amusing Ourselves to Death.* New York: Penguin, 1985. Print.

Pratkanis, Anthony, and Elliot Aronson. *Age of Propaganda.* Rev. ed. New York: W. H. Freeman, 2001. Print.

"Propaganda." *American Heritage College Dictionary.* 3rd ed. 1993. Print.

"Propaganda." *The New Encyclopedia Britannica.* 15th ed. 1982. Print.

Rogers, Everett M. *A History of Communication Study: A Biographical Approach.* New York: Free, 1997. Print.

Searle, John. *The Construction of Social Reality.* New York: Free, 1995. Print.

Shanahan, James. *Propaganda without Propagandists.* Cresskill, N.J.: Hampton, 2001. Print.

Skeat, Walter. *An Etymological Dictionary of the English Language.* Rev. ed. London: Oxford UP, 1909. Print.

Snow, Nancy. *Propaganda, Inc.* 2nd ed. New York: Seven Stories, 2002. Print.

Van Dijk, Teun A. "Discourse and Manipulation." *Discourse and Society* 17.2 (2006): 359–83. Print.

Webster's Dictionary. Merriam-Webster, Inc. 2015. Web. 6 May 2016.

Westen, Drew. *The Political Brain: The Role of Emotion in Deciding the Fate of the Nation.* New York: Public Affairs, 2007. Print.

Wolin, Sheldon. *Democracy, Inc.* Princeton: Princeton UP, 2008. Print.

A TAXONOMY OF BULLSHIT

GARY THOMPSON

MAGIC, n. An art of converting superstition into coin. There are other arts serving the same high purpose, but the discreet lexicographer does not name them.
—Ambrose Bierce, *The Devil's Dictionary*

There exists a category of statements, most familiar to us in the connected domains of public relations, advertising, and politics, that can be impolitely but justifiably called *bullshit*. As introduced to academic discussion via the 1986 article "On Bullshit" by the American philosopher Harry Frankfurt, the term offers an insight into some of the most pernicious forms of current propaganda.[1]

As commonly used, bullshit refers broadly to any statement, position, concept, or manner of treatment that is without value. In the specific meaning given by Frankfurt, however, bullshit is any communication made without reference to whether it is true or not, generally with the purpose of building a good impression of the speaker and whomever he or she represents. Frankfurt acknowledges that "the phenomenon of bullshit is . . . vast and amorphous" and restricts himself to discussing implications of the term itself rather than its "rhetorical uses and misuses" (2, 3). However, its rhetorical uses and misuses are very much relevant to discussions of propaganda: if rhetoric is properly considered to be the study and practice of persuasive communication, and if one of the dominant forms of persuasion is bullshit, then we need a better grasp of the phenomenon's rhetorical power, if only for self-defense.

If in 1986 it were true, as Frankfurt said, that there was "so much bullshit" (1), the problem has only worsened since, due to cable and satellite TV channels, the Internet, and other media mutations. Some bullshit may be innocuous or even entertaining; other forms, however, function as propaganda. In order to trace the relation between bullshit and propaganda, it will be necessary to do several things: extend Frankfurt's definition through a taxonomy of bullshit; discuss in more detail how bullshit and propaganda are related types of discourse; and discuss reasons why it is important but difficult to counter bullshit. Bullshit is a more varied phenomenon than "On Bullshit" can acknowledge and one that is ultimately corrosive to the modern public sphere. Frankfurt's definition and subsequent discussion can be developed into a heuristic device for a clearer understanding of the purposes and techniques of contemporary propaganda.

TAXONOMY

Most people use the term *bullshit* to refer uncategorically to anything without value: as there is no value in shit, there is no value in thinking too curiously on the matter. But if we want to understand the phenomenon more generally, definitions are a good place to start. Frankfurt connects bullshit to *humbug*, which in Max Black's parsing is "deceptive misrepresentation, short of lying, especially by pretentious word or deed, of somebody's own thoughts, feelings, or attitudes" (143).[2] Frankfurt takes issue with the "short of lying" part, suggesting that bullshit is analogous to shoddy goods, provided by speakers who care only about how they are perceived, not about whether what they are saying is true. According to Frankfurt, the essence of bullshit is its phoniness (47). The paradigm case for bullshit is a political leader speaking on a patriotic occasion: such a speaker does not intend to deceive anyone in talking about the Greatest Nation in the History of the World or otherwise wrapping himself in the flag; but neither he nor his audience think his resonant phrases describe anything real. He is speaking phrases detached from either truth or lies, and his purpose is to lead his audience to thinking well of him. Bullshit, in this formulation, is more dangerous than outright lies, since the liar at least respects the truth enough to lead people away from it. The bullshitter doesn't care.

As cogent as Frankfurt's analysis is, however, it does not cover all cases. Subsequent discussions, particularly that of G. A. Cohen, note that Frankfurt's definition does not account for much of what we term bullshit. Cohen's bête noire is poststructuralist academic writing, which he calls "unclarifiable nonsense" (332). Such writers may care deeply about the truth of their statements, but the jargon used makes the statements impenetrable. Another objection to Frankfurt's definition is that raised by Ben Kotzee: phrases such as *collateral damage* for unintended civilian deaths in war or *hexagonal fastening device* for a bolt do have some relation to truth, even though they may fairly be called bullshit because they disguise or inflate more normal usages (168). So we should look further into categories of bullshit, including but reaching beyond Frankfurt's definition to uncover some of the relations between bullshit and propaganda.

BULLSHIT RELATED TO PROPAGANDA

Lies

When we challenge an outrageous statement by saying, "Don't give me that bullshit," characteristically we are objecting to an outright falsehood. Cohen notes that Frankfurtian bullshit is not concerned with one of the most popular meanings of the term in use—that of outright lying. For example, in the Bush administration's statements leading up to the Iraq war, the assertion that Saddam Hussein's Iraq had "weapons of mass destruction" was called bullshit not primarily because of the phrase's deceptive imprecision but because it was almost entirely false, perhaps intentionally so. The usefulness of the neither-true-nor-false characterization should not obscure the fact that much propaganda simply furthers false claims (for example, consider the use of *death panels* during the 2010 debate over health care legislation).[3] These were bullshit as direct lies, with no apparent intention to promote the stature of the speaker.

Spin

Spin is a type of Frankfurtian bullshit clearly of use in propaganda. It may be regarded as an offhand label for *euphemism* or *dysphemism*, terms that modify the usual responses to words, phrases, or events by adding or taking away emotional connotation. Spin is best understood as what Andrew Aberdein (after the psychologist Charles Stevenson) calls *persuasive definition*, the use of a term that maintains the meaning and reference but alters the tone (154–56). For example, the denotative meaning of *the United States* and *America* is identical (though Canadians might disagree), but using *America* necessarily interjects an emotional connotation that is inescapably part of the meaning, designed to create a positive response.

We would probably not sing along to the music of Irving Berlin's stirring anthem "God Bless the United States."

Many examples of spin can be found in political discourse. Prior to announcing support for same-sex civil unions and marriages, President Obama let it be known that his position on these was "evolving" (so as to undercut opponents' charges that he was a "flip-flopper"). More serious euphemisms such as *ethnic cleansing* or *friendly fire* do the work denounced by George Orwell in "Politics and the English Language" of "mak[ing] lies sound truthful and murder respectable" (265). Other less lethal terms, such as *political correctness*, *downsizing*, and *outsourcing*, have become naturalized through repetition. The distinction between these spin terms and polite or joking euphemisms for sex, excretion, and death is that the latter are not usually offered for propagandistic purposes.

Equivocation

A special case of bullshit, related to both lies and spin, equivocation depends on alternative meanings of words and phrases, understood in one sense by the speaker or author of a source text, in another by the audience—and presented in such a way as to allow or even encourage the alternate interpretation. President Clinton proclaimed during the Monica Lewinsky scandal in 1998 that he did not "have sexual relations with that woman," with the key phrase *sexual relations* meaning vaginal intercourse rather than the more general definition, which would include oral sex. In equivocation, a word can function in two or more contexts. For example, *family* can mean the domestic social relation of parents, children, and other close relations, or it can refer to other, sometimes metaphorically close groupings (as in biology). The metaphor of family subsequently has been used by corporations to characterize their organizational structures through the language of human relations.

Of particular relevance to propaganda are god-terms such as *freedom* and *liberty* in political speeches. These are both spin and equivocation, used primarily to make the audience feel good by means of shifting definitions of key terms. *Freedom*, for example, may be understood by audiences to mean civil rights or free speech, when the speaker is using it to refer to unrestricted trade. A nonpolitical instance of equivocation is the term *excellence*, endemic to business and university mission statements (like thousands of other colleges and universities, Marquette University is devoted to "the fostering of personal and professional excellence" [Marquette]). Bill Readings's book *The University in Ruins* points to this god-term *excellence* as an empty signifier, symptomatic of the late twentieth-century corporatization of universities. As Readings notes, the term has no meaning outside of a specific context (excellence at swimming, accounting, and so on); its appropriation for PR purposes is a kind of equivocation. The recurrence of the term in universities' discourse is a reminder that bullshit pervades public discourse even in those institutions that proclaim their devotion to truth and accuracy in language.

Irrelevance

Both political discourse and advertising make a practice of offering possibly true but irrelevant claims. Irrelevance applies not only to claims that are provably true but unimportant but also to those that are essentially unprovable or impossibly subjective. Outbursts of appeals to patriotism are used to obscure questions about candidates' competence or policies. The fallacy of popular appeal—"America's best-selling beer"—diverts attention from questions of quality. Coca-Cola may be the world's most valuable brand name, but that is hardly a compelling reason to drink it. Irrelevance depends on isolating features of the topic and highlighting those in preference to others that may be more significant.

Irrelevant bullshit may come not from an individual but from a corporation (or individual representing a corporate viewpoint). If we ponder a phrase such as *America's fastest growing better burger concept,* we may be troubled by just how such a claim maps onto reality.[4] As with much bullshit, this statement offers impressive words as placeholders, leaving the audience to project positive associations.

Much irrelevant bullshit seems trivial. What is the point, after all, of complaining about advertising claims? If Anheuser-Busch tells us that Budweiser has *drinkability,* that is already a self-parody. Anyone who is taken in by such claims, we may think, deserves whatever minimal harm may follow. However, the danger is that such claims routinely advanced will erode the possibility of using language to convey truth.

NON-PROPAGANDISTIC BULLSHIT

However, not all bullshit is propaganda. Some types arise for innocent or even praiseworthy reasons.

Bluffing

Someone put on the spot to talk about a subject he or she knows nothing about may produce bullshit but not propaganda. Kotzee points to this usage, giving the example of an unprepared student attempting to bullshit his way through a difficult exam question. The unfortunate Miss South Carolina 2007 became a YouTube sensation when she was asked why so many U.S. students cannot find the United States on a world map:

> I personally believe, that U.S. Americans, are unable to do so, because uh, some, people out there, in our nation don't have maps. And uh, I believe that our education like such as in South Africa, and the Iraq, everywhere like such as . . . and, I believe that they should uh, our education over here, in the U.S. should help the U.S. or should help South Africa, and should help the Iraq and Asian countries so we will be able to build up our future, for us. (Miss Teen USA)

Something of a gray area between bluffing and propaganda is evident when a political candidate wants to stake out a position but is unprepared to do so. In November 2011, presidential candidate Herman Cain famously fumbled through a response to a question about President Obama's policy toward Libya (Cain). Such statements are best considered to be bluffing—definitely bullshit but not propaganda because they are not addressed to a mass audience, not distributed systematically, and not intended to gain advantage (beyond getting out of an uncomfortable situation). Both lies and bluffing do have some relation to the truth. As Frankfurt points out, the liar at least knows what the truth is and hopes to lead his or her audience away from it. Going on from Frankfurt's point, we can say that the bluffer knows that he or she does not know what the truth is and hopes to lead the audience away from that realization and on to firmer ground. Bluffing is therefore related to irrelevance—the difference being that the bluffer is usually surprised at being put on the spot, whereas bullshit based on irrelevance is often intentional.

Polite Bullshit

Most of us make statements daily that are bullshit, done for reasons of tact or social bonding. We may, for example, ask about a colleague's family members or express sympathy that is not deeply felt. We may introduce irrelevance through comments on weather or sports before getting to our real concerns. We may offer a harmless piece of flattery: *Have you been working out? You look like you've lost some weight.* Eulogies and comments about the recently departed are not necessarily truthful or expressive of our true thoughts.

Playful Bullshit

There is a ludic quality to much bullshit that should be acknowledged. Bullshitters are often playing with language, counting on collusion with the audience to cement a bond. This category can be split into what might be termed *counter-bullshit*, or a communication that takes bullshit's form but not its intent, for satirical purposes, and *ironic bullshit*, still meant to persuade (and thus possibly propaganda) but to do so by adopting a cool, insincere stance.

Stephen Colbert makes incisive use of counter-bullshit in his portrayal of a conservative blowhard on *The Colbert Report*: "Anyone can read the news to you. I promise to feel the news at you." Colbert established the paradigm with the term *truthiness*. Breaking character in an interview, he elaborated on the strategy: "'We're not talking about truth, we're talking about something that seems like truth—the truth we want to exist'" (Sternbergh). Examples of ironic bullshit would include advertisements that in effect wink at the audience, such as the Orbit gum ads that apparently produce impossibly gleaming teeth or the retro Mentos ads featuring hokey, ABBA-style music. Both truthiness and ironic ads point to a less-recognized problem with bullshit: our desire to blame the purveyors of bullshit without admitting our own complicity in buying in.

Another example of playful bullshit is that of comic speech, which is less satirically pointed. Professor Irwin Corey served as a stand-in, in 1974, for the reclusive novelist Thomas Pynchon in receiving the National Book Award.[5] This sort of bullshit is entertaining because it references and mocks the person who, as Frankfurt says, must say something owing to the context and unfortunately has no knowledge of the subject (and so must bluff). Depending on context, such satire can be more or less cruel, but because it depends on an unstated agreement between source and audience, it is hardly to be considered propaganda.

Variations on such harmless, non-propagandistic bullshit may be regarded as performative. Philip Eubanks and John D. Schaeffer point out that in some contexts, bullshit evokes a kind of sly affection and admiration, as in the saying "If you can't dazzle them with brilliance, baffle them with bullshit" (373). In fictional contexts, we may admire characters who extract themselves from difficult situations through verbal pyrotechnics (for example, Falstaff, or Ignatius J. Reilly from John Kennedy Toole's *A Confederacy of Dunces*). We may also admire the performance in propagandistic bullshit, and that performance can be yet another device to draw us in.

A GOOD WORD FOR PROPAGANDA?

Up to now, propaganda has functioned in this essay as a devil-term. But there may be circumstances in which propaganda (including bullshit) is desirable. The goal may be to motivate the public in a necessary war effort (as in propaganda during World War II), to stimulate economic activity, or to build support for social goods such as a better-educated public or improved public safety. And once we admit to such generally held public goals, making due allowance for ideology, we may tolerate the use of pro-pagandistic bullshit as well as rational discussion to further these goals.

Arguments have been advanced in favor of propaganda. Its most serious advocate, and one of bullshit's central practitioners as the godfather of public relations, was Edward Bernays.[6] His argument in *Propaganda* (1928) was that societies, whether democratic or totalitarian, always have leaders in charge, and those leaders must use persuasive methods to build public support, even when their citizens, having less information or different interests, do not recognize the reasons for their leaders' decisions. By and large, no public wants to go to war, pay taxes, or make other efforts that do not benefit them personally. So democratic societies in particular must make use of propaganda to maintain public order and build a strong economy. To think otherwise, he says, is to deny reality.

Bernays's argument elides good and bad rhetoric, or rhetoric and propaganda as commonly understood. Both propaganda and the harmful forms of bullshit are antidemocratic in that they seek to manipulate us to gain our consent without our understanding what it is that we are consenting to. Quite apart from the questionable ethics involved, to use bullshit as a basis of public support risks losing that support later.

Bernays's position had its opponents. The Institute for Propaganda Analysis was very active in the 1930s but lost support after the United States entered the war, partly because we needed to use our own propaganda in the war effort and partly because business leaders did not particularly want the public to be suspicious of their own sorts of propaganda. Any concerted effort to educate the public about bullshit has to reckon with opposition from those who deploy it.[7]

HOW DOES IT WORK?

Because at least some bullshit is commonly found in contemporary propaganda, and because a high quantity of bullshit can lessen the ability to appreciate and use cogent arguments, it is increasingly important to attempt to counter bullshit. It may be helpful to examine in more detail some of the ways in which propagandistic bullshit works.

Familiar models of propaganda derive from practices in totalitarian societies, such as those in Nazi Germany or the USSR, in which official media were controlled from the top down. In democratic societies, control from the top is less effective than that making use of communication from multiple sources (news media, advertising, free public discourse) to reinforce the message through appeals grounded in ideology. In societies in which media messages emanate from a single, top-down source, it is easier—though possibly physically dangerous—to counter propaganda through questions about that source; but with forms of propaganda as encountered in our own and other democratic cultures, frequently repeated messages appear to be simply the way things are. With contemporary technologies, propagandists can target messages more precisely to individual audiences rather than rely on mass media. Unlike totalitarian systems, democracies work less through brute force than through manufacturing consent.[8] Training ourselves to recognize these subtler forms of control is crucial to maintaining our own freedom of thought as well as the possibility of substantive public discourse.

We can see some of the devices designed to lead us to buy in through an example from advertising. Even though consumer goods are trivial in their social effects, their abundance contributes to the quantity of bullshit and thus to its assault on meaning. Television-saturated viewers of the late 1950s and early 1960s heard repeatedly a statement broadcast in innumerable toothpaste ads, a statement that resonates with phoniness:[9]

> *Crest has been shown to be an effective decay-preventive dentifrice that can be of significant value when used in a conscientiously applied program of oral hygiene and regular professional care.*

This slogan, prominently featured on the sides of toothpaste boxes and tubes, meets several criteria for bullshit:

has been shown—Note the use of passive voice, which conceals the agent of demonstration (perhaps the laboratories of Procter and Gamble).

an effective decay-preventive dentifrice—Pseudoscientific or pseudomedical language is useful for impressing the gullible.

> **that can be of significant value**—Vague terminology. Also of significant
> value would be rinsing your mouth out with tap water after eating.
> **when used in a conscientiously applied program**—Here we encounter
> the familiar *helps* motif: *A* helps to achieve *B*, and so all the benefits,
> not some, of *B* transfer to *A*. Nike basketball shoes help Michael
> Jordan on the basketball court, so (as Spike Lee says) "gotta be the
> shoes."
> **of oral hygiene and regular professional care**—Here is what's in it
> for the American Dental Association. To make Crest or any other
> toothpaste worth the price, you have to see your dentist regularly.

Bullshit originates through what we might call (adapting Aberdein's
term) *semantic negligence*. Statements in advertisements such as the toothpaste ad above take no responsibility for any meaning we may derive from
them. If we follow Frankfurt's limited definition, bullshitters neither know
nor care about the truth, so long as they achieve a positive impression with
their audience. This state of not-caring is comparable to negligence in professions: doctors, lawyers, and other professionals who fail to meet their
responsibilities face legal sanctions, and purveyors of bullshit, whether
deliberately or not, are neglecting their responsibilities to the language
that all of us rely upon for communication.

Such discipline is invoked by Orwell in "Politics and the English Language" as a means of correcting what he terms "bad usage." There is some
overlap between Orwell's targets and bullshit, and the remedies in both
cases may be necessary but are not sufficient: vigilance and sheer will are
likely to be exhausted nowadays by the volume of bullshit produced. However, it is difficult to see any alternative to continual, granular resistance to
bullshit. For this purpose, we need a better understanding of how bullshit
is used in propaganda.

In the case of spin, it may be less semantic negligence than semantic
malfeasance. Spin is the principal stock-in-trade of the public relations industry (*industry* may itself be euphemistic). When trying out titles for their
book about public relations, *Toxic Sludge Is Good for You*, John Stauber
and Sheldon Rampton were approached by a PR consultant for the Water
Environment Federation, the professional organization for waste-water
treatment facilities. She suggested a different title, since their organization
was trying to replace the term *sludge* (which she said is not toxic) with *biosolids* (100). According to the *HarperCollins Dictionary of Environmental
Science*, sludge is "a viscous semisolid mixture of bacteria- and virus-laden

organic matter, toxic metals, synthetic organic chemicals, and settled solids removed from domestic and industrial waste water at a sewage treatment plant'" (qtd. in Stauber and Rampton 104). Before arriving at *biosolids*, the Name Change Task Force considered other terms, such as "'all growth,' 'purenutri,' 'biolife,' 'bioslurp,' 'black gold,' 'geoslime,' 'sca-doo,' 'the end product,' 'humanure,' 'hu-doo,' 'organic residuals,' 'bioresidue,' 'urban biomass,' 'powergro,' 'organite,' 'recyclite,' 'nutri-cake' and 'R.O.S.E.,' short for 'recycling of solids environmentally'" (107).

Political consultants' careers thrive on bullshit. Among the best known of these is Frank Luntz, who advises Republicans on the most effective way to spin policy proposals. During the Occupy Wall Street movement in 2011, Luntz advised the Republican Governors' Association to substitute "economic freedom" or "the free market" for "capitalism"; to assert that government "takes from the rich" rather than "taxes the rich"; to speak about "hardworking taxpayers" rather than "the middle class"; and to invoke "government waste" rather than "government spending" (Tone).[10]

Political consultants generally work best in the background, but ego can get the better of them, as in the adviser—widely believed to be Karl Rove—who spoke to Ron Suskind about having moved ahead of the "reality-based community":

> "That's not the way the world really works anymore," he continued. "We're an empire now, and when we act, we create our own reality. And while you're studying that reality—judiciously, as you will—we'll act again, creating other new realities, which you can study too, and that's how things will sort out. We're history's actors . . . and you, all of you, will be left to just study what we do." (Suskind)

Bullshit surfaces even in the positive-sounding names devised for so-called astroturf groups, fake grassroots citizens' groups organized by public relations firms to exert political pressure. Some examples include Americans for Constitutional Freedom, bankrolled by *Playboy* and *Penthouse* to combat the Pornography Commission headed by former attorney general Ed Meese (Stauber and Rampton 14), and the Global Climate Coalition, an anti-environmental front group.[11] And in the post–Citizens United political climate, there are super PACs with spin-infused names: Restore Our Future (not to be confused with Winning Our Future), Make Us Great Again, Endorse Liberty, the Red White and Blue Fund, Freedomworks for America, and American Crossroads.[12] (These are parodied by Stephen Colbert's Americans for a Better Tomorrow, Tomorrow.)

In a democratic society, propagandists rely on the audience to buy in. One of the key devices to achieve this is *enthymemes*, phrases that come with embedded arguments. The most important aspect of enthymemes is that key parts of the argument are supplied by the audience, not stated by the source. Consequently, the source is not literally responsible for what we as the audience make of the statements. More important, we are more likely to buy into a candidate's message since we ourselves supplied the missing parts. President George H. W. Bush's phrase *a thousand points of light* can be elaborated into such a claim as this: *Support for the poor and disadvantaged is best accomplished not through government programs but through individual charitable work.* Labeling candidate Barack Obama's stylized image, such as in the familiar poster created by Shepard Fairey, with the single word *Hope* works similarly: *This candidate represents the positive value of hope for the future, in contrast to the politics of the recent past; therefore you should vote for him.* In the corporate world, references to *the bottom line* are abbreviated arguments that financial considerations trump humane concerns.

A type of communication related to the enthymeme is the visual argument: the image of a politician standing before a flag or of a candidate allowing a child to rub his hair may be phrased by audiences as a claim about her patriotism or his easy relations with the public, with the further, hidden claim that patriotic or friendly leaders are the best choices for high office. When phrased in this way, the claim's absurdity is evident, but images do not usually prompt such articulation.

CONCLUSION

To call something a *taxonomy* requires that we think of it as a system. Bullshit is too loose a concept, too colloquially designated, to have the same degree of rigor as the periodic table. However, there are varieties of bullshit, which vary widely in terms of their relevance to propaganda. According to the definition of propaganda advanced by Thomas Huckin in chapter 5 of this volume, "Propaganda is false or misleading information or ideas addressed to a mass audience by parties who thereby gain advantage. Propaganda is created and disseminated systematically and does not invite critical analysis or response." As described by Frankfurt, however, bullshit may or may not be deliberately false; it is advanced with no particular concern about whether it is true or not; it is likely to be misleading; it may or may not be advanced for purposes of gaining an advantage, beyond an attempt to create a good opinion of the speaker; it may or may not be systematic in its creation and distribution; and it clearly does not invite critical analysis or response. There is therefore some overlap between the two categories of discourse. At this point we should consider our responsibilities as the audience for both propaganda and bullshit: what makes us susceptible to propagandistic bullshit, and what hope do we have of countering its effects?

A necessary—but not sufficient—key to combating the influence of bullshit is a critical stance, not only toward the sources of much bullshit in political discourse, public relations, and advertising but also toward our own credulity and receptiveness. Labeling in itself does little to counteract the workings of propaganda; we have to *want* to resist its influence.[13]

The psychologist Joseph Jastrow suggested in 1935 "seven inclinations" that make audiences receptive to propaganda:

- credulity—or gullibility
- marvel—the urge to accept magic, which overwhelms us when we are in infancy and against which, in later life, rationalism can sometimes wage a losing struggle
- transcendence—the belief in powers that transcend the natural
- prepossession—the mental phenomenon whereby, when we seek evidence of our preconceptions, we find it
- congeniality of conclusion—whereby we reach the conclusion we *like* rather than the one dictated by evidence and logic
- vagary—the obsessive pursuit of a particular conclusion, decided upon early, whatever the contrary evidence
- rationalization—the intellectual art of piecing together valid evidence in such a way as to produce an invalid conclusion (qtd. in Grant 19–20).

As these are applicable to propaganda, they are also applicable to propagandistic bullshit.

We may become prone to tolerate bullshit through simple exhaustion. The more we become accustomed to bullshit as a normal means of communication, the less insistent we are likely to be that important communication be truthful. Moreover, as common as verbal bullshit is in contemporary culture, it may be outpaced by nonverbal forms such as visual bullshit. We are susceptible to bullshit, further, because its abundance creates an attitude of cynicism. Audience cynicism is a very helpful state of affairs for the propagandist. Ideally, propaganda would flourish best if, like young children, we believed everything we were told by our betters. Absent that, an audience of reflexive disbelievers is also useful, because we then will more easily believe false charges against opponents, or decide not to participate in public affairs since we assume that *they're all crooks*. Not all bullshit is equally problematic; we have to examine each utterance to determine its purpose. What is needed for responsible discussion in public life is careful, point-by-point, contextualized scrutiny of arguments.

Social media offer some promise of countering this corruption of language through their sheer numbers of presumably spontaneous, unpaid respondents. Yet even social media are being corrupted. In 2010, one anonymous Twitter account produced over ten thousand tweets from the end of June until mid-October; another such account, also anonymous and created ten minutes later, retweeted *all* those posts and produced none of its own. No matter what technology is invented, it can be turned to propagandistic use.[14]

We may be more accepting of propagandistic bullshit if it is *on our side*. This, however, is an ethically weak position. Olav Gjelsvik argues that "the defining trait of bullshit is not that the producer is unconcerned about truth, but that the producer is *unconcerned about knowledge*" (105). The same can be said about us on the receiving end of bullshit: as listeners and putative critical thinkers, we too may be unconcerned about knowledge and therefore receptive to bullshit.

So, if we are to have any hope of countering the effects of bullshit, what are our options? A series of questions about a statement may serve as a heuristic.

- What is the statement's apparent purpose?
- What are we being asked to do or believe?
- How would the bullshit be translated into a cogent argument? After such translation, is it in our interest to accept it?
- What is assumed but not argued?
- What are the emotional components?

Bullshit now can be dealt with primarily by shutting it out, limiting exposure to most media sources; by creating counter-bullshit, which can bring its own ethical problems; by satirizing it and thereby calling attention to it; or by recognizing that bullshit is unavoidable and social in nature and focusing instead on creating our own rational discourse so as to exhibit better rhetoric. Since language is social and contagious, many bullshitters are probably not aware that what they are speaking or writing is bullshit. The motive for critique is not to put others down but to raise the standard so as to think about the discourse we hear and recirculate ourselves.

We may think of the situation with respect to bullshit as analogous to currency. Calling a $100 bill counterfeit requires that we believe there are such things as real $100 bills. But if it should happen that we have no more confidence in U.S. currency than in counterfeits, then all money becomes in essence counterfeit. And if we come to believe that all communication is bullshit, then language itself is in danger of breaking down. Money and truth become, in Jean Baudrillard's term, simulacra, or copies without an original.[15] So we need to train ourselves, in effect, to inspect our verbal currency. To adapt a point from Black: bullshit is to lying as adulterated food is to poison. The latter is more directly harmful, but the former may go undetected and eventually wreak more harm. We are more likely to be on our guard against propaganda than bullshit, but we should be mindful of the latter as well.

Notes

1. "On Bullshit," first published in *Raritan* in 1986, was reprinted in 2005, when it attracted much wider public notice, holding a spot on the *New York Times* best-seller list for twenty-seven weeks.

2. Black notes that this applies to what he calls "first-degree humbug," not to degrees of self-deception.

3. The phrase *death panels* is an enthymeme containing the false assertion that optional end-of-life counseling would result in the government's deciding that the elderly could be put to death to save money.

4. PR slogan for Smashburger: http://www.qsrmagazine.com/category /chains/smashburger.

5. An excerpt from Corey's speech: "This in itself as an edifice of the great glory that has gone beyond, . . . based on the assumption that the intelligence not only as Mencken once said, 'He who underestimates the American pubic—public, will not go broke.' This is merely a small indication of this vast throng gathered here to once again behold and to perceive that which has gone behind and to that which might go forward into the future."

6. Bernays is discussed at length in this volume by Sharon J. Kirsch in chapter 1.

7. We can see such opposition most recently in a statement included in the 2012 Texas Republican platform, which maintained opposition to teaching critical thinking in K–12 classrooms:

We oppose the teaching of Higher Order Thinking Skills (HOTS) (values clarification), critical thinking skills and similar programs that are simply a relabeling of Outcome-Based Education (OBE) (mastery learning) which focus on behavior modification and have the purpose of challenging the student's fixed beliefs and undermining parental authority. (qtd. in Lach)

8. Edward S. Herman and Noam Chomsky's 1988 book, *Manufacturing Consent*, is a key text for this concept.

9. Sadly, I can recite this from memory.

10. Frankfurt notes that public relations (along with advertising and politics) "are replete with instances of bullshit so unmitigated that they can serve among the most indisputable and classic paradigms of the concept" (22).

11. The Global Climate Coalition's founding members included British Petroleum, Daimler/Chrysler (as it was then), Exxon, Ford, GM, and Shell Oil, as well as the American Highway Users Alliance, founded by GM and including highway construction companies. The Clean and Safe Energy Coalition was a front group that advocated for nuclear power construction in the face of concerns about disposal of nuclear waste and power plant meltdowns such as those at Three Mile Island, Chernobyl, and Fukushima.

12. Source for these super PAC names, along with other information, is the Sunlight Foundation, http://sunlightfoundation.com/superpacs/.

13. There appears to be a correlation between judging some bullshit as profound and support for conservative presidential candidates in 2016. Sample size and methodology in this study were limited, and the particular form of "pseudo-profound bullshit" investigated was defined as statements that "have a correct syntactic structure" but "lack content, logic, or truth from the perspective of natural science." See Pfattheicher and Schindler.

14. The researcher noted that "almost all of the more than 20,000 tweets from @HopeMarie_25 and @PeaceKaren_25 support Republican candidates, especially U.S. House GOP leader John Boehner, whose account @ GOPLeader is 'very frequently retweeted or mentioned.'" The team looked for examples from the political left but did not find any (Chaplin).

15. Another way to describe what has changed since mid-twentieth century is postmodernism. In some definitions, postmodernism is discourse that has become unmoored from its referent. Bullshit may be thought of as postmodernism that has escaped the academy.

Works Cited

Aberdein, Andrew. "Raising the Tone: Definition, Bullshit, and the Definition of Bullshit." *Bullshit and Philosophy.* Ed. Gary A. Hardcastle and George Reisch. Chicago: Open Court, 2006. 151–69. Print.

Baudrillard, Jean. *Simulacra and Simulation.* Trans. Shelia Faria Glaser. Ann Arbor: U of Michigan P, 1994. Print.

Bernays, Edward L. *Propaganda.* 1928. Port Washington: Kennikat, 1972. Print.

Black, Max. "The Prevalence of Humbug." *The Prevalence of Humbug and Other Essays.* Ithaca: Cornell UP, 1983. 115–43. Print.

Cain, Herman. "Herman Cain on Libya." Online video clip. YouTube. YouTube, 14 November 2011. Web. 18 July 2012.

Chaplin, Steve. "Busted: Astroturf Campaign on Twitter." *Futurity.* 25 October 2010. Web. 5 May 2016.

Cohen, G. A. "Deeper into Bullshit." *Contours of Agency.* Ed. S. Buss and L. Overton. Cambridge: MIT P, 2002. 321–39. Print.

Colbert, Stephen. *The Colbert Report.* Comedy Central. 17 October 2005. Television. http://www.cc.com/video-clips/63ite2/the-colbert-report-the -word---truthiness.

Corey, Irwin. "Professor Irwin Corey Accepts the National Book Award Fiction Citation for Thomas Pynchon and Gravity's Rainbow." Lincoln Center, New York. 18 April 1974. Professor Irwin Corey. Web. 24 May 2012.

"Crest Television Commercial #1 (1960s)." Online video clip. YouTube. YouTube, 31 December 2009. Web. 23 May 2012.

Eubanks, Philip, and John D. Schaeffer. "A Kind Word for Bullshit: The Problem of Academic Writing." *College Composition and Communication* 59.3 (2008): 372–88. Print.

Frankfurt, Harry. *On Bullshit.* Princeton: Princeton UP, 2005. Print.

Gjelsvik, Olav. "Bullshit Illuminated." *Understanding Choice, Explaining Behaviour: Essays in Honour of Ole-Jørgen Skog.* Ed. Jon Elster et al. Oslo: Unipub, 2006. 101–9. Print.

Grant, John. *Bogus Science: Or, Some People Really Believe These Things.* London: Facts, Figures and Fun, 2009. Print.

Herman, Edward S., and Noam Chomsky. *Manufacturing Consent: The Political Economy of the Mass Media.* New York: Pantheon, 1988. Print.

Kotzee, Ben. "Our Vision and Our Mission: Bullshit, Assertion and Belief." *South African Journal of Philosophy* 26.2 (2007): 163–75. Print.

Lach, Eric. "Texas GOP's 2012 Platform Opposes Teaching of 'Critical Thinking Skills.'" *Talking Points Memo*. TPM Media, 29 June 2012. Web. 1 July 2012.

"Marquette University Mission Statement." Marquette University. Web. 25 August 2015.

"Miss Teen USA 2007—South Carolina Answers a Question." Online video clip. YouTube. YouTube, 24 August 2007. Web. 23 May 2012.

"*Network* (1976): Quotes." IMDb. IMDb.com, n.d. Web. 21 May 2012.

Orwell, George. "Politics and the English Language." *Horizon* 13.76 (1946): 252–65. Print.

Pfattheicher, Stefan, and Simon Schindler. "Misperceiving Bullshit as Profound Is Associated with Favorable Views of Cruz, Rubio, Trump and Conservatism." *PLOS*. 29 April 2016. Web. 3 May 2016.

Readings, Bill. *The University in Ruins*. Cambridge, Mass.: Harvard UP, 1996. Print.

Stauber, John, and Sheldon Rampton. *Toxic Sludge Is Good for You: Lies, Damn Lies and the Public Relations Industry*. Monroe, Maine: Common Courage, 2002. Print.

Sternbergh, Adam. "Stephen Colbert Has America by the Ballots." *New York Magazine*. New York Media, 16 October 2006. Web. July 18, 2012.

Suskind, Ron. "Faith, Certainty, and the Presidency of George W. Bush." *New York Times*. New York Times, 17 October 2004. Web. 25 May 2012.

Tone, Jeff. "Strategist Frank Luntz Tells GOP How to Spin Occupy Movement." The Liberal Curmudgeon. N.p., 1 Dec. 2011. Web. 8 July 2012.

PART 2

PROPAGANDA'S CHALLENGE
TO DEMOCRACY: SITES AND
MECHANISMS OF SOCIAL CONTROL

POPULAR ECONOMICS: NEOLIBERAL PROPAGANDA AND ITS AFFECTIVITY

CATHERINE CHAPUT

> Virtually every feature of the built environment, virtually
> every feature of human and animal behavior, is the explicit
> or implicit result of the interplay of costs and benefits. There
> are rich textures and patterns in everyday experience that
> become visible to the practical eye of the economic naturalist.
> —Robert H. Frank, *The Economic Naturalist*

Every word, according to George Lakoff, comes to its audience conceptually packaged within a framework of other emotional and logical associations. This is not simply a discursive phenomenon but a physiological one—our brain learns words within contexts, and words imperceptibly index those contexts, giving power to a host of connotative associations. The example that Lakoff gives, not surprisingly, comes in the form of metaphor. Why is it that we think of a kind, generous person as warm and an unkind, selfish person as cold? The answer has to do with our cognitive framing. As infants, he says, we first perceive warmth while being held close to another body and being fed. The word *warm*, therefore, does not get arbitrarily linked to a nurturing individual; the two are neurologically coupled through repeated contextual associations so that the one indexes the other in the synaptic pathways and neurological circuits that give meaning to our experience.[1] Studying these frames helps speakers find the words that most likely result in the intended emotional and logical associations, a practice long employed by political and corporate campaigns.

Dedicated to just such inquiry, the Rockridge Institute (1997–2008), a small research center founded at the University of California, Berkeley, by

Lakoff and his colleagues, focused its studies on contemporary political debates. Its goal was to "reveal the deep frames—the moral values, political principles, and fundamental ideas, both progressive and conservative—that are implicit in political discourse" and to educate the public about the relationship between language choice and frames (Lakoff and Ferguson 1). Although committed to their left-of-center views, Lakoff and his colleagues contrasted the institute's "honest" work to the spin-doctoring of Frank Luntz, a well-known corporate and conservative strategist, because he "uses frames to mask information in the service of conservative ends" (2). Using framing theory to craft messages for the public, Lakoff and Ferguson purported to be transparent, while Luntz, they said, worked "to hide the ugly truth" (2). Luntz, of course, did not share this representation of his work. In an interview for the PBS documentary *The Persuaders,* he argued that his work on such notable campaigns as the conversion of estate tax to death tax "clarifies rather than obfuscates the issues." Regardless of the level of linguistic dissembling, both projects are squarely situated within the domain of propaganda: the crafting of messages intended to persuade the public to think and behave according to a preestablished agenda. Whether one seeks to eliminate the estate tax or decriminalize undocumented workers, the implementation of framing theory is the work of propaganda.

For me, the most effective way to understand the difference between these two agendas is not found in their content—whether one is right and the other wrong—nor in how transparent they are. The primary difference, the one that determines the effectiveness of each campaign, comes down to the affective energies—the unconscious physiological entities that undergird persuasive messages and enable bodies to receive or reject well-crafted arguments—circulated through their respective frames. Luntz energizes people through fear, fueling bodies that stand guard over the world as we imagine it is.[2] He asks that we watch out for those who might do us harm—illegal immigrants who take our jobs and commit crimes or governments that relentlessly tax our hard-earned dollars even at our deaths. This propaganda, according to Slavoj Žižek, does not use words to deceive the public; on the contrary, Luntz and other conservatives likely believe their own words as much as Lakoff and political progressives believe theirs. The conservative agenda is not one of malice as much as "a resigned conviction that the world we live in, even if not the best of all possible worlds, is the least bad, such that any radical change will only make it worse" (Žižek 28). This form of suspicious propaganda is self-protective and works, according to recent neurobehavioral research, with our own evolutionary makeup: it frames discursive debates according to our biochemical predispositions.[3] Alternatively, Lakoff advocates a form of propaganda that requires individuals to work against their embodied inclinations. He wants people to think and act differently. This not only requires increased commitment on the part of audiences but also seems to be less intuitive given that our biological and neurological structures predispose us to spend more time and energy on potential dangers than on potential possibilities (Anderson et al.). In short, the differences between these two kinds of propaganda require us to explore how individual bodies are inspired to move en masse, not only through language but also through the affective triggers that travel along with language, physiologically persuading us at an imperceptible level. Without investigating the physical motivations carried through semiotic systems, we are left to battle within an ideological field wherein disembodied psychological frames become the ground zero of our analysis; affective analysis, tied to language and its contexts, brings this ground zero to life in order to illuminate the material processes that empower propaganda.

Most propaganda theory has worked at the intersection of discourse and social psychology. Such foundational thinkers as Walter Lippmann and Edward Bernays, for instance, drew inspiration from crowd psychology, while their critics worked to undermine such theories. Across a chasm of differences, these theories support what Walter Ong long ago termed "the myth of myth" (144). Those who study myth—or, in our case, the psychology of propaganda—search out the unstated substructure of suppositions that fill in the voids and recesses of language. Thus, propaganda analysis proceeds from a belief that we can uncover the unformulated, mythical structures seeping into our discursive practices and shaping our material worlds. According to the myth of myth, propaganda masks our real interests, while its unveiling reveals those true material relations. Lakoff implies such a masking when he accuses Luntz of covering over issues and linguistically pandering to different audiences. Affect studies, however, observes that the conscious discursive act of unmasking does not necessarily change our lived behavior, which continues to operate unconsciously. Hinting at these unconscious operations and paraphrasing Alain Badiou, Žižek argues that propaganda "fights something regarding which it is itself unaware, something to which it is structurally blind" (27). From my perspective, we are blind to the autonomous physiological movements of affect that come along with language.[4] This structural blindness differs from the linguistic and psychological myths that inform earlier propaganda analysis because unconscious affective motivations are biologically inherent and cannot be removed.

To understand the role of propaganda in these different terms, we need to shift the conversation a notch on the analytical dial and explore how language motivates masses of people affectively as well as discursively. Lakoff's initial premise that all language functions within emotional and rational frames—social and psychological in practice but physiological in origin—offers a point of departure for such analysis. This chapter, therefore, begins by acknowledging that words have psychic ramifications because of physiological operations. As the next section will demonstrate, the material reality of affect lies conceptually untapped in early propaganda studies. After linking affect theory to propaganda analysis, I will model this alternative line of inquiry through an investigation into neoliberal economic thinking and its historical trajectory. In this way, I hope to reveal how the reading public has been molded into "economic naturalists" who see "every feature of human and animal behavior" in terms of cost-benefit analysis, as Robert Frank so clearly puts it in the epigraph to this chapter (204).

PROPAGANDA STUDIES AND THE MATERIALITY OF GROUP PSYCHOLOGY

Late nineteenth-century social psychologists such as Gustave Le Bon focused on the crowd and its collective mind. Living at a time when communication and political action took place primarily through physical gatherings, Le Bon noticed that "there are certain ideas and feelings which do not come into being, or do not transform themselves into acts except in the case of individuals forming a crowd" (27). In crowds, he says, "the power of words is bound up with the images they evoke, and is quite independent of their real significance" (102). Like so many theorists after him, Le Bon identifies the power of language within an undefined substructure, one he calls "the image." This nonverbalized entity travels throughout the crowd, gaining power and fueling individuals as it does. Its circulation creates mutual identification and inspires people to move and speak in step with others. Group psychology emerges when the image becomes so strong that the emotion of the crowd overtakes individual reason. Yet a group need not gather as a crowd to share emotional ties. Mass marketing, for instance, relies on group cohesion through discourse—print, visual, and audio—even though it does not necessarily gather people as a crowd. Thus, along with the crowd mentality, we must scrutinize "the image"—that thing that attaches itself to and travels with a range of semiotic content.

My contention is that what Le Bon calls "the image" can more precisely be understood as the affective energy transmitted through the words that bind groups together. The duality of semiotics—that it both denotes and connotes—serves as an indication that "a group can be cognitively responsive in relation to symbols" even as it is unconsciously responding to other affective stimuli (Brennan 66). Words index social and cultural contexts, but such indexing occurs physically as well as psychologically.[5] According to Teresa Brennan, affects "are there first, before we are. They preexist us; they are outside as well as inside us" (65). Words, images, and sounds cognitively signify a web of relationships, but they also come into our bodies through our various senses and thus trigger physiological processes that lay the foundation for how we engage others and their ideas.

While most propaganda theorists view "the image" as a structural myth embedded within our sacred cultural references, Lakoff's framing theory and Brennan's affect theory suggest that this mythology works physiologically as well as sociopolitically and culturally. As the raw material that precedes linguistic metaphors and social frames, affect transmits between people through sensual data, triggers particular synaptic pathways in our brains, and makes us more or less open to particular arguments. From this perspective, affect establishes the prelinguistic foundations that determine our receptivity to the persuasive quality of particular lines of argument. Indeed, Le Bon's conception of crowd mentality uses such a physiological metaphor. He explains that the changes constituted through the crowd formation function like chemical reactions: "just as in chemistry certain elements, when brought into contact—bases and acids, for example—combine to form a new body possessing properties quite different from those of the bodies that have served to form it" (30). The affect circulating with language production engages with bodies to reconstitute them, and those changes enable as well as disable specific kinds of future engagements.

The discourse of popular economics offers an excellent case study to explore the role of affect in propaganda. Most of us behave as though we believe in the invisible hand of the market, but this metaphor—if we follow Lakoff and Brennan—emerges in social contexts wherein affect literally seeps into our embodied experiences. The strength of the metaphor, subsequently, arises from its ability to initiate those affective connections. Because such connectivity is no match for rational argumentation, our analyses must explore the circulation of discourse as well as its ability to stimulate affective energies. As Badiou says, "Where all rationality risks crumbling beneath the immensity of propagandistic self-evidence, one must be careful to be sure of the details and, in particular, to examine the effects of the nominal chain induced by the passage" from the adjective to the substantive (19). We must ask, for instance, how we moved from neoliberal economics as a label describing one market theory among others to neoliberal economics as an orthodoxy akin to a subjective reality. The answer, it seems to me, lies in the dissemination of academic thinking into popular thinking, where material experiences become inscribed into linguistic practices.

THE HISTORY OF NEOLIBERALISM THOUGHT: FROM INTELLECTUAL INQUIRY TO MASS PROPAGANDA

The story of how neoliberal thought has become both a dominant form of economics as well as an ontological reality—the substantive structure of our world—is a complex one about which I can offer only a rough sketch. The sketch begins and ends at the crossroads of economics and propaganda. Famously coining the phrase "the manufacture of consent," Walter Lippmann's *Public Opinion* argues that increasingly technological and specialized societies require the production and dissemination of propaganda in order to educate the masses and steer them toward proper "democratic" decisions. One cadre of professionals determines the correct course and another group of professionals persuades the masses toward this end. In 1939, well after the publication of this work and just after the French translation of Lippmann's *Enquiry into the Principles of a Good Society,* Louis Rougier organized a gathering with the goal of tying classical liberal (that is, free market) and recent neoliberal economic thinking to legislative and juridical structures. This Walter Lippmann Colloquium, as it was called, was the first major attempt to define the terms and strategies of neoliberalism, with particular attention to the state's role in economic affairs. The event brought together those who specialized in shaping public opinion with those who studied neoliberalism in an effort to forge new economic and political practices (Foucault 161). Among the participants was Frederick Hayek, the Austrian economist who brought neoliberalism to the United States by way of the Chicago school and Milton Friedman. Although Friedman did not join the Lippmann event, he did attend the first meeting of the Mont Pèlerin Society in 1947 that was organized by Hayek to further the neoliberal strategies discussed at the earlier meeting. Hayek, while at the London School of Economics, met Aaron Director, who would later become a law professor at the University of Chicago. Director not only assisted Hayek in getting his now-famous *Road to Serfdom* published by the University of Chicago Press but also helped organize University of Chicago economics professors to attend the inaugural meeting of the Mont Pèlerin Society.

Unlike the prewar context of the Lippmann Colloquium, the post–World War II context in both the United States and Europe was deeply saturated in welfare state policies and Keynesian economics; it was situated at the opposite end of the economic spectrum from the kind of liberalism promoted by participants of the Mont Pèlerin Society. Thus, the group, consisting primarily of university professors and secondarily of journalists, had the ambitious task of preserving and deepening liberal thinking against a tidal wave of opposition (Hartwell 45–46). The best way to achieve this liberal renaissance, they surmised, was through intellectual dialogue among the most prominent neoliberal theorists across Europe and the United States. According to the history link on its website, the society

> did not intend to create an orthodoxy, to form or align itself with any political party or parties, or to conduct propaganda. Its sole objective was to facilitate an exchange of ideas between like-minded scholars in the hope of strengthening the principles and practices of a free society and to study the workings, virtues, and defects of market-oriented economic systems.

Given that the seeds for this society began with Walter Lippmann, it is not surprising that the group explicitly defined its project against the work of propaganda. While neoliberal ideology does eventually make its way into economic propaganda, its initial claim to a position outside the sphere of propaganda rings true. The Mont Pèlerin group as well as the Walter Lippmann Colloquium aimed at strengthening the relationship between the political state and the neoliberal market through academic inquiry. Because their mission focused on intellectual pursuits rather than on specific policy interventions, they steered clear of propaganda, which takes place within civil society and its apparatuses of mass communication.

The Chicago school of economics, however, grew to be not only a crucial site of academic training but also one deeply wedded to changing government policies in the United States and elsewhere. To take only the most famous example, Milton Friedman rose in popularity as a public intellectual from the 1960s until his death in 2006. His public work promoted the neoliberal ideals of Hayek and the Mont Pèlerin Society: politics and economics were intertwined, and political freedom could emerge only where economic markets were deracinated from government regulation. His most popular book, *Free to Choose* (1980), was aimed at a general audience and was accompanied by a ten-part PBS documentary series.[6] Through such public outreach, Friedman began to develop mass endorsement for the kind of neoliberal thinking that shaped British policy under Margaret Thatcher and American policy under Ronald Reagan (Harvey), as well as a host of countries worldwide—Chile, Argentina, Uruguay, Bolivia, Russia, South Africa, and Indonesia, to name only a few (Klein). Nearly synonymous with the Chicago school of economics and its influence, Milton Friedman earned his place as the most recognizable figure of neoliberalism. Nevertheless, different threads stand out in the tapestry of this neoliberal propaganda.

Just as Friedman took public policy to task through neoliberal economic beliefs, other Chicago school economists began to intervene in the social sphere. Among the earliest and most influential of these was Gary Becker. As a graduate student studying with Milton Friedman, Becker helped forge the practice of extending neoliberal economic thinking beyond economic and political realms. With book titles like *The Economics of Life: From Baseball to Affirmative Action to Immigration* and *How Real-World Issues Affect Our Everyday Life,* Becker initiated the habit of treating "the social as if it were or could be akin to perfectly working markets" (Fine and Milonakis 12). Treating the social within idealized economic models extended the boundaries of economics and produced interesting scholarship, but it failed to do justice to the complexity of social experiences because of its reliance on marginalist thinking. Marginalism—the economic model promoted by the Chicago school—predicts the value of incremental increases and decreases to production within an idealized market and, consequently, eschews the reality of a less-than-ideal social world. In addition to helping companies determine the perfect production scale, marginalism as employed by Becker and others helps explain individual consumption and behavior patterns. Applying marginalism to social phenomena means weighing the benefits (usually economic but also cultural) in relationship to the costs as production gradually alters. The ideal situation, of course, arises when the highest benefit-to-cost ratio emerges no matter what extraneous individual, cultural, or environmental factors might also emerge. Consequently, this neoliberal model of understanding everyday life effectively constitutes an asocial discourse on the social. At its most developed, this intervention into the social represents an economic encroachment on those subjects traditionally studied by other social sciences—one that Ben Fine and Dimitris Milonakis label *economics imperialism*. The universalization of economic thinking now known as freakonomics is, for them, the "natural progeny of economics imperialism" and an important form of promoting its neoliberal worldview across the social sphere inside and outside academic discourse (95).

To summarize this lineage, the popularization of neoliberalism that Hayek and Friedman began—with texts like *The Road to Serfdom* and *Free to Choose*, respectively—became diversified across a range of social issues within the work of Becker and emerged as full-fledged propaganda with the watershed publication of Steven D. Levitt and Stephen J. Dubner's *Freakonomics: A Rogue Economist Explores the Hidden Side of Everything.*[7] Levitt, another Chicago school economist, takes Becker's approach of studying the social from the perspective of marginalist economics and brings it to the masses. His three books (*Freakonomics*, *SuperFreakonomics*, and *Think like a Freak*) have been hugely popular, spawning other similar texts (such as Robert Frank's *The Economic Naturalist*) and facilitating new additions of older texts (Charles Wheelan's *Naked Economics*, for example). With the overwhelming reception of these mass-market books, we finally arrive within the terrain of propaganda—the shaping or manufacturing of mass public opinion.

AFFECT, PROPAGANDA, AND THE CASE OF FREAKONOMICS

As a field of inquiry, freakonomics trains the public to see the world exclusively through neoliberal frames.[8] The genre has less to tell us about its subject matter—breathtakingly sweeping in its scope and including such things as crack gangs, sumo wrestlers, prostitutes, school teachers, consumer production, and individual fashion, to only hint at its range of subjects—than it does about how to approach these and all other topics through economic self-interest and against collectivist intervention. While economic thinking includes heterodox approaches, such as the institutional, social, and historical schools, freakonomics presents the Chicago school of economic thought—the neoliberal approach—as the only form of economic thinking. This reductionism notwithstanding, the major triumph of this popular economic genre is the strength of its affective charge, making readers literally less able to engage alternative perspectives. Even though this affective habituation happens physically and materially, it does not operate neutrally. Our physical world is just as connected to power dynamics as is our ideological world. For this reason, we need a critical interpretive lens that weds affect theory to language theory. Consequently, a critical analysis of freakonomics requires an interpretive model that combines affect theory with an understanding of the political economic dynamics of language such as those formulated by Jean-Jacques Lecercle. According to Lecercle's six-part heuristic for interpreting discourse, one needs to understand language first as praxis, then as historical, social, material, and political, and finally as the building blocks of our subjectivity. His structure explains the ideological power of language (its epistemological function), and affect theory explains the socio-biological power of language (its ontological function). Both are needed to fully grasp the role of language as propaganda. Using these two theories, the following section offers an analysis of this economic propaganda and argues that the greater the discursive depletion of this historical, social, material, and political context, the greater its affective force.

Freakonomics as Neoliberal Praxis

Using Aristotle, Lecercle reproduces a tripartite structure among theory, practice, and praxis. Theory constitutes an abstract system that makes everything intelligible within that totality. Practice produces ideas and things according to that system, which, for language, requires a model of transparent representation—things naturally exist and language practices simply name them. Praxis, as action in common, does not create as much as it inspires, motivates, and fuels. As praxis, language "imports material force to the ideas that it embodies and which have no existence aside from the words that formulate them, which enable them to persuade the masses and rouse them to action" (151). Freakonomics functions as a form of praxis because it neither refers to an entity that exists outside this nomenclature nor creates concrete things from raw neoliberal theory. Instead, it provides the language through which proponents of neoliberal economics transmit energy or affectivity to the masses they wish to rouse. The very term *freakonomics* is, as Badiou says, "intrinsically propagandistic" as it simultaneously signifies nothing in particular and carries enough persuasive force to explain everything (19).[9]

Levitt unknowingly reinforces this propagandistic perspective when he claims that freakonomics reveals all underlying truths with no unifying theme. Although he considered focusing on the single topic of applied microeconomics, he settled on freakonomics, which "employs the best analytical tools that economics can offer, but allows us to follow whatever freakish curiosities may occur to us. . . . No subject, however offbeat, need be beyond its reach" (13). The book popularizes economics by showing its broad applicability, even though it has little to do with economics as it neither explains foundational economic concepts nor studies traditional economic terrain. According to the book's bonus material, the goal of this non-theme is to instruct readers in "how to look at the world like an economist" (263). Such a vantage point manifests consciousness as the art of "quantifying culture" (231). Freakonomics valorizes a way to think about and see the world. It propagandizes an entire ideology as it directs our attention to purportedly natural economic formulas that organize our world and make us suspicious of artificial interventions that disrupt the natural rhythms of this invisible apparatus. The material force of the book, therefore, habituates readers through repetitive methodological pathways that all arrive at neoliberal conclusions such as individualism, self-reliance, and self-responsibility; antagonism toward social programming and government regulation; and the financial empowerment of corporate classes, whose wealth will, as President Reagan famously said, trickle down. Moreover, these habituations come in the form of noneconomic, nonpolitical good humor, linking positive affective experiences with neoliberal "truths." So conceived, freakonomics is the praxis of neoliberal propaganda: without referencing any particularity, it nevertheless provides the motivating force for collective neoliberal actions across a seemingly endless terrain. As a praxis, freakonomics needs to be explored through Lecercle's four other linguistic tenets—historical, social, material, and political—all of which help interpellate the masses as neoliberal subjects.

Freakonomics as Ahistorical: Naturalizing Neoliberalism

As anyone who uses language knows, it evolves along with new historical conjectures. Always in progress, language "not only has a history, it *is* history" (Lecercle 158). Although in constant flux, language, like a palimpsest, manages to preserve its own historical traces. As Antonio Gramsci puts it, "Language is at the same time a living thing and a museum of fossils of life and civilization" (450). Similarly, our affective energies move through language and shift along with new historical conjunctures and collective experiences. This happens when, for instance, oppressed groups reappropriate the language of their subjugation, such as when gay people use the pejorative *queer* as a positive self-identification or when black people employ the word *nigger* as a sign of identification. New uses of words positively energize oppositional groups, but they do not deplete older uses of their negative affectivity. Always in process, language acquires new uses and meanings even as it carries the weight of its past energies and meanings. In short, the affective and semantic work of language constantly evolves, and thus the critic must study texts through their "tensions, contradictions, [and] power relations" (Lecercle 161). The historical contradiction at the heart of this popular movement is its origination myth. Freakonomics claims to be a natural and spontaneous burst of individual creativity rather than the result of a slow ossification of economic inquiry into a single, all-encompassing explanation of everything.

Freakonomics asserts itself as a decidedly new way of looking at the world; yet, as we have seen, it is the legitimate and welcomed offspring of a line of neoliberal thinking that has evolved over the last seventy-five years—from the Austrian school to the Walter Lippmann Colloquium to the Mont Pèlerin Society to the Chicago school theory to its sociological extension. Levitt distances himself from this history, ringing the alarm bells of propaganda, by stating repeatedly that he does not "know very much about the field of economics" (*Freakonomics* xxiv). Even as he is housed within the powerful Chicago school, he downplays this institutional allegiance. Dubner draws a clear distinction between Levitt and his academic colleagues: "Chicago is about theory, deep thinking and big ideas, while he is about empiricism, clever thinking and 'cute' but ultimately insubstantial ideas" (227). This disavowal of expert knowledge redoubles in Levitt's attack on professionals as those who manipulate people by using "their information advantage to serve their own agenda" (12). If economists are experts, he is not one of them. The natural, albeit unusual, musings of freakonomics are pitted against expert knowledge and its inevitable manipulations. Affectively, this closes down intellectual inquiry, leaving readers open only to their own natural instincts—instincts that have been carefully cultivated. Indeed, freakonomics redefines economics from a field of study led by what Robert H. Frank calls the "negligible fraction" of PhDs to an egalitarian terrain more inhabitable for those he calls "economic naturalists" (2).

In addition to severing its intellectual lineage, freakonomics dehistoricizes the entire field of economic inquiry. There is only one economics, and that is the neoliberal orthodoxy of the Chicago school. Levitt exemplifies this by presenting economic thinking as a coherent singularity rather than as a multiplicity of approaches. For instance, *SuperFreakonomics* describes microeconomist Keith Chen as a researcher who "after a brief infatuation with Marxism . . . made an about-face and took up economics" (212). In this structural frame, Marxism (a brand of economic thinking) stands opposed to economics proper (presumably neoliberalism). This opposition encourages a slippage from Marxism to Cold War enemy, fossilizing the dynamics of language and transmitting a palpable affective energy that narrows the living presence of economic practice. Furthermore, the description of turning "about-face" establishes an affective wall that prevents the reading public's ability to engage such oppositional arguments as those of Marxism and its critique of capitalism. With time and repetition, this affectivity creates a social context stripped of its sociality—people and ideas exist only in rigid identification or opposition.

Freakonomics as Asocial: Individualizing Neoliberalism

The multilayered sociality of language, as Lecercle interprets it, draws attention to its collective labor and its materiality. Language comes to us through material apparatuses and is spoken by socialized bodies. More than that, the life habits and internalized boundaries of speech are "linguistically material" in that they organize the "discourses and expressions, which speakers tirelessly repeat" (Lecercle 165). From this perspective, the language of freakonomics travels through institutions—the Chicago school, government apparatuses, and the media (including best-selling books, radio slots, and an extensive Internet site)—providing us with the affective and linguistic foundations on which we establish our material sensibilities. This sociality, simultaneously individual and collective, clings to the words we use regardless of our intentionality. Freakonomics promotes a different sociality as it frames its stories according to one simple truth: individual self-interest best suits society.

The repeated metaphors of stripping away and of cutting into the surface for truths that lie underneath exemplify the skewed sociality of freakonomics. In fact, the book cover announces this metaphor through its visual representation of an apple whose true content, once one slices into the flesh below, is an orange. This image encapsulates the book's fundamental project: "stripping a layer or two from the surface of modern life and seeing what is happening underneath" (Levitt and Dubner, *Freakonomics* 11). It is this archeological digging that allows Levitt to link decreased crime rates with legalized abortions, to compare crack dealers with McDonald's franchises, and to argue that both the Ku Klux Klan and real estate agents acquire power through information asymmetries. These intriguing comparisons support the neoliberal valorization of individual self-interest:

women who terminate unwanted pregnancies unintentionally contribute to the collective good of society; the individual rules of sole proprietorship are so innate that even illegal drug dealers follow them; and, consequently, expert knowledge impedes individual interests. The affective intensity of these lessons derives from the unexpected structural coherence attributed to a complex social world stripped of its complications. We delight in the peekaboo game that reveals neoliberalism behind even the most unusual cultural doors. The linguistic practice of redefining the world with simplistic neoliberal terms tethers the pleasure of effortless discovery (imprinted into our neurological pathways as children) to these worldviews, affectively sealing our intellectual curiosity according to one frame of reference.

This pattern of a true individuality hidden beneath the opacity of visible social dynamics equally permeates *SuperFreakonomics*. Levitt concedes, for instance, that "while gender discrimination may be a minor contributor to the male-female pay differential, it is desire—or lack thereof—that accounts for most of the wage gap" (45). The dual desires he references in this statement are that women love children whereas men love workplace power. The next obvious question about how desire becomes gendered in this way goes unanswered because freakonomics relies on regression analyses that reduce reality to the comparison of two "pure" variables, allowing Levitt to offer a social explanation to a question that denies the multidimensionality of social existence. He explains the social through essentialist definitions of individuals such that the solution to institutionalized sexism boils down to personal choice: children or workplace.

Using this same tactic, he later discusses the geopolitical impact of potential climate change solutions. In this discussion, Levitt claims that anti-carbon initiatives, aimed primarily at large industrial corporations, "will have a huge drag on the world economy. There are billions of poor people who will be greatly delayed, if not entirely precluded, from attaining a First World standard living" (199). He explores the initial inquiry into which climate change solutions seem most viable through a cost-benefit analysis stripped of various real-life factors. He discovers, without revealing the data, that it is cheaper to shoot 100,000 tons of sulfur annually into the stratosphere than to regulate corporate carbon emissions. Besides being more cost effective, such environmental engineering predictably reinforces neoliberalism's mantra of unfettered market forces conspiring to promote social good from individual self-interest. Corporations, as legal individuals, must be free to secure unlimited profit if society is to prosper. Similarly, the solution will protect economically disadvantaged individuals by allowing them, we are left to assume, to pursue work in carbon-emitting factories. Freakonomics presents individual self-interest as the solution to even the most pressing global issues. Yet the individual bodies seeking economic gain seem to be either absent (as in the corporate individual) or abstract (as in the billions of poor people). The individuated foundations of popular economics are not only asocial but also amaterial as they support decisions based exclusively in numerical data.

Freakonomics as Amaterial: Rationalizing Neoliberalism

For Lecercle, material bodies, and perhaps materiality itself, is "not only the seat of reason, but also of affects" (181). Reason combines with emotion—affectively induced—to form unpredictable and sometimes uncontainable material bodies. The materiality of freakonomics, conversely, relies on noncontradicting bodies of reason capable of predicting and containing society's material bodies. As a self-proclaimed empiricist, Levitt follows the Enlightenment legacy of separating unreliable emotions from reason supported by observable data. In this way, freakonomics interpellates its readers as subjects of interest rather than of passions. Although freakonomics presents its reason-based model as the means toward clear thinking about the material operations of society, the history of such reasonable economic-driven thinking connects this logic to the passive bodies of commercial society. According to Albert O. Hirschman's intellectual history, as avarice transformed into economic interest, it became empowered to produce passive, gentle bodies capable of rationally following their economic self-interest as opposed to their unpredictable embodied desires. This, claimed Enlightenment theorists, would produce a peaceful, progress-driven society (59–63). In other words, the purportedly unemotional material terrain of reason affectively prepares bodies as welcome recipients of neoliberal propaganda. This is not an argument about passivity, as the readers, viewers, and listeners who make up these economic case studies actively organized on a voluntary basis; instead, it is about the ways in which such participation constitutes rather than informs the neoliberal subject.

The material world of freakonomics establishes itself as rational, reasonable, and data-driven, opposed to the irrational, unreasonable, and emotion-driven discourse of others. Of course, for Levitt, the rationality inherent in empirical research is far from the utopian musings of moralists who merely deduce a hoped-for reality from ethical principles. For him, morality represents the way that people would like the world to work—whereas economics represents how it actually *does* work. Economics is above all a science of measurement. It comprises an extraordinarily powerful and flexible set of tools that can reliably assess a thicket of information to determine the effect of any one factor, or even the whole effect. (*Freakonomics* 11–12)

He goes on to say that if "the science of economics is primarily a set of tools, as opposed to a subject matter, then no subject, however offbeat, need be beyond its reach" (13). Responding to those who criticize its ability to explain everything, *SuperFreakonomics* contends that the authors are "sure reasonable people would view such a phrase as intentional hyperbole" (xiv). This defense stealthily elides responsibility for its linguistic materiality even as it reinforces the dissected material world on which it is based: critics are unreasonable while freakonomics remains squarely within the data-driven world of reason. As researchers, the individuals of this discourse are disembodied within the Enlightenment identity of impartial observer. Indeed, Levitt instructs the reader to "consider yourself, then, in the company of a third person . . . eager to explore the objective merits of interesting cases" (*Freakonomics* 14). In this framework, the limits to those objective merits and the boundaries of those cases disappear, affectively energizing neoliberalism as infallible and never-ending. Readers constituted by this discourse similarly pin their hopes on reason and its facility to explain all, producing the realities of the very claim it dismisses as hyperbole.

Against the prevailing discourse of freakonomics, affect theorists contend that individuals are not numbers but embodied persons whose biochemical makeup weds the emotional to the rational in all linguistic instances. Emotional content cannot help but seep into even the most rational claims of professedly emotionless economists. For instance, Levitt laments that "although economists are trained to be cold-blooded enough to sit around and calmly discuss the trade-offs involved in global catastrophe, the rest of us are a bit more excitable. And most people respond to uncertainty with more emotion—fear, blame, paralysis—than might be advisable" (*SuperFreakonomics* 169). He praises Robert McNamara as a rare economic-thinking politician who "tended to make decisions based on statistical analysis rather than emotion or political considerations" (146). Unstated in this celebration of McNamara, however, are the material devastations—human and otherwise—that resulted from his management of the Vietnam War. Instead, Levitt focuses on the former secretary of defense's role in helping Ford implement car seatbelts. He clearly prefers to highlight the anomalous and avoid dredging through explicitly political terrain. Perhaps it is not too far afield to suggest that this preference stems, at least partially, from Levitt's own emotional makeup and perhaps even his political affiliations.

Freakonomics as Apolitical: Neutralizing Neoliberalism

Just as language cannot avoid being emotional, it similarly cannot avoid being political. For Lecercle, language contains a politics because it carries affective energy capable of motivating individuals: "Ideas become material forces when they seize hold of the masses. They do so when they are embodied in language" (195). Replacing such political forces with the language of neutrality, freakonomics increases the affective receptivity of its worldview. Positioning oneself politically invites opposition and weakens the affective receptivity of one's messages; *Freakonomics,* therefore, draws affective strength from its repeated construction of Levitt as politically disinterested. In the bonus material, his coauthor describes Levitt as having "little taste for politics and less for moralizing" (221). Indeed, well-trained economists cannot be political. They are supposed "to think rationally and tell the truth about data," whereas "rationality and unvarnished data are practically forbidden on the campaign trail," where both politicians and voters prefer emotion (266). Yet, as Lecercle maintains, politics has a way of dwelling within even neutral statements meant to sidestep political contention. Freakonomics exemplifies such political neutrality as it claims to provide "a *method* of analysis, not an assumption about particular motivations" (12). In this vein, Levitt maintains that his claim about legalized abortion contributing to reduced crime rates has no politics. It is merely an interesting observation of how the world really works. Women do not abort pregnancies in hopes of reducing future crime rates; it is simply the serendipitous result of their self-interested choice. Nevertheless, their motivations do have a politics. Women who do not *feel* they can responsibly care for a child *know* that untended children make for troubled adults who, among other things, commit crimes. In this logical chain, feeling and knowing fuse as a political force that grabs hold of individuals and unconsciously motivates their decisions. Freakonomics supplants this political force with the neutral force of neoliberalism that esteems rationality as the sole, unbiased measuring stick of experience.

Levitt's discussion of cheating teachers and the 2002 investigation that resulted in dismissals of several instructors also claims to be apolitical while attesting to powerful political forces. By applying a computer algorithm to the standardized test scores of students, economists were able to detect suspicious consecutive correct answers at the end of tests (where several blanks might exist) and deduce that teachers filled in these answers to improve their students' results. Arne Duncan, CEO of the Chicago public schools, contacted the authors of this study, and they helped him implement additional tests to identify cheating teachers in his schools. Levitt praises this work as economic thinking oriented toward correct practices. He attributes Duncan's clearheadedness to the fact that his "allegiance lay more with schoolchildren and their families than with teachers and their union" (*Freakonomics* 33). The introduction of teachers' unions, however, signals Levitt's movement into political terrain. He introduces political antagonisms by pitting unionized teachers against the interests of schoolchildren and their families. Through this opposition, Levitt furthers the neoliberal agenda by making a nonunion issue politically antagonistic to unions while maintaining a position of political neutrality.

This move repeats itself in *SuperFreakonomics*, where Levitt lodges a wholesale attack on governments—another target of neoliberal derision. Governments, he says, "aren't exactly famous for cheap or simple solutions; they tend to prefer the costly-and-cumbersome route" (157). He goes on to say that none of the solutions he discusses arose from governments, which appears to be true. But equally true is that McNamara's car seatbelt—one of his earlier examples—became implemented only when the government enforced its use. Without mentioning politics in any traditional sense, Levitt promotes a specific agenda through linguistic choices that imply deep political antagonisms between the private and the public spheres. He repeatedly valorizes the clearheaded and simple solutions of the private sphere over the emotionally driven and complex solutions of the governmental sphere. These and other examples are political in two senses: first, they promote the anticollectivist agenda of neoliberalism, and second, they embolden political antagonisms with a linguistic repertoire of affectively potent truths. More important, they are political to the extent that they create the cultural poetics of a world in which private interests always trump public interests. Such neoliberal tenets require, of course, subjects to enact such politics.

Freakonomics as Neoliberal Subjectivity

Collectively, Lecercle's theory of language as a form of praxis that includes historical, social, material, and political dimensions culminates in his conclusion that language interpellates subjects. Subjects emerge from the "linguistic agôn that unites and opposes them, and which they do not pre-exist" (198). From this perspective, Levitt cultivates his readers as subjects of freakonomics rather than reveals their preexisting, economically self-interested individuality. Nevertheless, freakonomics addresses its readers as fully formed individuals rather than as interpellated subjects. Specifically, Levitt imagines his readers—and, indeed, all human beings—as autonomous, self-interested individuals who respond to incentives. His definition of incentives varies, however. In one place he says "an incentive is a bullet, a lever, a key: an often tiny object with astonishing power to change a situation" (*Freakonomics* 16); in another, "an incentive is simply a means of urging people to do more of a good thing and less of a bad thing" (17). Responding to incentives, he says, "is also known as rational behavior, which is what economics is all about" (*SuperFreakonomics* 122). People respond to their self-interests, and yet, because of emotional interferences, they require the layering of sociopolitical incentives to help direct them toward correct decisions. In this account, the supposedly natural force of the invisible hand that conducts equally natural self-interested individuals offers nothing more than a shorthand reference for a historically forged neoliberalism and the public it helps form.

Freakonomics interpellates these subjects through the continuous message that its mass-produced content originates naturally within self-interested individuals, affectively linking self-identity with neoliberal identity and creating a highly charged momentum. This strategy is nowhere more obvious than in Robert Frank's *Economic Naturalist*—a popular economic text riding the wave of the freakonomics craze. Frank's aptly titled book models itself on a pedagogical approach that asks students to pose and answer an "interesting question" from the perspective of an economist. Frank tells us and his students that the "answers don't have to be correct" (12). In other words, the value of the exercise does not derive from the truths it unveils but from its habituation into neoliberal economic thinking. Although Frank, unlike Levitt, admits that self-interest may be good for the individual but less good for the species, he nonetheless promotes the self-interested subject of freakonomics, as does an entire array of popular economic books. Indeed, he says that just by having read his book, one is "well on the road to becoming an economic naturalist," and "in relative terms, therefore, [that person is] already an economics expert" (201). Conflating instincts with expert knowledge is possible because freakonomics has so successfully propagandized neoliberal thinking that our instincts do naturally align with neoliberal doctrines. Once economic discourse sheds its history, sociality, materiality, and politics, everyone becomes an equal subject of neoliberalism.

Given this widespread public campaign to produce neoliberal economic thought as natural and intuitive, it is no wonder students feel empowered to pronounce judgment on such complex issues as public contracts, the mortgage crisis, and government spending without the slightest investigation into the issues. These questions, like so many others, entail explorations beyond cost-benefit analysis. The textures and patterns of lived experience are not, contrary to Frank's pronouncement in the epigraph to this chapter, visible to the practical eye (204). Indeed, as my concluding remarks indicate, the issues facing our society require different forms of seeing and more complex forms of analysis than those currently endorsed in popular economic literature.

PROPAGANDA, AFFECT, AND THE
MANUFACTURE OF MOTIVATION

The contemporary economic discourse of freakonomics habituates the public such that our internalized responses align with neoliberal tenets, even though we may have never studied them. This bodily response comes to us through the psychological and physical work of discourse. While propaganda theorists have explored the psychic life of linguistic experiences—often under the rubrics of ideology—they have yet to sink their collective teeth into the ways language scripts our bodies. To do this, we need to think more carefully about affect, physical sensation, and emotion as they relate to discourse. To some extent, Paul Turpin's *Moral Rhetoric of Political Economy* begins this work. Turpin offers a reading of Adam Smith and Milton Friedman. While both these economists fall within the long liberal tradition, their work diverges ideologically, politically, and historically. Nevertheless, Turpin identifies a common discursive tendency: they both eschew statements of virtuous behavior in favor of "enlisting the reader's identification with moral disapproval of those who thwart capitalism" (3). Smith and Friedman condemn behaviors that interfere with their understanding of a well-functioning market economy. Hence, they train readers to see the world in ways that align with economic liberalism. Such discourse, says Turpin, garners its persuasive force through a moralization that shapes "the reader's attitudes, to bring them more fully into the discourse community of economics" (4). He identifies a crucial persuasive feature at work in these texts, and yet we are still at a loss for explaining how this element works.

For such an understanding, I argue, we need to turn to cognitive linguists like Lakoff and cognitive psychologists like Brennan. In other words, we need to study the role of affect within language. This is not news to many of those who promote what I am calling a neoliberal propaganda. As Urs Stäheli has pointed out, behavior economics, with which freakonomics significantly intersects, "refers to Le Bon as one of its founding fathers," and excerpts from him are regularly anthologized in books on investment theory (271). Without citing the term *affect* as the connective tissue, economists are using propaganda theory to understand the relationship among arguments, individual bodies, and financial behavior. They know that language manufactures consent, while something else provides the motivating force behind such consent. As critics of propaganda, we will limit ourselves to its identification and to the way it prevents our ability to engage with and alter its driving forces until we better comprehend this force.

Notes

1. Lakoff explains the brain science behind framing theory in terms of contemporary politics. See, for instance, *Political Mind*.

2. For a range of perspectives on the persuasive value of fear, see Chaput, Braun, and Brown's *Entertaining Fear*.

3. Recent research shows that the social values embedded in language affect not only our attitudes about people and things but also our unconscious biological behaviors. For instance, studies indicate that people unconsciously spend more time viewing anonymous faces associated with negative linguistic descriptions than those with positive linguistic tags. Thus, they argue, our vision is affectively influenced in a top-down manner independent of our conscious decisions. See Anderson et al.

4. Riley argues that affect operates autonomously, seeping from words themselves. See, for instance, her *Impersonal Passion*.

5. Lakoff argues, as I mentioned, that this takes place through synoptic pathways in the brain. Others, such as Brennan, believe it occurs through a range of sensory exchanges—we take affect into our bodies through smell, taste, touch, sight, and hearing, all of which are embodied processes that alter our chemical and biological states.

6. The television series as well as the book were conscious responses to John Kenneth Galbraith's BBC series and book, both titled *The Age of Uncertainty*, which offered a different take on the history and current state of capitalism.

7. The *Freakonomics* books are coauthored by Levitt and Dubner. Their authorial relationship emerged when Dubner, a journalist, wrote an article on Levitt. The two fast developed a personal and an intellectual camaraderie from which these best-selling books emerged. Because Levitt is the economist, I attribute the book's economic content to him.

8. I will refer to freakonomics as a discursive field separate from, but emerging through, Levitt and Dubner's *Freakonomics*. As testimony to the range of this discursive terrain, see their website: http://www.freakonomics .com/.

9. The belief that some words, especially abstract ones, better suit the work of propaganda is not uncommon. According to Le Bon, for instance, "Words whose sense is the most ill-defined are sometimes those that possess the most influence" (102). Donna Haraway, following Kenneth Burke's "god-terms," calls such words a "god-trick" (Burke 107–8; Haraway 189); Žižek calls them "empty signifiers" (29); and Arjun Appadurai says they are "concept-metaphors" (36) All agree that the value of such terms stems from their ability to signify nothing in particular at the same time that they represent the most deeply held beliefs of a group. This paradoxical character places such words above investigation and gives them significant power.

Works Cited

Anderson, Eric, Erik H. Siegel, Eliza Bliss-Moreau, and Lisa F. Barrett. "The Visual Impact of Gossip." *Science* 332.6036 (2011): 1446–48. Print.

Appadurai, Arjun. *Modernity at Large: Cultural Dimensions of Globalization*. Minneapolis: U of Minnesota P, 1996. Print.

Badiou, Alain. *Polemics*. London: Verso, 2006. Print.

Brennan, Teresa. *The Transmission of Affect*. Ithaca: Cornell UP, 2004. Print.

Burke, Kenneth. *A Rhetoric of Motives*. Berkeley: U of California P, 1969. Print.

Chaput, Catherine, M. J. Braun, and Danika Brown. *Entertaining Fear: Rhetoric and the Political Economy of Social Control*. New York: Peter Lang, 2009. Print.

Fine, Ben, and Dimitris Milonakis. *From Economics Imperialism to Freakonomics: The Shifting Boundaries between Economics and Other Social Sciences*. New York: Routledge, 2009. Print.

Foucault, Michel. *The Birth of Biopolitics: Lectures at the Collège de France, 1978–1979*. New York: Palgrave, 2008. Print.

Frank, Robert H. *The Economic Naturalist: In Search of Explanations for Everyday Enigmas*. New York: Basic, 2008. Print.

Gramsci, Antonio. *Selections from the Prison Notebooks.* Ed. and trans. Quintin Hoare and Geoffrey Nowell Smith. New York: International, 1992. Print.

Haraway, Donna. *Simians, Cyborgs and Women: The Reinvention of Nature.* New York: Routledge, 1991. Print.

Hartwell, Max. *A History of the Mont Pelerin Society.* Indianapolis: Liberty Fund, 1995. Print.

Harvey, David. *A Short History of Neoliberalism.* Oxford: Oxford UP, 2005. Print.

Hirschman, Albert O. *The Passions and the Interests: Political Arguments for Capitalism before Its Triumph.* Princeton: Princeton UP, 1997. Print.

Klein, Naomi. *The Shock Doctrine: The Rise of Disaster Capitalism.* New York: Metropolitan, 2007. Print.

Lakoff, George. *The Political Mind: A Cognitive Scientist's Guide to Your Brain and Its Politics.* New York: Penguin, 2009. Print.

Lakoff, George, and Sam Ferguson. "Framing versus Spin: Rockridge as Opposed to Luntz." George Lakoff. The Rockridge Institute, 12 June 2006. Web.

Le Bon, Gustave. *The Crowd: A Study of the Popular Mind.* London: Ernest Benn, 1952. Print.

Lecercle, Jean-Jacques. *A Marxist Philosophy of Language.* Trans. Gregory Elliott. Chicago: Haymarket Books, 2009. Print.

Levitt, Steven D., and Stephen J. Dubner. *Freakonomics: A Rogue Economist Explores the Hidden Side of Everything.* New York: Harper, 2009. Print.

———. *SuperFreakonomics: Global Cooling, Patriotic Prostitutes and Why Suicide Bombers Should Buy Life Insurance.* New York: Harper, 2009. Print.

———. *Think Like a Freak.* New York: Harper, 2014. Print.

Lippmann, Walter. *Public Opinion.* 1922. New York: Free, 1997. Print.

The Mont Pelerin Society. "About MPS: History." The Mont Pelerin Society. Mont Pelerin Soc., n.d. Web. 28 May 2011.

Ong, Walter J. *The Barbarian Within and Other Fugitive Essays and Studies.* New York: Macmillan, 1962. Print.

The Persuaders. Dir. Barak Goodman and Rachel Dretzin. PBS, 2005. DVD.

Riley, Denise. *Impersonal Passion: Language as Affect.* Durham: Duke UP, 2005. Print.

Stäheli, Urs. "Market Crowds." *Crowds.* Ed. Jeffrey T. Schnapp and Matthew Tiews. Stanford: Stanford UP, 2006. 271–87. Print.

Turpin, Paul. *The Moral Rhetoric of Political Economy: Justice and Modern Economic Thought.* New York: Routledge, 2011. Print.

Wheelan, Charles. *Naked Economics: Undressing the Dismal Science.* 2002. New York: Norton, 2010. Print.

Žižek, Slavoj. *First as Tragedy, Then as Farce.* London: Verso, 2009. Print.

———. "Multiculturalism, or, the Cultural Logic of Multinational Capitalism." *New Left Review* 225 (1997): 28–51. Print.

PRIVATIZED PROPAGANDA AND BROADCAST NEWS: LEGITIMIZING THE CALL TO ARMS

JOHN ODDO AND PATRICIA DUNMIRE

> Our government need not pursue a policy of stamping out
> dissidence—the uniformity imposed on opinion by the
> "private" media conglomerates performs that job efficiently.
> —Sheldon S. Wolin, *Democracy Incorporated*

On 7 October 2002, President George W. Bush presented to the American public his argument for "confronting" Saddam Hussein. The president contended that Iraq posed a significant threat not only because it was reconstituting its nuclear weapons program but also because it had links to Al Qaeda. The speech was rife with inaccuracies and distortions. In fact, according to a congressional report, Bush's speech contained eleven "misleading statements," more than any other address by an administration official before the Iraq War (Waxman ii). Before the speech, the public had not yet been convinced that the "threat" from Iraq required military action. Most believed the conflict could be solved diplomatically through weapons inspections (Pew Research Center). Thus, President Bush aimed his speech primarily at persuading Americans that war, rather than inspections, would be necessary to "disarm" Saddam Hussein.

Interestingly, while cable channels carried Bush's speech live, the major networks—NBC, ABC, and CBS—elected not to broadcast it, "despite . . . the growing sense that the nation may soon be at war." Network officials reasoned that, since the president had been arguing to confront Iraq for months, it was unnecessary to broadcast his address. Besides, they argued, "any news that came out of his speech would be shown on their regular newscasts" (Rutenberg). This suggests that, while many were able to watch

Bush's speech, millions of others relied on television news to learn about and assess the president's arguments for war.

In this chapter we consider how the media's treatment of the president's speech participated in what Noam Chomsky has identified as the *privatized* system of propaganda (68). We are interested in how the news media, a key component of this system, disseminate meanings that legitimate and perpetuate "values and beliefs and codes of behavior" for the general populace to internalize (1) and, moreover, orient the public toward identifying with elite interests (Herman and Chomsky xi).

ANALYTIC FRAMEWORK

We examine the agenda-setting function of the media (Jowett and O'Donnell 188) from a critical discourse analytic perspective, drawing primarily on Jan Blommaert's conception of voice and James R. Martin and Peter R. R. White's appraisal theory. Blommaert identifies voice—the ways in which people attempt to make themselves heard and understood, or fail to do so— as the crucial discursive site in which power and inequality manifest and, thus, as the key object of study for those interested in critically examining discourse and society (4). The ability to "make sense" within a particular context, Blommaert explains, resides in a speaker/writer's ability to formulate an utterance in such a way that his or her intended meaning is recognized and accepted by the audience (68). If a speaker/writer fails to meet the "conditions of use" specified for a particular context, it is unlikely that his or her text will be rhetorically effective (5). To avoid such failures, speakers/writers deploy a range of linguistic and semiotic resources designed to orient audiences toward the preferred meanings of their utterances (15). It is through this discursive orchestration of uptake, Blommaert argues, that social actors attempt to realize their desired ends through language (68).

Martin and White's appraisal theory provides useful analytic tools for examining how speakers/writers orchestrate uptake by inserting themselves into the text in particular ways and by positioning their audiences with respect to the meanings embedded in those texts (1). Simply put, appraisal theory is concerned with the affective dimension of discourse, with how speakers/writers positively or negatively evaluate various aspects of the social world, and, importantly, with how they attempt to position audiences to supply similar evaluations (2).

Martin and White's framework comprises three interacting domains: attitude, engagement, and graduation. Attitude concerns evaluations, including emotional reactions (happy/sad), judgments of human behavior (right/

wrong), and assessments of artistic objects, texts, and speeches (compelling/unconvincing) (35). Engagement concerns the sourcing of attitudes and the interactions of voices around particular issues and opinions (35). Resources of engagement (for example, quoting, denial, affirmation) position the speaker/writer vis-à-vis both the values being advanced in a text and audiences' potential responses to the speaker/writer's position (36). Graduation concerns the ways in which speakers/writers "grade" particular phenomena by amplifying or dampening their feelings toward a given phenomenon, event, or entity and/or by manipulating associated category boundaries (35).

Analyzing the presentation and management of voice through the appraisal theory framework enables us to consider how the news media support and/or challenge different opinions concerning the events, people, and institutions they report on. That is, we understand the news media to serve as what Blommaert terms a "centring institution": a "real or imagined" social actor or institution that provides "authoritative attributes to which one should orient in order to have a voice" on a given issue or within a particular context (172). In the analysis that follows, we examine the ways in which President Bush's 7 October 2002 Iraq War speech was represented by ABC, CBS, and NBC. We identify the specific voices incorporated into the broadcasts and examine how the news organizations positioned these voices relative to one another and to the president's case for war. We argue that as "centring institutions," the broadcast news outlets mediated (Fairclough 30) the president's voice in such a way as to enhance his capacity to make himself heard and to achieve a successful uptake of his message concerning war with Iraq. In so doing, they fulfilled their function as part of the United States' privatized propaganda system.

ANALYSIS

An important premise of our analysis is that *evaluative discourse*—discourse conveying positive and negative attitudes—provides a partial window into a given speaker's ideology (van Dijk 33). Thus, in the table below, we not only enumerate the prominent voices featured in the newscasts but also chart the types of linguistic and visual evaluations they produced about key social agents and events (Martin; Martin and White). Following Martin and White, we distinguish between two general kinds of voices: authorial voices and nonauthorial voices. Briefly, **authorial voices** are those that speak or write directly to the audience, those that we recognize as the "narrators" of a given message (for example, *I oppose the war*). Meanwhile, **nonauthorial voices** are cited voices: represented voices that are "implanted" in a text and that we recognize as separate from the authorial voice (for example, _John Edwards said_ he supports the _war_). Thus, we distinguish between the authorial voices of journalists (dark gray) and the nonauthorial voices of other textual speakers (light gray), that is, the sources the journalists brought into their stories "from the outside." We examine whether these voices expressed positive or negative attitudes about (1) the prospect of violence in Iraq; (2) President Bush and his speech; (3) Saddam Hussein and the Iraqi government; and (4) those political institutions considering nonviolent alternatives to war (for example, the United Nations, France, and so on).

This tabulation is necessarily "blind" to textual details, but it will serve as a useful reference point. We can see that the newscasts included an array of voices espousing different ideological attitudes about the social and material world. Generally, however, both journalists and other textual speakers _positively_ evaluated the president and his desired war in Iraq while _negatively_ evaluating Saddam Hussein and those exploring peaceful alternatives to violence.

The subsequent analysis provides a more detailed account of this phenomenon. In the first half, we focus on the authorial voices of journalists and their attitudes. Here, we concentrate on how the journalists themselves explicitly evaluated the various "targets" listed in the top row of the table. In the second half, we turn our attention to nonauthorial voices and their attitudes. Here, we are interested in the kinds of attitudes attributed to nonauthorial speakers like George W. Bush, U.S. lawmakers, and American citizens. Even more so, we are interested in the different ways these nonauthorial voices were _framed_ by the journalists (Fairclough 53). Indeed, we show that journalists do not just frame other textual speakers by _explicitly evaluating_ them. They also endorse and delegitimize nonauthorial speakers (and their attitudes) more subtly, depending on how frequently and extensively they feature those speakers, how faithfully they report the utterances attributed to those speakers, and how evenhandedly they _engage_ with those speakers, that is, how they signal their tolerance for different speakers and position audiences to regard certain voices as more "natural and legitimate" than others (Martin and White 96).

Authorial Voices: Journalists Promote the "Showdown"

The journalists in our study were not impartial chroniclers of events but ideological agents who expressed clear attitudes about the characters and events in their stories. First, the authorial voices of journalists expressed _negative judgments_ about Saddam Hussein and Iraq (_n_ = 14). Typically, this judgment entailed assuming that Iraq possessed weapons of mass

Attitudes Expressed by Different Voices in News Narratives

TARGETS OF EXPRESSED ATTITUDES

Textual Voices	Potential Violence		Bush and His Speech		Hussein and Iraq		Proponents of Nonviolent Alternatives	
	POS	NEG	POS	NEG	POS	NEG	POS	NEG
NBC (10/7)								
Journalists (authorial)	1	0	6	0	0	4	0	0
Bush	0	0	1	0	0	1	0	0
Admin. Officials	0	0	4	0	0	2	0	0
U.S. Congress	0	0	1	4	0	0	0	0
U.S. Citizens	0	0	2	1	0	0	0	0
Other	0	1	1	3	0	0	0	0
TOTALS	1	1	15	8	0	7	0	0
ABC (10/7)								
Journalists (authorial)	0	0	4	0	0	3	0	0
Bush	0	0	0	0	0	6	0	0
Admin. Officials	0	0	1	0	0	0	0	0
U.S. Congress	—	—	—	—	—	—	—	—
U.S. Citizens	1	4	4	7	0	0	0	0
Other	—	—	—	—	—	—	—	—
TOTALS	1	4	9	7	0	9	0	0
CBS (10/7)								
Journalists (authorial)	3	0	4	0	0	6	0	1
Bush	1	0	0	0	0	7	0	0
Admin. Officials	0	0	2	0	0	0	0	0
U.S. Congress	1	0	0	4	0	0	0	0
U.S. Citizens	1	2	0	0	0	0	0	0
Other	0	1	0	0	0	0	0	0
TOTALS	6	3	6	4	0	13	0	1
CBS (10/8)								
Journalists (authorial)	6	0	7	0	0	1	1	3
Bush	7	0	0	0	0	12	0	1
Admin. Officials	0	0	2	0	0	2	0	1
U.S. Congress	1	1	0	0	0	1	0	0
U.S. Citizens	—	—	—	—	—	—	—	—
Other	0	0	0	0	1	2	0	0
TOTALS	14	1	9	0	1	18	1	5
GRAND TOTAL	22	9	39	19	1	47	1	6

destruction and posed a threat to the United States. For example, CBS anchor Dan Rather reported on 8 October about "the concern that pressuring Saddam could make him **more dangerous,**" presupposing that Mr. Hussein was *already* dangerous. Meanwhile, NBC's David Gregory referred on 7 October to "**the Iraqi threat,**" presenting a negative judgment of Iraq as a taken-for-granted aspect of reality and failing to engage with (or even acknowledge) any alternative views on the subject. In fact, Gregory transformed an arguable and alleged clausal process (someone says that Iraq *threatens* people) into an objectified and seemingly non-negotiable nominalization (the Iraqi *threat*).[1]

The journalists also included negative visual evaluations of Iraq. For example, on CBS on 7 October, John Roberts reported that, according to "the White House," the president would describe[2]

Excerpt 1

Saddam's weapons capabilities

and his potential to use them.

Verbally, Roberts presupposes that Hussein *has* "weapons capabilities"; he does not clarify that these are *alleged* weapons capabilities. Meanwhile, in the visual track, CBS displayed consecutive shots of giant missiles, which, given Roberts's verbal report, could only be interpreted as *Saddam's* missiles. Thus, CBS not only verbally presupposed that Iraq had weapons of mass destruction but also visually endowed these weapons with seemingly unchallengeable rhetorical *presence* (Perelman and Olbrechts-Tyteca 117).

Meanwhile, ABC's Terry Moran reported the following:

Excerpt 2

. . . the President claims Iraq poses a special **danger** to the U.S.

In terms of linguistic engagement, Moran employs a distancing verbal process (*claims*) in order to separate himself from President Bush's assertion that "Iraq poses a special danger." But in the visual track, we see stock footage of Saddam Hussein blasting a shotgun while wearing a gangster-like trench coat and fedora. In selecting this image, ABC opted to portray Saddam Hussein in the least flattering light possible, as an aggressive figure who casually discharged weapons to display his power. Thus, even as Moran verbally distanced himself from Bush's assertion, ABC's visual presented an image of Hussein that supported the notion that the Iraqi leader was "dangerous."

Along with these negative portraits of Hussein and his country, the journalists also produced positive attitudes about President Bush and his address (*n* = 21). For example, ABC's Charlie Gibson offered the following endorsement of the president's speech: "President Bush is **laying out his case** for war against Iraq" (7 October) Here, the verb and its complement index the legitimacy of Bush's address. The reporting phrase (*laying out*)

188 ☆ JOHN ODDO AND PATRICIA DUNMIRE

suggests a detailed arrangement of arguments, while the complement (*his case*) indicates a comprehensive body of evidence brought against someone already arrested and charged with a crime (that is, Hussein). If Gibson had chosen different engagement resources, he might have projected a much more neutral assessment of the president's discourse: "President Bush is *making a speech* for war against Iraq."

Even when the journalists did not explicitly praise Bush's speech, they included other positive evaluations of Bush—sourced to *no one in particular*. These positive evaluations were placed in the "Other" category in the table, but they were so vaguely attributed that they almost seemed like "factual reports." For example, NBC's David Gregory reported that "Mr. Bush **is expected to speak . . . in detail** about what Saddam Hussein has done to develop his weapons stockpile." Note, first, that Gregory refers to Hussein's "weapons stockpile," presupposing that the Iraqi leader has weapons and that his supply of these is substantial. Equally important, the words "in detail" indicate a positive evaluation of the complexity of Bush's address: Bush will not speak "superficially" on the subject of Saddam Hussein but will thoroughly explain Hussein's weapons development. Significantly, the source of this positive evaluation is unspecified, since Gregory employs a passive verb (*is expected*) without identifying the agent responsible for "performing" this verb. We do not know precisely *who* expects Bush to speak "in detail." Indeed, this passive construction seems to imply a *universal* agent (Robinson 440); Bush is expected to speak in detail *by everyone*—or, at least, by everyone whose opinion on the subject *matters*. Thus, Gregory "universalizes" a particular and contentious evaluation by transforming one person or group's expectation about the future into a universal assessment (Fairclough 45). In a sense, Gregory positions his audience to believe in an apparent consensus about Bush's speech, to envision along with "everyone" else Bush's detailed account of Iraq's "weapons stockpiles."

Overall, then, journalists exhibited ideological polarization (van Dijk 67), portraying Saddam Hussein as dangerous, while representing Bush and his speech as legitimate. This was epitomized on the 8 October CBS broadcast, where Dan Rather established a "covert 'antagonist-protagonist'" structure (Fairclough 54), pitting the "untrustworthy" assertions of Saddam Hussein (covert antagonist) against the "authoritative" assertions of the president (covert protagonist). The news segment opened as follows:

Excerpt 3

In Baghdad today, Saddam Hussein again denied he has weapons of mass destruction. . . . But in his speech last night in Cincinnati, President Bush carefully laid out his arguments for a decisive showdown soon with Saddam.

Here, we see how one speaker's denial can be undermined in a journalistic context that supports the contrary affirmative assertion (Dunmire 246). Rather initially reports that Saddam Hussein "denied he has weapons of mass destruction." However, the denial sourced to Hussein is countered with appreciative evaluations of Bush's discourse. First, the coordinating conjunction "but" establishes that Bush's speech is to be taken as a counterstatement to Hussein's denials. And this counterstatement is ornamented with positive attitudes about Bush's meticulousness (*carefully*) and the compelling arrangement of his arguments (*laid out*). Thus, while Rather merely acknowledges Hussein's denial, he engages with the president's voice quite differently, explicitly endorsing Bush's speech.

This example also illustrates another notable finding: journalists positively evaluated a *future confrontation* with Saddam Hussein ($n = 10$). Above, Rather accomplishes this both verbally and visually. First, notice that Rather refers to a future confrontation with Saddam as "decisive," a positive judgment that construes potential violence against Iraq as the end of a conflict (rather than, say, the beginning of a more serious humanitarian catastrophe). Meanwhile, the multimodal image behind Rather's shoulder features the words "SHOWDOWN WITH SADDAM" in bold yellow font. Of course, the term "showdown"—also uttered by Rather—evokes western gunfights in which a hero (that is, Bush) faces off against some villain (that is, Saddam). Thus, potential war is construed as a kind of exhilarating melodrama featuring just two people, a melodrama that will presumably end with the "decisive" defeat of Saddam Hussein. Behind the words

"Showdown With Saddam," one can discern a circular "lens" split into four quadrants by a cross—what amounts to a view through the scope of a rifle. And what is this "rifle"—and, by extension, the viewer—targeting? Well, the American flag fills the top half of crosshairs, and the Iraqi flag fills the bottom half. Thus, CBS is not just reporting about the *possibility* of a confrontation between two nations; it is "aiming at" this confrontation. Again, future violence is construed as desirable for the viewer.

A similar pattern emerged on NBC, as Tom Brokaw introduced Bush's speech:

Excerpt 4

Tonight in Cincinnati, President Bush is making what his aides say is his most comprehensive case yet on the reasons to remove Saddam Hussein from power in Iraq.

In NBC's multimodal slogan, Iraq is framed linguistically as the "Target." It is hard to think of a word that would better promote the idea that Iraq needed to be attacked. What is more, the word "Target" is also super-imposed over the image of Saddam Hussein's face, indicating that he, too, is a legitimate object of attack. Meanwhile, President Bush's face appears in the top left quadrant above Hussein's. Once again, Hussein and Bush are pitted against one another in a kind of personalized conflict, but Bush is positioned in the "idealized" position—higher than Saddam Hussein (Kress and Van Leeuwen 193–202). Against this visual backdrop, the positive valuation of Bush's speech (*comprehensive*)—a valuation sourced to anonymous aides—takes on greater authority. Insofar as NBC glorifies Bush over the Iraqi "target," it positions viewers to regard other positive evaluations of Bush's case as legitimate.

Except for CBS, the journalists rarely expressed such explicitly positive attitudes about potential violence (see table). But even when they did not openly endorse violence, they frequently *euphemized* violence (Chilton 12–14), sanitizing it of its unpleasantness ($n = 9$). So, if the journalists fell short of overtly legitimizing war, they at least helped to make such war seem more palatable. In excerpt 4 above, for instance, note that Brokaw refers to Bush's reasons "**to remove** Saddam Hussein from power." The nasty business of *violently forcing* Hussein out of his presidential palaces is rendered more tolerable when it is constructed innocuously as "removing him from power." Indeed, Brokaw's language reproduces the "surgical" metaphor prevalent in contemporary military discourse: bombing Saddam Hussein from thirty thousand feet is akin to the "hygienic" operation of removing a tumor (Lakoff).

Similarly, on NBC, David Gregory reported that "the President is not expected to address . . . how the United States will rebuild Iraq after a **regime change** is achieved." The noun phrase *regime change* represents an extraordinary euphemism. In particular, the nominalization *change* suggests a straightforward exchange: substituting one government for another without bloodshed. We get no sense of the violence needed to create this change—the armed invasion required to overpower an existing government. Nor do we get any sense of the complicated political processes needed to supplant the original government with a new "legitimate" one.[3] Furthermore, the passive verb *is achieved* connotes *success* and *achievement*—indeed we only "achieve" things that are positive. Thus, Gregory suggests that "regime change" is—or rather will be—a legitimate accomplishment. Importantly, Gregory does not specify the actors responsible for "achieving regime change." Presumably, U.S. troops will be the ones to invade Iraq and drive out its leaders. But Gregory is careful not to implicate them—and certainly not in such "negative" terms. By contrast, the "positive" future action in Gregory's report is expressed in a full transactive clause[4] where the responsible actor *is* clearly specified: "the **United States** will **rebuild** Iraq." Thus, a potentially unpleasant action (overthrowing a government) is encased in a euphemistic noun phrase (*regime change*) that conceals the responsible Americans, while a relatively positive action (*rebuilding*) is stated directly in a full clause that highlights the responsible Americans. Of course, what is missing—except by implication—is that for Iraq to be rebuilt, it would first need to be destroyed.

Aside from legitimizing and euphemizing violence, the CBS journalists also offered negative evaluations of those political institutions that were exploring peaceful alternatives to war (*n* = 4). Correspondent John Roberts portrayed those opposed to immediate militarization as obstacles standing in the way of progress. He reports, for instance, that "France is **holding up** the UN measure [a resolution to disarm Saddam Hussein]" (8

October). By using the verb phrase *is holding up*, Roberts evokes a negative judgment of France, portraying a country with questions about war as a hindrance bent on "getting in the way." Roberts continues:

> President Bush will telephone French president Chirac tomorrow to try to **move the UN process along**, but now there's a possible delay in the Senate with West Virginia's Robert Byrd **threatening to block the resolution there**. That **could hold up** a vote on the measure until next week.

Notice that while France's action (*holding up*) is dilatory, Bush's action (*moving the process along*) is proactive. However, this positive judgment of Bush is countered (via the word *but*) with the "bad news" that even in the U.S. Senate there is another "possible delay." Here, Robert Byrd's arguments[5] for opposing the congressional war resolution are transformed into a single, negatively charged nominalization: "delay." Indeed, Byrd is construed as "threatening to block" the congressional resolution, a metaphorical representation that portrays Byrd as a kind of aggressor who intimidates (*threatens*) others to get his way. Just as France "*is holding up* the UN measure," Byrd "*could hold up*" the congressional vote. Note that both Byrd and France can only "slow down" the momentum for war. They may "delay" but not stop the political rituals that generate violence, rituals that, in the CBS newscasts, represent "forward progress."

Framing Nonauthorial Voices: Legitimizing War Talk

Generally, the authorial voices of journalists discredited Saddam Hussein, commended President Bush's address, legitimized violence against Iraq, and disapproved of those considering peaceful alternatives. These journalistic attitudes served as crucial "sign-posts" (Martin and White 64), indicating how audiences should regard the other voices and ideological positions featured in the newscasts. Thus, for example, audiences could infer that other textual voices discrediting Iraq were "on the same side" as the journalists, while textual voices opposing war were "at odds" with the reporters.

In this section of the analysis, we focus more closely on nonauthorial voices and investigate how they were framed by the journalists in their October 2002 broadcasts. That is, we examine how the authorial voices of journalists *entextualized* and *recontextualized* the voices and ideological positions of other speakers in their narratives (Bauman and Briggs 73–78). By entextualization, we mean the act of turning a stretch of discourse into a textual unit, so that it may be extracted from one context and recontextualized, that is, re-presented, in another (73). Importantly, entextualization and recontextualization are not neutral processes but political acts with implications for the "construction and exercise of power" (77). Journalists, in particular, hold the power to appropriate others' discourse, to alter this discourse as they recontextualize it, and to claim legitimacy for their recontextualizations (76–77). Indeed, given that they reach enormous public audiences, journalists serve "important gate-keeping positions": they have a unique capacity "to select, endorse and . . . re-perspectivize" other people's words and the authority to "*subdue or silence voices*" before they reach the public sphere (Linell 151).

The most prominent nonauthorial voice featured in the newscasts was that of President Bush. As shown in the table, speech attributed to Bush was featured in every news narrative, and this speech was teeming with negative judgments of Saddam Hussein and Iraq (*n* = 26). Importantly, Bush's voice was always given priority over other textual voices in three important ways. First, his speech was almost always featured before any other voices in the news segments. That is, the journalists began their newscasts with Bush's speech, implying the overriding importance and legitimacy of the president's opinions. For example, NBC's David Gregory opened his 7 October segment with a roughly fifty-second preview of Bush's address—complete with a description of the speech's purpose (*to detail the threat posed by Saddam*) and a presentation of several key assertions (for example, *the president will call the Iraqi threat to the U.S. "unique"*). In this way, the president's discourse became the predominant frame for all subsequent material in the newscasts. Thus, when Gregory went on to report that "Congress is about to vote on a war resolution," the viewer had already been positioned to understand this vote in the president's terms—that is, as a vote over whether to authorize a war that confronted "the Iraqi threat to the U.S." and not, say, as a vote over whether to sanction illegal aggression.

Second, the journalists frequently recontextualized the president's speech in *televised clips* and *direct quotations* (*n* = 9). This suggests that the journalists wished to remain as faithful as possible to the president's "authoritative" utterances—that is, they sought to resist any "compromising transformation" of the president's discourse as they recontextualized it in their reports (Bauman and Briggs 77). For instance, CBS on 8 October played four consecutive clips of President Bush delivering his address—just after Dan Rather offered his legitimizing introductory remarks (see excerpt 3). In these clips, Bush appears in a close shot behind a podium adorned with the official presidential seal. Speaking uninterrupted to the viewer for almost a full minute, Bush offers no fewer than twelve negative judgments of Iraq, declaring that Saddam Hussein could have a nuclear weapon "in less than a year" and even raising the specter of a "mushroom cloud." No other speaker in the newscast received this much unfettered coverage; no other speaker's oration was featured so saliently and endowed with such rhetorical presence (Perelman and Olbrechts-Tyteca 117).

The quotations of Bush's address are also remarkable given that they were presented in newscasts *before* Bush spoke. Bush's discourse was regarded as so important that it was actually "pre-quoted." For example, ABC's Terry Moran *precontextualized* Bush's future utterance (Oddo), endowing it with presence in the here-and-now:

Excerpt 5

[Bush] will say, "By its past and present actions, by its technological capabilities, by the merciless nature of its regime, Iraq is unique."

This excerpt also reveals the third way that Bush's voice was prioritized above others in the newscasts: his speech was consistently endowed with verbal *and* visual presence (Perelman and Olbrechts-Tyteca 117). Note that ABC not only *voiced* Bush's speech but also *printed* it on-screen, working in two modes to increase the salience of Bush's remarks. Moreover, ABC supplemented Bush's words with a symbol of his authority (Van Leeuwen 106–10, 120): an image of the presidential seal, shimmering as it rotated behind his head like a glowing Christian halo.

The networks also recontextualized utterances attributed to unnamed members of Bush's political team—variously referred to as *aides, White House sources,* or *officials* (see excerpts 1 and 4). The chief function of these voices, as the table indicates, was to express positive attitudes about the president and negative attitudes about Saddam Hussein. Thus, we find officials calling Bush's speech *comprehensive* (ABC, NBC), *compelling* (CBS 7 October), *detailed* (NBC, CBS 7 October), and *never-before-seen* (NBC) and, conversely, reaffirming that Saddam Hussein had *weapons* (NBC, CBS 7 October) and posed a *threat* (NBC). As Patricia Dunmire explains, these administration sources represent an ambiguous group of speakers whose anonymity and self-legitimizing ("official") titles make them relatively "impervious to criticism" (230). Thus, the newscasts not only presented the president's speech in ways that indexed his authority but also included relatively unchallengeable voices that further endorsed the president and his arguments.

Of course, the newscasts also featured other nonauthorial voices, voices not always as friendly to the president and his wartime agenda. Most prominent in this category were the voices of *U.S. lawmakers* and *U.S. citizens*, respectively.[6] As we show below, while these recontextualized voices sometimes expressed dissent regarding the president's plans for war, very few expressed unqualified disapproval—indeed, most actually *supported* the notion of going to war in Iraq. And those voices that did express clear antiwar arguments were subtly delegitimized in the context of the news narratives.

We see in the table that when U.S. congressional voices appeared in the newscasts, they expressed more negative attitudes ($n = 8$) about President Bush than positive ones ($n = 1$). But this statistic requires additional explanation. First, seven of the eight negative attitudes expressed about the president were attributed to just one person—Senator John Edwards (D-N.C.)—who appeared in two different newscasts. Second, if we look closely at the content of Edwards's reported speech, we see that he was not really opposed to war in Iraq per se but to Bush's unilateral approach to war.

In the 7 October CBS newscast, for instance, John Roberts first explains that "Edwards supports a congressional resolution authorizing force," making clear that the Democratic senator favored war in Iraq. Only then does he go on to report that Edwards "sharply **criticized** what he sees as the President's gratuitous **unilateralism, a determination to act alone for the sake of acting alone**." Here, Edwards's reported speech is infused with some rather intense language: he *sharply* criticized the president for his *gratuitous* unilateralism. Oddly though, as Roberts reports on Edwards's stance, the visual track features an American fighter jet taking off from an aircraft carrier and zipping through the sky. Edward's reported criticisms are undercut by this arresting image, which arguably suggests to the viewer that, regardless of the political noise, the American military is about to "blast off."

A moment later, when Edwards appears on-screen talking at a press conference, he again uses strongly negative terms to describe Bush: "the administration's policy projects . . . **arrogance without purpose**." But notice that Edwards's negative evaluations, however forceful they may be, concern not the correctness of invading Iraq but the manner in which the invasion will be executed (*unilateralism*) and the ethos that this manner of warfare projects (*arrogance without purpose*). Thus, while the newscasts feature a politician disputing the president, the dispute concerns only *how* the war should be carried out, not *whether* it should be. And visual data (such as the fighter jet) only reinforce the notion that war is imminent.

The final category of nonauthorial speakers, U.S. citizens, also expressed more negative than positive attitudes about President Bush (8:6) and the prospect of war in Iraq (6:2). Again, these "raw numbers" require further explanation. First, like the lawmakers, even when citizens expressed negative attitudes about potential war, they did not necessarily *object* to the war. For example, on NBC, a Cincinnati reporter named David Wells appeared on-screen, pretending to speak to President Bush: "All right, you've **convinced** us we need to do this. Now **tell us how we're going to do it, and how much it's going to cost us**." Wells expresses conviction about the necessity of war and suggests that the president has been very persuasive in making his arguments. Specifically, he asserts that all of "us" have been *convinced* that we *need to* invade Iraq. The only negative attitudes are communicated implicitly as Wells projects *feelings of insecurity* about how the war will be prosecuted and how much it will cost. Of course, he also suggests that this insecurity will be lessened once the president "tells us" his plans for war.

Second, with the exception of Wells, citizens who appeared on-screen to discuss Bush were never identified for the viewer. For example, on 7 October ABC played four brief clips of Cincinnatians opining about the president's upcoming speech. While these citizens were "permitted" to speak, they remained anonymous and were never given credentials. Thus, in contrast to the president, citizen voices were treated as relatively indistinguishable and unauthoritative.

Finally, the citizen-speakers were framed by journalists such that those who criticized the president were consistently "counteracted" by a stronger group of Bush's supporters. For instance, in this same ABC broadcast, an anonymous woman calls the president's war-talk "**diversionary**" and complains that Bush "**isn't concerned enough with the economy, with what's happening in our country**." These are decidedly negative judgments of Bush's plans for war and his (lack of) attention to domestic matters. On the heels of these negative evaluations, however, Terry Moran intervenes, saying, "But for many there is an underlying **trust** in the commander in chief." Here, lest we assume that the woman criticizing the president represents the entire city of Cincinnati, Moran steps in to engage with her voice, countering her assertion (via the word *but*) with the information that the majority of people still trust Bush. Note Moran's use of "quantification," the imprecise reckoning of numbers and amounts (Martin and White 148). Specifically, the up-scaled quantification—*many*—clearly "trumps" the unique opinions of one woman. To further stack the deck against the anti-Bush sentiment, Moran describes the "trust" for Bush as *underlying,* that is, as more fundamental than any superficial anxieties about the war. And, of course, Bush is designated not by name but with the authoritative military title *commander in chief.* With this, a different male citizen appears on the screen declaring that, if Bush "feels like he needs to [go to war]," then "I'm **backing [the president] up**." Given Moran's framing, we immediately understand that the man "backing up" the president represents the "many," unlike the woman who represents "the few."

The woman who called the president's speech "diversionary" was the only citizen who spoke on camera offering not just vague reservations about potential violence (for example, *I get nervous anytime I hear somebody talking about wars*) but direct criticisms of the president and his military agenda. This is remarkable considering that on the day of Bush's speech, roughly *five thousand citizens* gathered at the site of the address specifically to oppose a future war in Iraq (La Botz). The antiwar demonstration would seem to be newsworthy, but, in fact, protesters were referenced only once by John Roberts on CBS on 7 October:

Excerpt 6

[the President's] speech is intended to help . . . convince a growing chorus of antiwar protesters that it [war] is the right thing to do.

Here, the "voice" of antiwar protesters is given some visibility, since the sign reading "No Blood for Oil" is salient. Obviously, this represents a negative attitude about the propriety of war. Moreover, Roberts uses a metaphor (*chorus*) that amplifies the quantity and unity of the protesters. However, this "chorus" of protesters appears on-screen for all of three seconds (and only in this report). Moreover, in his verbal report, Roberts "passivates" the protesters (Van Leeuwen 33). That is, they are not represented as agents actively resisting the war but as objects being acted upon by Bush—and potentially being "convinced" that war is the "right thing to do." Thus, Americans truly opposing war were scarcely visible in the news, and when they did appear, they were portrayed not as thoughtful speakers with legitimate arguments for peace but as potential "converts" who could yet be persuaded to accept violence.

CONCLUSION

To us, it seems obvious that democracy is hindered in significant ways by the privatized system of propaganda. How, for instance, can members of the public have an informed, democratic debate about war when they are bombarded almost exclusively with the voices of elite warmongers, voices that are legitimated and naturalized by corporate mass media? Perhaps it is too radical to suggest that citizens should opt out of corporate news media *altogether*. But, at the very least, they should seek out alternative news media—perhaps as a first option—so that they can encounter and consider the voices of dissent. Moreover, we believe that rhetoricians should play a more significant role in helping to foster "critical media literacy," empowering students to both recognize and resist the media's role in propagating unjust rhetoric and policies (Kellner and Share). The privatized system of propaganda is pernicious—and it can have deadly consequences. Concerned rhetoricians must do their part to oppose its influence and to ensure that voices committed to social justice—voices on the margins—are heard and heeded.

Notes

1. *Nominalization* is a grammatical concept that generally refers to the process of transforming a verb into a noun (for example, *She grew quickly* → *Her growth was quick*).

2. In this and other excerpts, we have deleted some frames to save space.

3. We also note that the word *regime* represents a negative judgment of the Iraqi leadership, since this epithet is used almost exclusively to describe dictatorial governments.

4. A transactive clause includes an *actor,* a *verbal process,* and an *affected entity* (for example: The U.S. [actor] will rebuild [process] Iraq [affected]). Transactive clauses make clear who does what to whom (Hodge and Kress 19).

5. Byrd voted against the resolution authorizing President Bush to attack Iraq. Three days after Bush's address, he said the following on the Senate floor:

> The president is hoping to secure power under the Constitution that no president has ever claimed before, never. . . . The Bush administration wants (the) president to have the power to launch this nation into war—without provocation and without clear evidence of an imminent attack on the United States. And we're going to be foolish enough to give it to him. (qtd. in Kelly)

6. This represents a rather narrow field of textual voices from the U.S. political spectrum and citizenry. Other relevant voices were simply not included. For instance, in these newscasts, we never encounter speech from UN representatives, weapons inspectors, or international leaders—except for Saddam Hussein, whose discourse is featured only once, as a kind of illegitimate counterpoint to the president's address (see excerpt 3).

Works Cited

Bauman, Richard, and Charles L. Briggs. "Poetics and Performance as Critical Perspectives on Language and Social Life." *Annual Review of Anthropology* 19 (1990): 59–88. Print.

Blommaert, Jan. *Discourse: A Critical Introduction.* Cambridge: Cambridge UP, 2005. Print.

Bush, George W. "President Bush Outlines Iraqi Threat." The White House: President George W. Bush. 7 October 2002. Web. 10 June 2014.

Chilton, Paul. "Metaphor, Euphemism and the Militarization of Language." *Current Research on Peace and Violence* 10.1 (1987): 7–19. Print.

Chomsky, Noam. Interview with David Barsamian. "Language in the Service of Propaganda." *Chronicles of Dissent.* Monroe, Maine: Common Courage, 1992. 63–85. Print.

Dunmire, Patricia. "Naturalizing the Future in Factual Discourse: A Critical Linguistic Analysis of a Projected Event." *Written Communication* 14.2 (1997): 221–63. Print.

Fairclough, Norman. *Analyzing Discourse: Textual Analysis for Social Research*. London: Routledge, 2003. Print.

Herman, Edward, and Noam Chomsky. *Manufacturing Consent: The Political Economy of the Mass Media*. New York: Pantheon, 1988. Print.

Hodge, Robert, and Gunther Kress. *Language as Ideology*. London: Routledge and Kegan Paul, 1979. Print.

Jowett, Garth, and Victoria O'Donnell. *Propaganda and Persuasion*. Thousand Oaks, Calif.: Sage, 2006. Print.

Kellner, Douglas, and Jeff Share. "Toward Critical Media Literacy: Core Concepts, Debates, Organizations, and Policy." *Discourse: Studies in the Cultural Politics of Education* 26.3 (2005): 369–86. Print.

Kelly, Mary Louise. "Byrd's Legacy: 18,000 Votes Later, He Loved His Job." NPR.org. National Public Radio, 28 June 2010. Web. 10 June 2014.

Kress, Gunther R., and Theo Van Leeuwen. *Reading Images: The Grammar of Visual Design*. London: Routledge, 1996. Print.

La Botz, Paul. "Thousands in Cincinnati Protest Bush's Call for War in Iraq." *Baltimore Independent Media Center*. 9 October 2002. Web. 10 June 2014.

Lakoff, George. "Metaphor and War: The Metaphor System Used to Justify War in the Gulf." *Vietnam Generation Journal and Newsletter*. November 1991. Web. 10 June 2014.

Linell, Per. "Discourse across Boundaries: On Recontextualizations and the Blending of Voices in Professional Discourse." *Text* 18.2 (1998): 143–57. Print.

Martin, James R. "Fair Trade: Negotiating Meaning in Multimodal Texts." *The Semiotics of Writing: Transdisciplinary Perspectives on the Technology of Writing*. Ed. Patrick Coppock. Turnhout, Belgium: Brepols, 2002. 311–38. Print.

Martin, James R., and Peter R. R. White. *The Language of Evaluation: Appraisal in English*. New York: Palgrave Macmillan, 2005. Print.

Oddo, John. "Precontextualization and the Rhetoric of Futurity: Foretelling Colin Powell's U.N. Address on NBC News." *Discourse and Communication* 7.1 (2013): 25–53. Print.

Perelman, Chaim, and Lucie Olbrechts-Tyteca. *The New Rhetoric: A Treatise on Argumentation*. Trans. John Wilkinson and Purcell Weaver. Notre Dame: U of Notre Dame P, 1969. Print.

Pew Research Center for the People and the Press. *Midterm Election Preview: Americans Thinking about Iraq but Focused on the Economy*. 10 October 2002. Web. 10 June 2014.

Robinson, William S. "Sentence Focus, Cohesion, and the Active and Passive Voices." *Teaching English in the Two-Year College* 27.4 (2000): 440–45. Print.

Rutenberg, Jim. "Threats and Responses: The Networks; 3 Networks Skip Bush's Talk, Citing Absence of Request." *New York Times* 8 October 2002: A13. Print.

Van Dijk, Teun A. *Ideology: A Multidisciplinary Approach.* London: Sage, 1998. Print.

Van Leeuwen, Theo. *Discourse and Practice: New Tools for Critical Discourse Analysis.* New York: Oxford UP, 2008. Print.

Waxman, Henry A. *Iraq on the Record: The Bush Administration's Public Statements on Iraq.* Washington: United States House of Representatives Committee on Government Reform, Minority Staff, Special Investigations Division, 2004. Print.

Wolin, Sheldon S. *Democracy Incorporated: Managed Democracy and the Specter of Inverted Totalitarianism.* Princeton: Princeton UP, 2008. Print.

ATTENTION! RUMOR BOMBS, AFFECT, AND MANAGED DEMOCRACY

JAYSON HARSIN

> The nature, indeed the very notion, of actuality . . . becomes
> virtual at worst, abstract at best. These unprecedented pow-
> ers and the scales they can command appear as especially fa-
> vorable to elitism, to the quick-witted and manipulative, but
> uncongenial to democratic values and deliberative practices.
> —Sheldon Wolin, *Democracy Inc.*

The elite projects of steering mass communication, especially journalism, through an increasing professionalization of politics via marketing,
advertising, and public relations have met serious obstacles in the new
digital culture era. However, immense resources have been invested in
studying the new digital culture and adapting propaganda methods to
the new challenges. Political rumor (in addition to rumor generally) is a
site where one can study the struggles to manage communication flows in
the present. More precisely, what I call rumor bombs (Harsin, "Diffusing"
and "Rumour Bomb") have produced a crisis of verification resulting in
what I call vertiginous democracy, which benefits elites more than citizens
(such confusion could potentially destabilize or harm elite interests and
projects, too, but empirical examples tend to favor the contrary). In this
chapter, I offer a convergence theory of rumor bombs that explains their
current historical ubiquity while also employing recent insights from affect theory, neuroscience, and Tardean sociology of influence to explain
their powerful viral efficacy—all of which have no small consequences
for democracy.

CONVERGENCE CULTURE AND THE
PROBLEM/WEAPON OF RUMOR

Both the Walter Lippman/Edward Bernays technocratic project of managed democracy (between public relations, psychology, and professionalization of politics) and communication research itself—evidenced by
the work of pioneers such as Harold Lasswell and Robert Knapp on the
control of information and the authority to separate rumor from fact—
shared the concern regarding potentially dangerous public claims and
their power in a mass-communication age (Simpson 17–23; Knapp; Allport
608). Leaving aside the historical differences in Western managed democracy projects (and objectionist alternatives offered by theorists like John
Dewey), the technocratic project of managed democracy was especially
successful in the United States, aided by various "states of exception" in
the Cold War. The civil rights, student, and antiwar movements of the
1950s through 1970s nevertheless periodically destabilized it. Still, new
challenges emerged for managed democracy in the last three decades of the
twentieth century (Curtis). They were hastened by the arrival of new digital
technologies, from the cell phone and digital camera and photo editing
to the Internet, accompanied by the splintering of mass communication
audiences (and thus informational gatekeeping) with the rise of cable and
satellite TV—all in the context of increasingly negative or "dirty" politics.
The new digital technologies found their place in a long history of hopeful
responses to new communication technologies as tools for more effective
democracy that somehow never fulfilled their potential (Mattelart). With
the rise of the Internet, Lippmann's "pictures in our heads" (Ewen 147)
returned as a problem for technocrats and citizens alike, as was evidenced
in the growth of rumor-debunking sites on the Internet, such as Snopes.
com and TruthOrFiction.com, followed at the debut of the twenty-first
century by the emergence of the fact-checking movement (including Fact-
Check.org, for example), left- and right-wing media watchdog groups, and
the first-ever American presidential candidate's rumor-debunking site,
Barack Obama's Fight the Smears in 2008. These conditions constitute
an era of vertiginous democracy—participating in democratic political
communication has, more than ever, become confusing, dizzyingly so.
Rumor emerges as one of the primary sources of epistemic and political
vertigo marked by increasing distrust of all major institutions of society:
government, media, and business.

RUMOR, POLITICS, AND CONVERGENCE CULTURE

Henry Jenkins's concept of "convergence culture" has become a keyword for our present conjuncture, where new and old media content, production, and consumption collide in vexingly new ways. Though gatekeeping practices in news and cultural production have weakened, creating new production opportunities, rumor rises to new levels of importance in this postmodern political context.

Despite digital divides, cases of rumor exploding into public scandal are fairly global. They have prompted suicides, imprisonments, stock plunges, resignations, and government investigations. For example, on Friday, 3 October 2008, on CNN's Citizen Journalism website, a post appeared stating that Apple CEO Steve Jobs had suffered a heart attack. Apple stock plunged immediately, though the rumor was debunked an hour later, leaving suspicions that it was planted by a short-seller after quick gains (Harsin, "Rumor Bomb").

However, rumors have assumed a very special role in professionalized politics, where communication experts shrewdly read the new convergence culture and try to use rumor to steer political discourse via intermedia agendas, again in an impressively global range. In February 2006, the Democratic Party of Japan admitted that one of its politicians used a hoax e-mail producing a scandal that implicated a senior official of the governing Liberal Democratic Party, who allegedly received large sums of money from a publicly disgraced Internet startup. In 2005, a political consultant in South Africa was paid to fabricate e-mails to sow division and contribute to the succession battle in the African National Congress. In Nigeria in September 2008, an entire TV station was closed after it repeated an Internet claim that Nigeria's president would resign due to illness (Harsin, "Rumor Bomb").

New photo-editing technologies have led to visual rumors. Recall the doctored photo of John Kerry with "Hanoi" Jane Fonda that made its way into the *New York Times* and countless war journalism examples (Mikkelson and Mikkelson).

Perhaps the most common recent American political rumor concerns Barack Obama, and it illustrates the interplay of professional communication and amateur new media in managed democracy. When it was clear that Obama would be a contender for the 2008 presidential nomination, opponents launched the rumor that he was a Muslim on new online media (NM), which landed in old broadcast and print media (OM) when a Clinton campaign volunteer was caught forwarding it. Filmed McCain supporters (on NM) also announced dread of an "Arab" President Obama, a statement that again appeared on news agendas, pressuring McCain to respond that Obama was a "decent family man" (not an Arab). Meanwhile, these rumors have complements that imply Obama was/is a terrorist because he allegedly "pals around with terrorists," referring to acquaintance Bill Ayers.

Rumor, then, is a keyword of contemporary politics and culture. I have theorized the concept of rumor bombs to distinguish a particular use of rumor from other related notions. I begin with rumor's common definition: a claim whose truthfulness is in doubt and which often has no clear source, even if its ideological or partisan origins and intents are clear. I then treat it as a particular rhetorical strategy in current contexts of political communication.

While rumors have often been seen as troublesome social and political phenomena regarding unverifiable claims, they are not necessarily about lying or misleading deliberately. Thus, rumor bombs may be viewed within theories of propaganda as Thomas Huckin has defined the term (see chapter 5 of this volume), with characteristics such as false or misleading information, a mass target audience, a design that is advantageous to the propagandist, a specific sociopolitical context and system of dissemination, and goals of noncritical reception. Yet, as we shall see, rumor bombs complicate traditional theories of propaganda, especially in that they depend on an NM communication ecology, where creating noise as much as meaning, blocking channels and distracting, and producing disagreement about their propositions is just as key as producing acceptance (Harsin, "Public Argument").

The rumor bomb extends the definition of rumor into a media/politics concept with the following features:

1. A crisis of verification: This feature is perhaps the most salient and politically dangerous aspect of rumor. Rumor is classically defined as a kind of persuasive message involving a proposition that lacks secure standards of evidence (Pendleton 69). Obama is a Muslim, an Arab, a terrorist. In each of these cases, the verification is dependent on the definition of the term the subject is accused of embodying, its persuasive impact depending on its strategic ambiguity and on the desire of the receiver to interpret it in a particular way. If Obama spent important formative years in a country where Islam was a dominant religion, does that make him in some way "Muslim," even if he identifies with Christianity? The very fact that some will debate it suggests the rumor bomb's political capital.

2. A context of public uncertainty or anxiety about a political group, figure, or cause, which the rumor bomb overcomes or transfers onto an opponent: The United States has been in the greatest financial crisis since the 1930s and is fighting two wars that have been marketed as a "war on terror" or a "war on terrorism," and the once popular post-9/11 Bush became one of the least-liked presidents in recent history. All reflect public uncertainty and anxiety about a country's leadership and future. Enter the rumor bomb "Obama is a Muslim"—similar to "John Kerry is French" in the context of "freedom fries" and images of supposedly mass protests against French "treason" by Americans pouring out their Beaujolais. Anxiety and uncertainty can be created, and encouraged, perhaps resulting in "panics," via what has been described as bipolitical projects of modulating affect.

3. A clearly partisan, even if anonymous, source (for example, "an unnamed adviser to the president"), which seeks political profit from the rumor bomb's diffusion: Examples include Jerome Corsi, who was proud to make a book out of the Swift Boat rumor and the "Obama is a Muslim" rumor; the Clinton campaign volunteer who happily circulated the viral e-rumor about Obama being a Muslim; and the "unnamed White House official" who, during the 2003 declarations of Democratic presidential candidacy, told the *New York Times* that John Kerry was "French-looking" (Nagourney and Stevenson).

4. A rapid electronic diffusion and contagion (that is, a "convergence culture" where news travels fast).

Of course, democracy's communication managers do not always create rumor bombs themselves (in the French Kerry case, an unnamed White House official was the apparent source; in the case of "Obama is a Muslim," a citizen on NM). Thus, rumor bombs may just as often be about communication experts exploiting the immaterial labor of new prosumers who, with their own motives, create and launch rumor bombs into the digital ether. In that case, the new power is not just production but the cybernetic role of researching (data mining, code, constant surveillance of social media trends) communication networks to intervene and block unwanted information and rhetorical ploys (noise), permitting preferred messages a privileged, repeated circulation and target contact (Hofstetter; Terranova 10–20). Controlling circulation and attention are top priorities of managed democracy in convergence culture.

While it may appear that communication experts of managed democracy have managed a technology-driven cultural shift, the emergence of rumor bombs in the present conjuncture is in fact more complicated. I have discussed this complexity in a theory of cultural convergence (Harsin, "Diffusing" and "Rumor Bomb"). Three converging historical trends have privileged the emergence of rumor bombs as popular political communication (or propaganda, if you prefer) strategy.

THREE CONVERGENT FACTORS EXPLAINING RUMOR BOMBS

Three major phenomena have converged into a highly formative conjuncture for political communication and the use of rumor: (1) changing news values and news-gathering practices, influenced by new communication technologies—namely the Internet, e-mail and blogs, and a shift in ownership of news organizations (for example, Time-Warner, Disney/ABC, and GE/NBC); (2) increasing influence of public relations on political communication, especially executive branch information and news management; and (3) new stages of affective contagion and the new attention economy, both partly shaped by the codes and protocols of NM interfaces.

News Media Market and News-Gathering Practices

Corporate mergers have increased pressures of speed and expanding viewerships and readerships for ever-increasing profit (even while the readerships and viewerships of particular publications and shows have often decreased with the fragmentation of audiences and the proliferation of channels and information). The phenomena of horizontal and vertical media convergences and strategies of synergy have helped blur the boundaries between news and entertainment. Entertainment and tabloid reporting have long been characterized by rumors. Thus, the traditional codes of ethics and standards of news-gathering are more frequently bowing to the dictates of profit in a market where "serious" and "soft" news categories are less clearly demarcated. Briefly, I will note some major reasons why contemporary media market pressures produce conditions of news-gathering and presentation practices favorable to rumor.

The first important explanation of rumor explosion in news today can be attributed to cuts in staff and financial resources for investigation and editing. As Lance Bennett has noted, market forces encourage a growing acceptance of public relations material (including that of governments) in the news (175). I will return to this trend later when I note the importance of political public relations in rumor launching and circulation illustrated by recent stories about the Bush administration's use of "fake news" video releases, staged press conference questions, and "fake reporters."

Combined with shrinking resources and cost cutting is the market drive for/by speed in a news world operating in real time. Real-time reporting came with the new technology of satellite broadcasting and then the Internet's up-to-the-minute stories so that events could be covered as they happened. The explosion of cable and satellite in the late 1980s and early 1990s combined with the Internet to produce a more fiercely competitive news market. Newspaper reading and major network news have been experiencing trends of decreasing readerships and viewerships for several years now. This has resulted in new news values and marketing strategies "running newsrooms" (Underwood). Pressures of speed and real-time reporting sometimes end up in "the use of unattributed sources, [indulgence] in idle speculation or [production of] slanted reports influenced by rumour" (Thussu 121; Seib). The Internet's production of information renewed in seconds has created strong competition for OM, which responds by trying to continually update stories and headlines on their sites or by e-mailing headlines to interested netizens. Thus, the Internet's acceleration of information renewal has pressured OM to follow suit or be left behind. According to David Bohrman, CNN White House bureau chief, "The media is doing the fact-checking it can . . . [but] more sources seem to be stepping up to speak who haven't spoken in the past, and the [news] cycle on cable news is so fast, it's immediate" (qtd. in Deggans). Yet the effect of the Internet is not just a faster OM with laxer editing standards and gatekeeping. The Internet is also increasingly the *source* of OM agendas.

If the Internet and NM such as e-mail contribute to dwindling audiences for OM, they are also increasingly playing an agenda-setting role for OM. Some political communication scholars trace the trend to the influence of Matt Drudge's blog-like *Drudge Report,* which broke the Clinton-Lewinsky affair before traditional elite news media followed suit (Bennett 8). Blogs and e-mail have played an increasingly powerful agenda-setting role (sometimes an alternative agenda to the OM and sometimes an intermedia agenda setting) vis-à-vis OM. Their influence is attributed to speed and low cost, both of which OM imitate (Drezner and Farrell). The same is true of e-mail and electronic discussion boards. Examples of this new network of influence abound.

But this intermedia agenda setting has also favored the circulation of rumor. As Todd Gitlin has pointed out in the 2004 American presidential campaign, this phenomenon has resulted in an increase in rumor circulation in the elite OM because the Internet is, among other things, a bottomless archive of rumors and lies. A rumor bomb circulated in early February 2004 that alleged John Kerry, while married, had an affair with an intern in her twenties demonstrates this phenomenon. Further alleged was that Kerry sequestered her in Africa to suppress the circulation of the story and that her parents found Kerry "sleazy" (Gitlin). It happened that the *Drudge Report* and then Rupert Murdoch's London-based *Sun* and *Times* had posted on their websites a claim that Kerry had had an affair with an intern. Soon the *Wall Street Journal*'s website followed suit. While other major newspapers avoided the story, on 13 February CNN featured a discussion on what the media should do about the accusations. In that discussion, commentator Jeff Greenfield claimed it did not matter whether the mainstream traditional media tried to play gatekeeper, because the Internet had dissolved such gates: "In this brave new world of instant communications, literally tens of millions of people will know about the story no matter what the networks and top tier newspapers do." However, Gitlin notes, there was no evidence anything in the story was true! "Three days later, the woman in question declared, 'I have never had a relationship with Senator Kerry, and the rumors in the press are completely false.'" The problem with this—as well as with the rumors about Al Qaeda and Saddam Hussein, weapons of mass destruction (WMDs), WMDs moved to Syria, and so forth—is that it demonstrates the greatest truism of rumor in today's global media environment: it is much easier to launch a rumor than to retrieve or defuse it. One by no means finds shelter from the rumor bomb by heading to the Internet. On the contrary, it is often a force influencing the circulation of rumor in OM.

Indeed, there is ample evidence that the Internet and the blogosphere are combining with the pressures of 24/7 cable news to influence the OM and political agendas. In some cases, the convergence is more "watchdog"—as in the case of Senator Trent Lott's racially volatile comments at Strom Thurmond's birthday party, which was kept alive in the blogosphere until OM took notice (Drezner and Farrell). E-mail circulation, blogs, and social media increasingly play an agenda-setting function. Yet sometimes the agenda is also fueled by rumor. Consider, for example, the debate in October 2000 between New York senate contenders Hillary Clinton and Rick Lazio. Moderator Marcia Kramer of WCBS asked the candidates about Bill 602p, "now before Congress," which would allow the U.S. Postal Service to tax people five cents for each e-mail they sent. Both candidates fell for the hoax, stressing that they would not vote for this bill—when in fact they could not vote for it, as it did not exist. It was a hoax circulating around the Internet and e-mailed as a question to the moderator, who, like the candidates, did not know any better (Collins). Other such rumors making their way into OM via the Internet or leaks include the Center for American Progress's claim that White House press secretary Scott McClellan referred to Iraq as an "imminent threat" (Fritz, Keefer, and Nyhan 243); the Swift Boat Veterans for Truth rumors that John Kerry lied about his heroism; the 2000 Republican primaries rumor that John McCain was mentally unfit; and conspiracy rumors about the Clintons' role in the alleged murder of aide and friend Vince Foster.

Furthermore, amid journalism's institutional crisis, the conflation of fact and fiction therein serves as further evidence of a crisis of verification susceptible to rumor bombs. In 2003, *New York Times* reporter Jayson Blair was found to have plagiarized significant parts of several stories and to have faked quotes in others. A year later, it was discovered that *USA Today's* Jack Kelly had fabricated parts of multiple stories over a ten-year period. These examples combined with rumor infiltrations of OM create a gnawing sense of uncertainty for consumers of information on websites, in e-mails, on TV, on the radio, and in newspapers and magazines. They are a product of the collapsing authority for agenda setting and gatekeeping displaced onto the Internet, an information culture characterized by speed, abundance, and fiduciary anxiety. The Project for Excellence in Journalism's annual report for 2005 emphasized that a major new trend in "models of journalism" was "toward those that are faster, looser, and cheaper. The traditional press model," it continued, "the journalism of verification—is one in which journalists are concerned first with trying to substantiate the facts. It has ceded ground for years on talk shows and cable to a new journalism of assertion, where information is offered with *little time* and *little attempt* to independently verify its veracity" (Project for Excellence in Journalism, emphasis added).[1] The free-for-all blogosphere's news, it concluded, "exponentially" worsened the problem, publishing anything and leaving the rest of us to verify.

The vast exhibit of resignations, firings, apologies, and scandals attests further to OM's crisis: Jeff Gannon and Karen Ryan (fake reporters); Eason Jordan's resignation from CNN; *New York Times* and *Washington Post* apologies for cheerleading the Iraq war; and *Times* reporter Judith Miller's particular role in cheerleading. One notable scandal involves Journatic, a company that provides content for local news outlets. An employee discovered stories outsourced to the Philippines and bylines of nonexistent reporters (Zuckerman).

Journalism's agenda-setting crisis—that what people find entertaining on the Internet may set journalistic agendas, rather than vice-versa—also raises the issue of how entertainment values have become increasingly important in the news business. As briefly mentioned above, trends of tabloidization and infotainment have crept into OM as a way to retain viewers and deliver them to lucrative advertisers. Infotainment is "journalism in which entertainment values take precedence over information content" (McNair 4) (which may or may not refer to political agendas). Extended further to politics, "politicotainment" is defined as "the way the political is represented or negotiated by entertainment formats" (Riegert 3). Like my concept of rumor bombs, politicotainment stresses a political economy of news and new "promotional machinery" applied equally to policies, celebrities, and politicians (Riegert 3; McNair 63).

Tabloid and entertainment trends have been growing in mainstream American news throughout the late twentieth century (reversing the 1920s attempt to distinguish between journalism and tabloids) but even more so recently with the fragmentation of a mass audience due to the explosion of cable and the Internet and less and less interest in OM generally. OM's content has thus been driven closer to other entertainment genres. As noted ten years ago, MBAs are ruling the newsrooms with a different set of values and institutional goals (Underwood). Some editors and publishers openly declare a market crisis for newspapers and a desire to simply give customers/readers whatever they want. In a recent interview with the *Online Journalism Review,* former *San Francisco Chronicle* vice president Bob Cauthorn blamed the financial hardships of newspapers on the reporters and editors who, he believes, "insulate themselves from the public," are not "aligned" with their readers, and instead believe their readers are not smart enough to determine what sort of news product they want. Speaking of trends toward celebrity news and "trash," Cauthorn proclaims, "If that's what readers want, great. Serve the reader" (qtd. in LaFontaine). Such views are also present in elite journalism schools such as Northwestern and Columbia.[2] Not only does the unidimensional reduction of journalism to marketing raise serious questions for journalism's relationship to democracy, but it also suggests how news values of entertainment and profit are a breeding ground for rumor. To embrace tabloid news values is to embrace and encourage rumor and scandal in general. Tabloid news does not aspire to fact-based journalism and values of objectivity; it seeks to be entertaining. It is no surprise then that with tabloid market trends, one should find an accompanying pervasiveness of rumor (Bennett 33; Kovach and Rosenstiel 40).

But in addition to new market and intermedia pressures, is it possible to see the problem of rumor as rooted more deeply in the very foundations of journalistic professional culture: in its dependence on official sources? To be sure, this is an ongoing problem, especially in the middle of wars; however, if we are to allow that journalism cannot be held to any standards of playing sources one against another, fact-checking, and disregarding strategically ambiguous and provocative claims, then the possibility of active democratic citizenship becomes foreclosed in the whirl of sensational appeals and permanent incredulity. Aside from declining interest in fact-checking in exchange for entertainment, an overdependence on official, possibly manipulative sources is certainly a problem that critics of American professional journalism have long noted (Bennett 125) and plays a role in the convergence of forces that have produced rumor bombs. The dependence on official sources goes hand-in-hand with news management and growing PR strategies in political communication over the long twentieth century.[3]

These concerns with belief and news market trends have brought us inevitably to the domain of politics and the professionalization of political communication. Thus, while a consideration of new market pressures and journalistic norms helps explain the proliferation of rumor in especially American news media today, it needs to be viewed in relation to at least two other major factors with which it importantly converges: the professionalization of political communication, and the new cultural conditions of prosumerism, viral networks, and the attention economy.

Professionalization of Political Communication

Rumor is a political communication strategy that issues out of the ideology of a technocratic representative democracy and its increasing PR-driven tendency toward simulating events, questions, and reporters in a controlled environment and has twentieth-century origins, discussed in the beginning of this chapter. Further, rumor is partly an obvious political strategy in response to changing political media (from oral to radio to TV/cable) and their particular technological constraints on content and style. Rumor bombs are common in this highly technocratic political culture through leaks and deliberately unverifiable accusations/claims in a climate of increasingly protected secrecy. Last, rumor bombs follow recent developments in political communication and cognitive sciences, taking lessons from neuro-marketing and consumer psychology.

The professionalization of political communication is encouraged by long-term media market trends discussed above, which converged with a new kind of managerial rhetoric or the PR-ification of political discourse in the late twentieth-century United States. A managerial political communication style has been developing since the early twentieth century, and more specific PR-managed politics since the Eisenhower years (Maarek 11). With the rise of mass electronic media and an elite need to direct a national political agenda came an increasing executive dependence on ever-larger White House staffs for communication-management purposes (Perloff 28–30). The need for strategic political communication on the model of public relations also corresponds to the twentieth-century growth of executive power, a phenomenon described as "the rhetorical presidency" and "going public" (Tulis). John W. Tebbel and Sarah M. Watts suggest that Theodore Roosevelt was the first to use news media to manage public opinion in aggressive new ways. Roosevelt expanded the White House pressroom, gave reporters phones, and talked openly with them. But perhaps more important, he controlled access by dividing the White House press into two groups: those who gave him favorable press and those who did not, treating them accordingly (330–35).

Though political public relations have played a great role in campaign politics for several decades, their constant presence in White House communications is more recent. The Bush administration used PR and propaganda to a greater degree than any of its predecessors. Its ability to launch rumors was especially achieved through a cultural project of secrecy and unaccountability/mystery. That project has taken two major forms: the anonymous leak and the front group.

While the White House increasingly tried to produce a kind of public relations staff to help manage the media and set the public agenda, it was only in the 1950s that presidents and their opponents began to use public relations firms to sell their agendas (Maarek 11). Campaign strategists moved into the White House permanently (Grann). Not only are campaign tactics normalized for governing, but also the communication tactics are themselves institutionally influenced by the twenty-four-hour cable and Internet news cycle. While the Clinton administration routinely used public relations to push its agenda, many observers claim that the George W. Bush administration only expanded such activities. As George Stephanopoulos commented with regard to the changes between Clinton and Bush, "Everyone said that our campaign war room in 1991 was the fastest. Now it would be considered Paleolithic" (qtd. in Grann).

Recently, cognitive science, neuro-marketing, and consumer psychology have begun to influence political communication. In *The Political Brain,* Drew Westen implores Democrats to stop using rational policy arguments in elections and governance; emotion is what works. Some cognitive science would even suggest going pre-emotional or affective (as a matter of response without having time to think) based on brain scan experiments with focus groups (Plassman, Ramsøy, and Milosavljevic). I will return to these developments in neuro-politics in my consideration of the third factor of new cultural interfaces: networks, imitation, and the attention economy. One need not be nostalgic for a time when an unbridled watchdog press and a full participatory democracy existed (of course they have not) to note clear differences in the way U.S. (and international) political discourse has been practiced and covered by news media from the nineteenth to the end of the twentieth century. What have been the results of increasing political public relations in media and politics combined with changing news market pressures and values? In 1988, Kathleen Jamieson argued that contemporary public discourse was most characterized by its mediated time compression. From 1968 to 1988, the average American TV news sound bite afforded to presidential candidates dropped from forty-two seconds to ten seconds. It dropped even lower in 2000 (Paletz 223). Politicians no longer go through histories of public problems, their causes, and considerations of proposed solutions. They prefer negative politics.

Thus, says Jamieson, audiences are often left with the likelihood of simply embracing positions that are already theirs, or they may embrace a politician and his or her claims out of blind partisan loyalty (trust, invoking the problem of space-time compression for deliberation and the trends toward politics as branding) (10–12; Swanson 50–51).

Jamieson's conclusion speaks loudly to the findings of a 2004 study by the Program on International Policy Attitudes/Knowledge Networks (PIPA) at the University of Maryland. The findings of this study on American beliefs about Iraq/Al Qaeda links and the evidence of WMDs came only *one month* prior to the 2004 American presidential election. According to this study, 75 percent of Bush supporters had the impression that Iraq had direct involvement in, or gave substantial support to, Al Qaeda's 9/11 attacks. In contrast, only 8 percent of Kerry supporters had the impression of direct involvement by Iraq, and only 22 percent had the impression that there was "substantial support" given to Al Qaeda.

The differences in misperception are similar on the issue of WMDs. According to the PIPA study, the majority of Bush voters believed that Iraq had WMDs and that the Bush administration and independent experts confirmed it. Kerry voters believed the opposite. There was no great discrepancy between Kerry and Bush supporters' understanding of what Bush *meant*. That is, the data seem to suggest an explanation for the differences in belief was not *polysemy* but *polyvalence*.[4] Value, not meaning, was the difference, resulting in (dis)trust.

The deliberate repetition of rumor bombs such as Iraq–Al Qaeda links to 9/11 by former vice president Dick Cheney (as recently as 2007) (Kessler) or that WMDs were moved to Syria are well documented ("Cheney Asserts"; Pavlus). Such studies as that by PIPA suggest rumor bombs are not without considerable effects on public perceptions and beliefs, which can provide consent for public policy as grave as war.

Many of these developments that Jamieson and the PIPA study outline are the result of advocates and politicians adapting to NM business values, structures, and news-gathering practices on which the circulation of new compressed public address depends. However, they would hardly be possible if it were not for major changes in an increasingly balkanized information and propaganda news culture that overlaps between older OM and NM, from blogs to Facebook, Twitter, and YouTube.

New Participation, Attention, and Managed Imitation

Today *attention economy* has become a buzzword. A 1997 *Wired* article observed that attention was a scarce commodity amid information abundance (Goldhaber). Businesses invest great resources in trying to capture and monetize it, while political communication experts attempt to capture and steer it, sometimes to persuade, other times simply to distract, by occupying intermedia agendas.

Understanding the condition of attention as shaped by new technologies and their programming protocols is key to understanding how managed democracy projects are evolving and how rumor bombs are part of them. First, attention is now estimated to be at twenty minutes maximum before a person shifts focus to something else. But market researchers estimate most Web users spend no more than ten seconds on a page (Lake). For online videos, it is estimated between thirty seconds and five minutes. Further, the short temporal frame in which people pay attention may result in quick affective, pre- and unconscious responses—clicks, deletes, shares, likes, retweets, forwards, PayPal donations.

The most powerful rumor bombs function through symbolic condensation. Sigmund Freud's dream condensation theory has been applied outside of psychoanalysis to symbols generally, theorized as condensation symbols by Doris Graber and Murray Edelman. Graber writes, "A condensation symbol is a name, word, phrase, or maxim which stirs vivid impressions involving the listener's most basic values" (289). They have often been primed over years.

Condensation has no doubt been central to humans' social life for eons. Gabriel Tarde argues, "With regard to these slow acquisitions of our senses we take the transformation of reiterated judgments into ideas and of ideas into sensations at face value" (204). Through observation and experience, our senses judge, or infer. Through repetition, we form ideas and beliefs, though mere "sensations at face value" condense the entire history of our sensing and judging. However, condensation is more relevant for analyzing convergence culture, imitation, and contagion because of the way time and space have been altered by the invention of digital technologies, routinely appropriated for political and especially economic purposes. Memes (repeated cultural units) travel faster than ever before, and condensation is key to that process. The condensation triggers are not always met with cognitive linguistic processing but with affective reactions.

When I speak of rumor bombs' affective qualities, I am making reference to a concept of growing importance in the contemporary humanities and social sciences. According to Silvan Tomkins, there are eight or nine innate affects that are primary motives. He divides them into "negative" and "positive" affects. The negative ones are fear-terror, distress-grief, anger-rage, shame-humiliation, and contempt-disgust (later divided into two, disgust and dissmell). The positive ones are interest-excitement and enjoyment-joy and the reorienting affect of surprise-startle (185). In addition, affect is contagious: depression, for example, is contagious, as are smiles and nervousness (Gibbs 191). Someone else's bodily signs and actions can produce affects in us, or affective effects. Furthermore, though less studied than in interpersonal relations, affect transmission has also been demonstrated in the epoch of mass media. One of the most famous cases is, of course, the mass panic that followed Orson Welles's broadcast of *War of the Worlds*. But it is not just panic that is contagious. Both contemporary neuroscience and Tardean social theory suggest that imitation and innovation are at the very basis of social life: "'Action observation implies action simulation' . . . engendering in us at the very least a kind of empathy and often contagious behavior" (Ravven 73). Other scientists suggest "the other is experienced as another being like oneself through an appreciation of similarity" (73). Thus, our networks are often connected to those with whom we identify and are likely to imitate through empathy and trust.

Thus, when some Americans see the statement "Obama is a Muslim," an affective response has been primed via associations with the anger, fear, and shock experienced by radical Islamic terrorists on 9/11 and the resulting discourse that conflated Muslims with terrorism.[5] When some see "Obama has a fake birth certificate," it likely reinforces the rumor bomb that he is Muslim, further triggering the affective condensations just mentioned. One could make similar claims of the condensation of historical Francophobia (Harsin, "Diffusing") and the Bush administration's construction of French betrayal, spectacularized by calls to rename French fries "freedom fries" and by widely circulated images of Americans emptying French wine, protesting the alleged betrayal. They primed many responses to the rumor bomb that John Kerry was French-looking.[6]

Yet we cannot understand how affective contagion via rumor bombs is achieved by managed democracy without also considering how it is importantly facilitated by the new cultural norms of participation and consensual monitoring (such as cookies permitting data mining) that have been appropriated by communication consulting, marketing, and their political and governmental equivalents (Hofstetter; Howard). As Steven Best and Douglas Kellner observe, "One is never totally free of social influences and in cyberspace all technologically-mediated communication is structured to some extent by computer protocols, codes, and programs" (152). Networks today are mechanisms of control (though with openings), with nodes and their spokes, biological and informatic, which are "leveraged as value-laden biomedia for proprietary interests" (Galloway and Thacker 22). Networks we inhabit through Internet sites personalize our paths, which is to say limit them. As Internet sites increasingly tailor "their 'services' to the idiosyncrasies of individual users, queries for 'climate change,' 'stem cells' and even 'pizza' yield different individual" results and facts (Morozov): truthiness, in comedian Stephen Colbert's term ("Merriam-Webster"). Affect and networks are the objects of constant attempted management.

Key to structured, though not totally controlled or closed, attention networks is encouragement if not exigency of "participation." The political economy of social media (what practically allows us to have these NM "sites" of communication) revolves around value created through attention in networks. Again, it is not simply belief in rumor bombs but even argument about them that gives them attention capital and power in contemporary managed democracy.

Rumor bombs help explain issue salience in networked convergence culture, where more accessible productive and distributive agency afforded by NM technologies converges with globalizing news business trends (infotainment) and negative politics and where character and trust direct consent and support. This fiduciary, often affectively mediated rapport may refer to both the proposition of the rumor and the media form providing the encounter, whether on a blog, website, radio or TV talk show, prestige press story, YouTube/Facebook/Twitter post, or personal e-mail from friends, family, organization, or unfamiliar source. Yet in error would we focus entirely on the logical propositions of rumor bombs. They are sometimes backed by a (poor) logic/narrative, such as WMDs were moved to Syria, Obama grew up in a Muslim culture, or John Kerry grew up vacationing in France, has a French cousin, and speaks fluent French. But they are just as likely not to be examined as claims, serving rather as affective condensations, unleashing powerful associations. The likelihood is even stronger considering evidence on short attention spans and quickly shifting digital interfaces.

In addition to the Obama rumor bombs, recent ones about alleged "death panels" enabled by the Affordable Care Act and the one stating "Shirley Sherrod is a racist" (resulting in her firing/resignation) suggest that this phenomenon applies to understanding not just the political vertigo of campaigns in OM/NM convergence culture but also the dynamics of governing in it—to say nothing of watching, processing, even influencing it. Let us engage the geometries of circulation, attention, belief, and confusion that constitute a new era of managed democracy.

Notes

1. The gatekeeping anxiety is pervasive. *Columbia Journalism Review*'s managing editor Steve Lovelady reiterates, "We've said it before and we'll say it again: The great thing about the Internet is that anyone can start a blog—and the terrible thing about the Internet is that anyone can start a blog" (Lovelady).

2. Northwestern's Medill School of Journalism dean Janet Castro, public lecture at the American University of Paris, "International Perspectives and the One-Minute News Cycle," 19 September 2005.

3. Also during the Bush administration but beginning with Clinton, the unquestioning use of "fake news" video releases, which are actually PR fakes

originating in the executive branch, by NM is telling. See www.prwatch.org /tazonomy/term/120/9.

4. See Condit.

5. On the conflation of Muslim, Arab, and terrorist, especially post-9/11, see Saeed.

6. Another way of thinking about this priming is through the "cultivation theory" tradition of media effects. Repetition of the same messages "cultivates" a particular condensed perception and possibly un- or pre-conscious response. For an introduction to cultivation theory, see Morgan and Shanahan.

Works Cited

Allport, Gordon W. "Restoring Morale in Occupied Territory." *Public Opinion Quarterly* 7.4 (1943): 606–17. Print.

Bennett, W. Lance. *News: The Politics of Illusion.* New York: Longman, 2003. Print.

Best, Steven, and Douglas Kellner. "Debord, Cybersituations, and the Interactive Spectacle." *SubStance* 28.3 (1999): 129–56. *JSTOR.* Web. 15 May 2015.

"Cheney Asserts Iraq–Al Qaeda Link." *BBC News.* BBC, 4 June 2007. Web. 6 December 2009.

Collins, Gail. "Public Interests; Inside George's Web." *New York Times Opinion.* The New York Times Co., 10 October 2000. Web. 3 May 2015.

Condit, Celeste M. "The Rhetorical Limits of Polysemy." *Critical Studies in Mass Communication* 6.2 (1989): 103–22. Print.

Curtis, Adam, dir. *The Century of the Self.* Perf. Adam Curtis. BBC Four, 2002. DVD.

Deggans, Eric. "The Truth Is Out There." *St. Petersburg Times* 19 September 2004: 1P. Print.

Drezner, Daniel W., and Henry Farrell. "Web of Influence." *FP.* The Foreign Policy Group, 26 October 2009. Web. 22 July 2014.

Edelman, Murray. *The Symbolic Uses of Politics.* Urbana: U of Illinois P, 1967. Print.

Ewen, Stuart. *PR! A Social History of Spin.* New York: Basic, 1996. Print.

Fritz, Ben, Bryan Keefer, and Brendan Nyhan. "Spinsanity." *Philly.com.* 2014. Web. 15 September 2016.

Galloway, Alexander R., and Eugene Thacker. *The Exploit: A Theory of Networks.* Minneapolis: U of Minnesota P, 2007. Print.

Gibbs, Anna. "After Affect." *The Affect Theory Reader.* Ed. Melissa Gregg and Gregory J. Seigworth. Durham: Duke UP, 2010. 186–205. Print.

Gitlin, Todd. "Lying about Kerry." openDemocracy. openDemocracy Limited, 19 February 2004. Web. 5 March 2004.

Goldhaber, Michael H. "Attention Shoppers!" *Wired* 5.12 (1997): n.p. Web. 5 June 2005.

Graber, Doris A. *Verbal Behavior and Politics.* Urbana: U of Illinois P, 1976. Print.

Grann, David. "Inside Dope: Mark Halperin and the Transformation of the Washington Establishment." *New Yorker.* Condé Nast, 25 October 2004. Web. 3 May 2015.

Harsin, Jayson. "Diffusing the Rumor Bomb: 'John Kerry Is French.'" *The Diffusion of Social Movements: Actors, Mechanisms, and Political Effects.* Ed. Rebecca K. Givan, Kenneth M. Roberts, and Sarah A. Soule. Cambridge: Cambridge UP, 2010. 163–84. Print.

———. "Public Argument in the New Media Ecology." *Journal of Argumentation in Context* 3.1 (2014): 7–34. Print.

———. "The Rumor Bomb: On Convergence Culture and Politics." *Flow* 9.4 (2008): n.p. Web. 3 May 2015.

———. "The Rumour Bomb: Theorising the Convergence of New and Old Trends in Mediated US Politics." *Southern Review: Communication, Politics and Culture* 39.1 (2006): 84–110. Print.

Hofstetter, Sarah. "Six Ways the Social Web Is Revolutionizing Market Research." *iMedia Connection.* iMedia Communications, 2 February 2012. Web. 2 May 2013.

Howard, Philip N. *New Media Campaigns and the Managed Citizen.* Cambridge: Cambridge UP, 2006. Print.

Jamieson, Kathleen Hall. *Eloquence in the Electronic Age.* New York: Oxford UP, 1988. Print.

Jenkins, Henry. *Convergence Culture.* New York: NYU P, 2006. Print.

Kessler, Glenn. "The Cheneys' Claim of a 'Deep, Longstanding, Far-Reaching Relationship' between Al-Qaeda and Saddam." Fact Checker. The Washington Post, 17 July 2014. Web. 2 May 2015.

Knapp, Robert H. "A Psychology of Rumor." *Public Opinion Quarterly* 8.1 (1944): 22–37. Print.

Kovach, Bill, and Tom Rosenstiel. *Blur: How to Know What's True in the Age of Information Overload.* New York: Bloomsbury, 2010. Print.

LaFontaine, David. "Old-School Community Journalism Shows: It's a Wonderful 'Light.'" *Online Journalism Review.* 25 August 2005. Web. 15 May 2015.

Lake, Chris. "22 More Reasons Why I'll Leave Your Website in 10 Seconds." Econsultancy. 8 August 2013. Web. 15 May 2015.

Lovelady, Steve. "Exit Polls and Other Temptations of the Wild West." *Columbia Journalism Review*. 6 February 2004. Web. 6 May 2016.

Maarek, Philippe J. *Campaign Communication and Political Marketing*. Hoboken: Wiley-Blackwell, 2011. Print.

Mattelart, Armand. *Networking the World, 1794–2000*. Minneapolis: U of Minnesota P, 2000. Print.

McNair, Brian. *Journalism and Democracy: An Evaluation of the Political Public Sphere*. London: Routledge, 2000. Print.

"Merriam-Webster 2006 Word of the Year." N.p., n.d. Web. 15 May 2015.

Mikkelson, Barbara, and David P. Mikkelson. "Claim: Photograph Shows Senator John Kerry and Jane Fonda Sharing a Speaker's Platform at an Anti-war Rally." Snopes.com. 1 March 2004. Web. 5 December 2004.

Morgan, Michael, and James Shanahan. "The State of Cultivation." *Journal of Broadcasting and Electronic Media* 54.2 (2010): 337–55. Print.

Morozov, Evgeny. "Your Own Facts." *Sunday Book Review*. The New York Times Co., 10 June 2011. Web. 1 May 2012.

Nagourney, Adam, and Richard W. Stevenson. "For 2004, Bush's Aides Plan Late Sprint for Re-election." *New York Times* 22 April 2003. NYTimes. com. Web. 15 May 2015.

Paletz, David L. *The Media in American Politics*. Reading, Pa.: Addison-Wesley, 2002. Print.

Pavlus, Sarah. "Citing No Evidence, Hannity Maintains Iraqi WMDs 'Were Moved.'" MediaMatters. Media Matters for America, 4 January 2007. Web. 30 April 2016.

Pendleton, Susan C. "Rumor Research Revisited and Expanded." *Language and Communication* 18.1 (1998): 69–86. Print.

Perloff, Richard. *Political Communication Politics, Press, and Public in America*. Mahwah, N.J.: Lawrence Erlbaum, 1998. Print.

Plassmann, Hilke, Thomas Zoëga Ramsøy, and Milica Milosavljevic. "Branding the Brain." *Journal of Consumer Psychology* 22.1 (2012): 18–36. Web. 3 May 2015.

Project for Excellence in Journalism. "Five Major Trends." *The State of the News Media 2005*. N.p., n.d. Web. 15 May 2015.

Ravven, H. "Spinozistic Approaches to Evolutionary Naturalism." *Politics and Life Sciences* 22.1 (2003): 70–74. Print.

Riegert, Kristina. *Politicotainment*. New York: Peter Lang, 2003. Print.

Saeed, Amir. "Media, Racism and Islamophobia: The Representation of Islam and Muslims in the Media." *Sociology Compass* 1.2 (2007): 443–62. Print.

Seib, Philip. *Beyond the Front Lines*. New York: Palgrave, 2004. Print.

Simpson, Christopher. *Science of Coercion*. New York: Oxford UP, 1996. Print.

Swanson, David. "Transnational Trends in Political Communication." *Comparing Political Communication*. Ed. Frank Esser and Barbara Pfetsch. Cambridge: Cambridge UP, 2004. 45–63. Print.

Tarde, Gabriel. *Gabriel Tarde on Communication and Social Influence: Selected Papers*. Chicago: U of Chicago P, 2010. Print.

Tebbel, John W., and Sarah M. Watts. *The Press and the Presidency*. New York: Oxford UP, 1985. Print.

Terranova, Tiziana. *Network Culture: Politics for the Information Age*. London: Pluto, 2004. Print.

Thussu, Daya. "War, Infotainment and 24/7 News." *War and the Media: Reporting Conflict 24/7*. Ed. Daya Thussu and Des Freedman. London: Sage, 2003. 17–132. Print.

Tomkins, Silvan S. *Affect, Imagery, Consciousness*. New York: Springer, 2008. Web. 3 May 2015.

Tulis, Jeffrey. *The Rhetorical Presidency*. Princeton: Princeton UP, 1987. Print.

Underwood, Doug. *When MBAs Rule the Newsroom*. New York: Columbia UP, 1995. Print.

Westen, Drew. *The Political Brain: The Role of Emotion in Deciding the Fate of the Nation*. New York: Public Affairs, 2007. Print.

Zuckerman, Esther. "Faked Bylines and Outsourced Writers." *The Wire*. The Atlantic Monthly Group, 2 July 2012. Web. 2 Aug. 2012.

THE *CONTRACT WITH AMERICA*: A LEGAL, SOCIAL, AND RHETORICAL CONTRACTUAL OBLIGATION

MEG H. KUNDE

> There is no subjection so perfect as that which keeps the
> appearance of freedom.
>
> —Jean-Jacques Rousseau, *The Social Contract*

In 1994, soon to be Speaker of the House Newt Gingrich (Ga.), along with fellow Republican representative Dick Armey (Tex.) and the rest of the House Republicans, put forth a legislative plan called the Contract with America. The contract included a document, signed by 367 Republican candidates running in the midterm elections, that promised to reform government and to restore the "bonds of trust" (*Contract* 13) between the people of the United States and their legislators. It detailed ten legislative acts for passage in the first one hundred days of the 104th Congress. That November, Republicans gained control of both the House and Senate for the first time in forty years and went on to use the contract as their platform for change. The contract was a "detailed agenda for national renewal" (7). Kerry Knott, Armey's chief of staff and the executive director of the House Republican Conference, first gave the contract its name: "I don't even know where it came from. I think we just talked about it enough. It can't just be a promise. It needs to be more than that, and the word 'contract' came from somewhere, and we just eventually put it together" (qtd. in Garrett 76). Shortly after the midterm elections, the House Republicans, spearheaded by Gingrich and Armey, released the book *Contract with America* as a symbol of their "promise" and "detailed agenda."

A close analysis of the book *Contract with America* reveals that the plan was, indeed, more than a "promise" and both more and less than a "detailed agenda"; it was a tool of propaganda that gained depth and power from its conceptual, structural, and stylistic layering of generic form. I argue that the *Contract* drew on the public's conceptual understanding of social and legal contracts to call for efficiency and transparency in government and to provide citizens with more autonomy. At the same time, the style and the structure of the *Contract*'s form and message presented a well-thought-out, tightly confined, and substantial plan through which these expectations could be fulfilled. Yet while the *Contract* provided the reader with a sense of legitimacy, certainty, and comfort, it simultaneously acted as a barrier against ideas that lay outside the plan. As a result, the *Contract*'s multiple layering of generic form and contractual obligation created a space of "participation" that was free of legislative uncertainty and public dissatisfaction.

To begin, I first describe the political environment out of which the contract arose. Second, I analyze how the book *Contract with America* drew on both legal and social contract theory to substantiate and define its conceptual relationship with the people of the United States. Next, I describe how the *Contract*'s structural and stylistic forms further bolstered its promise of contractual certainty and coherence and provided the plan with a sense of urgency and expedience. Furthermore, I show how several of the *Contract*'s messages about legislation, Republican legislators, and policy were embedded within, or were iconic of, its structure and style. Finally, I discuss the implications of the way the *Contract* used form as propaganda to make arguments about the legislative process.

THE CONTEXT OF THE CONTRACT:
ENGENDERED CERTAINTY

House Republicans began to develop the Contract with America in early 1994 and presented it to the public during the campaign season later that year. It evolved from a unique set of circumstances: the defeat of President George H. W. Bush in 1992, the ascension of Gingrich to House Majority leader, and declining support for President Bill Clinton (Bader). Moreover, public opinion polls and the Republican Party's independent public opinion research indicated growing cynicism and much dissatisfaction with the legislative practices of the time (Bader; Garrett; Gimpel).[1] In January 1994, Gingrich invited the contract's future leadership team to dinner: Dick Armey, Tom DeLay (Tex.), Bob Walker (Pa.), and Bill Paxon (N.Y.). At a Republican conference in February, Gingrich introduced the idea of a national platform. As the contract developed, Armey was responsible for the "ideas," while Gingrich was responsible for the "selling" (Garrett 69–70).[2] On 27 September 1994, exactly six weeks before the election, 367 Republican House members and candidates convened at the Capitol to reveal the plan and sign the Contract with America document. It was orchestrated to be a major media event. Speakers were shuttled from platform to platform on the West Front Lawn of the Capitol to explain the different components of the contract while television cameras filmed the action. Press packets and copies of the proposed bills were handed out to present the contract as more than a fleeting campaign event.[3]

Although Republican unity was strong, it was not seamless. Even though Bob Michel (Ill.) no longer served as House minority leader, there were still a lot of "old guard" Republican representatives who believed that the notion of a minority party proposing its own budget was unfathomable (Garrett 53). The bold and revolutionary initiatives proposed by Gingrich and the "young Turks," a group of newer representatives who were ready to change the rules and pave the way for a new type of Republican leadership, alarmed some of the "old guard" representatives. In addition, some representatives felt as if they were not given enough input into the plan, the more socially conservative representatives wanted the contract to take a firmer stance on social issues,[4] and there was concern over how the more moderate Republicans in the Senate would respond to the plan. On the campaign trail, most candidates used the contract in a piecemeal fashion, its support ranging from passive to enthusiastic. Incumbents and challengers with previous experience tended to emphasize it less than newcomers in need of a platform. The candidates who had been running on contract themes before it was revealed tended to continue to do so, while others found it much harder to change their campaign midseason. Despite these internal divisions, only seven Republican representatives who were elected in November did not sign the contract (Gimpel 19–28).[5]

After Republican candidates were voted into office on Election Day, the promise to fulfill the contract became a reality. The midterm elections of 1994 brought a dramatic shift of power to Congress. There was a fifty-four-seat swing in the House, giving the Republicans a 230 to 176 majority.[6] Although it is far from agreed upon that the Contract with America was the key to this Republican takeover, Gingrich and other contract stalwarts assumed voters had endorsed the plan and provided a mandate for its implementation. Accordingly, congressional Republicans were now under contract to perform and needed to maintain the support of those both inside and outside of the Beltway in order to translate the plan's proposals into legislative bills.

PROPAGANDA AND GENERIC FORM

The book *Contract with America*[7] became a physical symbol of what voters had agreed to on Election Day and a reminder to congressional Republicans about what they had promised. It became the tool by which the uncertainty that existed within Washington about the general plan and the cynicism that existed throughout the nation about government in general could be replaced by a more decisive and clearer direction. The utility of this tool, however, was predicated on the maintenance of the relationship between the people of the United States and the Republican legislators who would vote on and pass the plan's bills. The rest of this analysis will investigate how the *Contract* utilized a multitude of forms to create a binding relationship among the Republican representatives and between the Republican representatives and the people of the United States.

Generic form can be described as "a group of acts unified by a constellation of forms that recurs in each of its members" (Campbell and Jamieson 20). In other words, generic form provides a predictable pattern of elements that are often utilized in similar circumstances for similar purposes and are met with similar reactions. In this chapter, I demonstrate how the *Contract* used generic form to offer a sense of coherence and certainty out of a complex and bureaucratic legislative system and to offer an answer to citizens' frustration over the partisan gridlock of the preceding years. The *Contract* provides an example of how conventional forms that are familiar and unobtrusive can be used to bolster the completeness and impermeability of a message or plan. Republican consultant and pollster Frank Luntz wrote in a memo, "The Contract works not because of the individual components but because it is a complete package. In other words, the sum is greater than the parts. Remove a single component and you destroy the entire effort" (qtd. in Garrett 96). Thus, Luntz highlighted the *Contract*'s form in order to posit it as a unifying political device or package. He also recognized the unique elements that made up its composition.

Yet, as Karlyn Kohrs Campbell and Kathleen Hall Jamieson point out, genre "classification is justified only by the critical illumination it produces[,] not by the neatness of a classificatory schema" (18). As such, this chapter will focus not only on how generic forms of contract were used but also on why they were used and how they helped to "assert or seek a unity of meaning . . . between author and reader" (Aichele 91), or, in this case, between the Republican representatives and the people of the United States. Furthermore, I examine how the *Contract* used genre as "a rhetorical means for mediating private intentions and social exigence; [how] it motivates by connecting the private with the public, the singular with the recurrent" (Miller 163).[8] In other words, I examine how genre is used to facilitate an interaction between political representatives and their constituents. Genres can be used to construct and maintain institutional spaces within which actors are ascribed designated roles. In the case of the *Contract,* although the use of generic form became constraining at times, it maintained the integrity of the overall contractual package. It also constituted Republican legislators and the people of the United States as contractual parties with designated obligations to uphold. This analysis demonstrates how political relationships are structured through genre not only institutionally but also rhetorically.

In the same way that rhetors are always situated in ideological spaces influenced by "specific historical, social, cultural, and political circumstances" (Bjork 215), Anis S. Bawarshi argues that no genre is exempt from an ideological framework. He explains that genres "define and organize kinds of situations and social actions, situations and actions that the genres, through their use, rhetorically make possible" (17–18), and become a "dynamic site for the production and regulation of textured, ideological activities (a site in which habitual language practices enact and reproduce situated relations, commitments, and actions)" (18). Accordingly, genre can become a way to package a desired message or doctrine and deliver it to a mass audience.

In this way, the choice of using a particular genre can become a tool of propaganda if the "ideological activities" implied in the genre are misapplied or concealed. The notion of propaganda is often connoted negatively; as opposed to news or information, propaganda carries with it elements of power and bias. Or, as Thomas Huckin states in chapter 5 of this volume, "Propaganda is *false or misleading* information or ideas addressed to a *mass audience* by parties who thereby gain *advantage.* Propaganda is created and disseminated *systematically* and *does not invite critical analysis or response.*" To use genre as a tool of propaganda is to create a package of rhetorical trappings that not only protects that which is inside from extraneous ideas but also normalizes the procedures and discourse inside that generic space.

Accordingly, I demonstrate how the *Contract* used its multiple layering of genre and form as a tool of propaganda to naturalize its message and garner simple acquiescence for its plan. The *Contract* assured the people of the United States that their Republican representatives would take care of them. The people, then, became part of the overall propaganda package that had already been sealed with their consent. Thus, although a survey conducted in late October 1994 by the Times Mirror Center for the People and the Press, now the Pew Research Center, found that only 29 percent of people polled knew what the *Contract with America* was ("Democrats Recover" 6), the *Contract* assumed full-scale support. Ironically, then, the consent that the Republican legislators rhetorically created within the *Contract* was, simultaneously, the evidence upon which they legitimated their policies and actions.

THE LEGAL CONTRACT WITH AMERICA

In what follows, I demonstrate how the *Contract* emphasized its formalistic qualities to substantiate its contractual relationship with the people of the United States, attempting to make up in form that which it might have lacked in content. To begin, although the *Contract* was not actually a legally binding document, it described itself as such. It pulled from the idea that a legal contract includes a promise (Gardner; Cohen; Fried) and a consideration that something of legal value be exchanged by each party entered in the contract (Blum; Gardner; Cohen; Joseph and Hiller). Like a legal document, the *Contract* asserted that the Republican Congress would make all promises and considerations transparent and solve the problems of secrecy and violation of law fostered under Democratic leadership:

> The Democrats' iron-handed, one-party rule of the House of Representatives over the last four decades led to arcane, arbitrary, and often secretive procedures that disenfranchised millions of Americans from representation in Congress. . . . The result was a Congress held in contempt not only for failing to act on crucial issues but also for holding itself above the law and operating in secret. (13)

The *Contract*'s comparative language suggested that betraying public confidence was like breaking the law. It affirmed the fact that the Democrats had failed to uphold their commitment to the people and, thus, behaved illegally. As such, the Democrats had broken their contractual promise to the people and relieved them of any reciprocal obligations.

The *Contract* argued that Republicans, on the other hand, understood that something more than an informal agreement was needed to reveal the transactions between the people and their leaders. It used legal form to reconceptualize the political relationship between the people of the United States and their Republican legislators. The *Contract* stated that the House Republicans recognized that "public confidence in Congress and other institutions had reached its lowest point in twenty years. The feeling among voters that elected officials are not accountable to the same rules as everyone else and do not understand their frustration with a political process that doesn't work for them had to be addressed" (5). Rather than allow Congress to operate "above the law," a mechanism had to be put in place to ensure accountability and trust: "Returning accountability, and the faith and trust that come with it, was the very reason for creating this contract" (4).

The *Contract* presented itself as "an instrument to help repair a fundamental distinction between citizens and their elected officials" (5). It promised that on the first day of the 104th Congress, Republicans would immediately pass a reform to "require [that] all laws that apply to the rest of the country also apply equally to Congress" (8). That Republican legislators were voluntarily making the decision to change how legislation was conducted further bolstered the commitment and trustworthiness of the new Republican Congress. The *Contract* used its description of the wrongful behavior of Democrats in Congress to demonstrate that every legislator had a choice; Democrats had made the wrong one, but Republicans were making the right one. Unlike Democratic representatives who "ignored" the people (23), were "unwilling" to take action (25), and "refused to get tough" (37), the *Contract with America* promised that Republican representatives were willing to make the tough decisions and be held accountable because they wanted the best for the people.

That Republican representatives would follow the law and uphold their contractual obligations was highlighted by the *Contract*'s provision of a visible agenda on which they could be judged: "That is why, in this era of official evasion and posturing, we offer instead a detailed agenda for national renewal, a written commitment with no fine print" (7). Although legal contracts do not have to be written, a contract often takes written form, includes signatures, and is copied and preserved as a formal record (Joseph and Hiller). Joel Joseph and Jeffrey Hiller advise, "Putting your agreements into writing minimizes the likelihood of dispute. . . . Thousands of lawsuits can be avoided by making agreements in the form of clear, understandable, written documents" (2). Accordingly, the *Contract* used the physicality and formality of its agreement as evidence that it was willing to go on permanent "record" (22). It stressed that "for the first time in memory, American citizens have a document they can refer to as a means of holding Congress accountable" (4).

The physical signatures contained within the *Contract* also provided a formal record of the legislators' commitment. The signatures of the 367

Republican candidates in the 1994 midterm elections who signed the *Contract* take up twelve pages in the appendix of the book (169–80). The *Contract* promised that "the candidates who signed on the *dotted line* carry a responsibility to do what they can to make the principles of the *Contract* a *reality*" (6, emphasis added) and that they "pledge to honor" the "pact that was *signed* on September 27, 1994" (7, emphasis added). Furthermore, in the acknowledgments at the beginning of the book, the *Contract* states, "The 367 Republican candidates who signed their names on the dotted line to help change the nation . . . should be recognized for accepting the responsibility of putting forward a bold agenda" (vii).

The use of the formal components of a document and signatures provided evidence that the *Contract* understood that the justification of a legal contract rested on the idea that a breach of contract has consequences and calls forth remedies to protect the interests of each involved party (Gardner; Cohen). The *Contract* employed the idea that the "chief role of contract law is to provide a framework for the enforcement of promises" (Chirelstein 12). According to the *Contract,* "To rebuild the faith that is needed for representative government to really work, it was necessary to produce a signed, written contract that states explicitly, 'If we break the contract, throw us out'" (13). Similarly, the *Contract* also acknowledged, "If we fail, we know we will be shown the door in much the same way the Democrats were in this past election" (22). By explicitly recognizing their punishment if they went back on their contractual promises, the signatories of the *Contract* underscored their authenticity and sincerity in delivering on their end of the bargain.

The legal form the *Contract* took became significant because it implied both obligations and consequences. Republican legislators were obligated to keep their promises and serve the citizens of the United States. Furthermore, readers were implicated into the *Contract* because they were given the obligation to oversee the legislative process and put pressure on their legislators to uphold the *Contract*. This pressure, in turn, provided a reason for Republicans to move forward in a united fashion, bound to one another in success or failure. Republican consultant and pollster Frank Luntz wrote, "To those voters who have had an opportunity to take part in the market testing, *the Contract represents the willingness of certain politicians to come together over a set of important issues and put their names and their careers on the line. This is an exercise in unity and integrity not seen in recent political memory*" (qtd. in Garrett 96, emphasis Luntz's). Thus, not only did the Republican legislators have an obligation to the people to uphold the *Contract,* but also they had an obligation to one another. If either of these obligations was broken, the consequence was clear: the *Contract* would fail and Republicans would be removed from office.

THE SOCIAL AND LEGAL CONCEPTUAL FRAMEWORK

The Republican legislators' acknowledgment of their punishment if they did not deliver on their promise brought into focus the other party in the *Contract with America,* the people of the United States. Once the people were implicated in the process, the *Contract* conceptualized the relationship between them and their legislators so that the people's rights did not appear to be usurped. As Bawarshi points out, "Genres are the conceptual realms within which individuals recognize and experience situations at the same time as they are the rhetorical instruments by and through which individuals participate within and enact situations" (113). Accordingly, the *Contract* relied on the generic form of both legal and social contract to make two significant rhetorical moves regarding citizens' role in the contractual process.

First, the *Contract* emphasized that its contractual bond was a mutual endeavor. It depicted a relationship between legislators and the people of the United States that is similar to the reciprocal and equivalent relationship formed between two parties in a legal contract, into which each party enters by their own free will (Friedman; Cohen; Blum; Fried). That a legal contract is supposed to protect each party's own autonomy has its roots in the liberal idea that "all restraint is evil and that the government is best which governs least" and in the "classical economic optimism that there is a sort of pre-established harmony between the good of all and the pursuit by each of his own selfish economic gain" (Cohen 558).[9] Second, the *Contract* also drew on the more naturalized form of a social contract to underscore the idea that the best type of government is one that "seeks to renew the American Dream by promoting individual liberty, economic opportunity, and personal responsibility through limited and effective government" ("Contract" 5). Social contract theory, as expressed in the philosophical and political thought of Thomas Hobbes, John Locke, and Jean-Jacques Rousseau, addresses the tension between natural society and social order and rests on the assumption that a fraction of natural rights are necessarily given up for a type of civil and political protection that extends rather than impedes individual autonomy.

The *Contract* suggested that the people of the United States, like their legislators, must make a choice to uphold the *Contract* because it consisted of an "exchange relationship" (Blum 2). The text makes this clear: "This is two-way contract. The American people are being asked to join the fight in order to pass these common-sense reforms" (*Contract* 166). The suggestion that the *Contract* was two-way involved the people in the process. At the same time, however, it was a proposition that had to be substantiated because the *Contract* was not signed or created by the people of the United States but by the Republican Congress. As such, the *Contract* had to define rhetorically the role the people were to play and make them feel as if they must uphold their contractual obligation as well.

The *Contract* did so by arguing that the people had entered into a contract through their own actions. In the introduction, the *Contract* states, "Voters sent a clear, undeniable message" (3) of their acceptance of the *Contract*. The *Contract* equated the people's votes to an endorsement of the *Contract*'s agenda. The voters, according to the *Contract,* indicated their acceptance through the mandate they delivered on Election Day: "Nothing written before or after the campaign better defines the difference between the two parties than the document you now hold in your hands—the *Contract with America*. Rarely has such a meaningful mandate been delivered by the voters" (3). Thus, the *Contract* cemented the public's commitment to the plan and celebrated the people's right to vote as evidence of their decision to enter the contract of their own volition and free will.

Once the people of the United States entered into this contractual agreement, the *Contract* explained their role in the process. Just as the *Contract* spelled out the obligations of the Republican legislators, it gave the people several obligations to fulfill as well. First, they had to oversee the legislative process, which entailed becoming informed about the *Contract*'s bills and pressuring their legislators, both Republican and Democrat, to pass the bills. As they would a formal contract, the people were encouraged to read all of its clauses and details. Yet, also as with a contract, it was likely that the people would not do so, giving the Republican legislators more control than implied. The *Contract* states,

> Part of the responsibility for [the bills'] passage rests with the American people. In a Republican House it will be easier for the public to obtain information (all the bills in the Contract with America are currently on the Internet system) and have their views represented (we pledge to allow more amendments). That provides people greater opportunity for participating in the legislative process. (21–22)

In addition to bringing the public into the legislative and deliberative process, this statement ensured a future relationship between the contractual parties.

In remarks given at the end of the *Contract,* Gingrich explained that Republican legislators wanted to hear the people's ideas and views and urged citizens to call 1-800-T-O-R-E-N-E-W (192–93). The *Contract* further recommended, "Whether you agree or disagree with any or all of the bills that make up the *Contract with America,* please make your voice heard. We made a point of letting the people know where we stood on these important issues, and now it is up to you to let your representatives know where you stand on them" (22). Although the *Contract* suggested that people share their views regardless of what they were, it seemed to assume that citizens would speak out in support of its proposals and did rhetorical work to make sure of it. By associating the people's votes with support of the *Contract,* Republicans pulled citizens closer to their cause: "Voters have once again voiced their concerns and their issues at the ballot box by entrusting Republicans with control of the House of Representatives" (20). Thus, the *Contract* implied that the only way for voters to remain consistent and to fulfill the obligation they had voluntarily entered into was to continue to support the *Contract* rather than to voice any doubts about it.

The other way that the *Contract* rhetorically constructed citizens' role in the contractual process was by proclaiming that the people had an obligation to enact the *Contract*'s call for accountability outside of the political sphere and back in their homes: "You have to accept greater responsibility back home. We are going to have to be partners. This is going to have to be a team in which we work together to renew American civilization" (192). At the same time the *Contract* stressed mutual agreement and partnership with the people, it made a clear statement that autonomy would be preserved and called on the people to enact it. On both a legal and social level, the *Contract* carefully balanced its desire to enter into a contract with the people of the United States with its conservative political position that the government should not interfere with citizens' private lives. The way in which the *Contract*'s agreement was structured adheres to Rousseau's 1762 definition of government: "An intermediate body set up between the subjects and the sovereign, to secure their mutual correspondence, charged with the execution of the laws and the maintenance of liberty, both civil and political" (48). The *Contract* similarly stated, "Republican legislators recognize the innate ability of every American to make decisions around the kitchen table without some dictum handed down from Washington" (21). Not only did the *Contract* demonstrate that it did not want to overstretch its bounds, it also showed its reverence for the sanctity of family life and the intimate space around the dinner table.

The *Contract* promised that its bills would strive to "restore a proper balance between government and personal responsibility" (14) and made responsibility, along with accountability and opportunity, a core principle. One of its ten bills was the "Personal Responsibility Act," which overhauled the welfare system (66). The *Contract* held that it could not and would not attempt to do the job best left to individuals and families who were under the attack of a "government that's grown larger than ever imagined by our Founding Fathers" (14). The *Contract* asserted, "The belief that you can trust Americans to make valid judgments permeates Republican initiatives from the smallest hamlet to the halls of the U.S. Congress" (21). The *Contract* implied, then, that just as Republican legislators trusted the people to govern themselves, the people should trust the Republican legislators to fulfill the *Contract*'s potential. If the people did not, they were letting themselves down and failing to take responsibility; hence, the *Contract*'s failure became the people's failure as well.

THE RHETORICAL CONTRACTUAL FORM

Thus far I have shown how the *Contract* grounded itself in particular genres in order to legitimize itself, manufacture support, and, most important, constitute the people of the United States and their legislators into a contractual relationship. In what follows, I show how the *Contract*'s structural and stylistic form supported and substantiated the pact it had established. Its narrative form had a certain rhetorical function (Lucaites and Condit) that added to its use of generic form as a tool of propaganda: it offered a sense of certainty regarding the overall coherence of its plan and its ability to deliver definitive legislative answers. According to John L. Lucaites and Celeste M. Condit, "Because the rhetorical narrative functions in general to compel the audience to a particular understanding of the facts of the case, to a particular point of view, it must project a voice that underscores the unity of direction of the discourse" (98). Specifically, the *Contract* used visual anchors, the juxtaposition of binaries, and the repetition of an organizational pattern to mark its plan with certainty and structure and simultaneously push the prose and its readers forward. As Morton W. Bloomfield states, "A literary work is not just the addition of sentence to sentence, not just a string of sentences, but has some viability as a whole, though not necessarily an organic whole" (285). Accordingly, as each chapter of the *Contract* was presented, the narrative form was familiar, and the prose advanced almost habitually. The movement of this text was important for two paradoxical reasons: it continued the flow if the information became too complicated, and it continued the flow if the explanation given was too shallow.

The *Contract* made repeated use of visual anchors such as italicized headings, bullet points, and parenthetical numbers. For example, in chapter 2, the "Balanced Budget Amendment and Line-Item Veto" and the "two powerful, common sense ways to control Congress's penchant for spending" (24) were laid out in bullet points. Then two bullet points outlined the way in which Congress had formerly tried to "circumvent the few budgetary restraints it has set for itself" (26). Similarly, the most recent debate regarding the proposed balanced budget amendment was described by its twofold requirements in the House debate—(1) and (2)—and by the four reasons why the Senate rejected its own resolution, (1), (2), (3), and (4). Although the language within the chapter was highly technical and would need further explication for its full comprehension, the frequency of visual anchors promised a sense of completeness that urged the reader to move forward. Accordingly, there was no time and no reason to ponder what an "up-or-down vote," a "package of rescissions" (24), or "exempting Social Security" (28) meant.

The stylistic certainty and movement of the *Contract* also relied on the setting up of binaries. Whereas binaries might act as stumbling blocks in an otherwise stagnant prose style, in the case of the *Contract* they became an expected and repeated anchor in the discourse and created an up-and-down rhythmic tide that the reader was invited to ride forward. The middle chapters were organized similarly. They began with a section that justified and elevated the legislative act in question. Next, a history surrounding the act was provided, which detailed how the people of the United States had been let down by the government. Then, the text quickly returned to the *Contract*'s legislative plan as the answer to citizens' frustrations. The transition between the dichotomies of past and future was represented by such phrases as "Here's what (our) Contract with America proposes" (43, 70, 100) or "Here's what we propose" (85, 126). After the legislative act was explicated in each chapter, the chapters concluded with the "Myths versus Facts" section. Each "myth" was put forward to "challenge" the plan and immediately countered by "fact" that set the record straight. Hence, an up-and-down rhythmic tide of binaries created a bridge from past to present, from ambiguity to clarity, and from the problem to the solution.

At the same time the forward-moving prose depended on the binaries, the effectiveness of these binaries depended on the forward-moving prose. In the "Myths versus Facts" section, dichotomous readings of the legislative act were offered, with the "facts" succinctly clearing up any misreading or misunderstanding that might have occurred. Similarly, the paired questions and answers in the "Questions and Answers" chapter at the end of the book worked much like the "Myths versus Facts" sections. The way in which a question was asked and a short, usually paragraph-length, answer provided gave the impression that there was one clear and "right" answer to each question. Overall, the movement of the text flowed through the binaries before "conversation" or dialogue between the two sides was considered.

LEVELS OF ICONICITY IN THE *CONTRACT*

The narrative form established the tone and set up the ideological framework within which the legislative process could be situated and ingested by the *Contract*'s readers. The process of creating and passing legislation is often cumbersome and complicated. The *Contract,* however, used its mutually reinforcing form and message to suggest otherwise. Many of its key messages about legislation and Republican legislators were iconic of the straightforward, systematic, and momentum-driven flow of prose that constituted the *Contract*'s stylistic and structural form. According to Michael Leff, iconicity occurs when form and content "blend together within the unfolding development of a discourse, a development that simultaneously holds the discourse together and holds it out as a way of influencing the world in which it appears" (277) and of influencing the auditors who receive it.[10]

That the momentum on the physical page of the *Contract* quickly moved from one visual anchor to another without hesitation was iconic of the pace and efficiency of legislative action offered in the *Contract*'s message. The *Contract* argued that the public would no longer have to impatiently wait for results as the onerous task of legislation unfolded. Accordingly, the *Contract* presented the plan as providing "a dramatic change in the direction of federal policy-making. The pace of ten major bills in the first hundred days indicates the magnitude of change to come" (15). In this statement, emphasis is placed on the "pace" of legislation, which becomes the corollary by which "magnitude" is measured. The *Contract* stressed that its ten proposed bills would be voted on within the first one hundred days. In each of the ten chapters that outline the ten legislative proposals, the *Contract* reiterated the significance of this duration of time with statements such as "That's why in the first one hundred days of a Republican House we will vote on the Fiscal Responsibility Act" (23). Ultimately, this message of legislative speed and finality is iconic of the *Contract*'s flowing prose, which pushed a reader through the legislative bills regardless of the specifics of the information presented.

The way in which Republicans presented themselves via the *Contract* is also iconic of its form. In addition to showing that Republicans preferred order and, thus, would ensure that legislation moved forward efficiently, Republicans used the *Contract* to define themselves as the forward-moving and action-oriented party. By repeatedly stressing that the House would vote on all of its proposed bills in one hundred days, the *Contract* emphasized that Republican legislators would actively work to propel legislation forward. This approach was posited in contrast to that of the Democrats, who conducted "business as usual" (22) and waited for legislation to passively unfold. Moreover, by differentiating "deed" from "word," the *Contract* promised that its plan would not stand still:

> The notion for such a contract was born on a snowy weekend in February 1994, if not by *word* then by *deed*. At a conference of House Republicans in Salisbury, Maryland, a *direction was set* for making sure citizens could clearly understand what the Republican Party stood for and meant to *deliver* if ever given a chance to *control* the federal legislative process. (4, emphasis added)

Although the *Contract*'s plan was written down, it would be carried out and moved forward in "deed" by the legislators. The *Contract* also laid out a clear "direction" that Republicans would take. Furthermore, Republicans were described as the party who would "set" the direction, have "control," and "deliver." The association of the word "Republican" with active verbs discursively equipped Republicans with a sense of agency and power and connoted them as the drivers of policy.

THE ONE-WAY, TWO-WAY *CONTRACT*:
IRRECONCILABLE DIFFERENCES

The *Contract*'s adherence to the generic forms of the legal and social contract and the cohesiveness that was achieved by its marriage with structural and stylistic forms created a sense of completeness. Although the *Contract* implied that it was adhering to certain generic forms and conventions and was offering a thorough inspection of the legislative process, it promoted its own agenda. The *Contract* used genre as a propaganda tool to contain legislative possibilities and restrict citizens' opportunities to evaluate legislation, perform politically, and negotiate their relationships with their Republican legislators. As a result, the *Contract* stripped agency away from the reader and freedom away from the individual citizen, asking for little more than acquiescence from the people of the United States despite its claim to "make us all proud again of the way free people govern themselves" (8). What was presented as a reciprocal relationship between representatives and citizens, then, is better described as unidirectional. Although the "father" of propaganda studies, Edward Bernays, states that propaganda is neutral because it "is simply the establishing of reciprocal understanding between an individual and a group" (161), this analysis of the *Contract* acts as a reminder of the importance of taking a deeper look at the processes that establish the assumed understanding and reciprocity of a work of propaganda.

More specifically, this chapter demonstrates the importance of exploring how generic form can be a carrier of ideology, which, when misapplied, can be used as a tool of propaganda that imposes and conceals ideology rather than negotiates or exposes it. In many ways, the overall rhetorical forms become the evidence for why a certain course of action should be taken rather than policy reasons or the results of deliberation. In other words, the basis for the bond that the *Contract* sealed was generically constructed rather than materially provided. Despite the *Contract*'s promise to give "rebirth to an open political process that provides substantive debates and votes upon issues of common agreement among the vast majority of Americans" (6), the legislative process was generically situated to make the *Contract*'s agenda feel like the only "right" way to conduct legislation. The *Contract* argued that its "common-sense agenda" (3–4), "common-sense changes" (164), and "common-sense reforms" (166) were natural and universal and could be objectively understood. Hence, the *Contract*'s "naturalness" stood in for the actual details of policy making, while the practical implementation of policy fell to the wayside.

In this sense, the *Contract*'s message became naturalized and ingrained within the legislative institutions the *Contract* constructed using genre. According to Norman Fairclough, "Naturalization gives to particular ideological representatives the status of common sense, and thereby makes them opaque, i.e. no longer visible as ideologies" (42). Hence, at the same time the *Contract* used genre and its narrative form to substantiate its plan and legitimize itself in common conventions, the form also became a type of facade behind which the *Contract* could hide its ideology and motives. Once legislation becomes naturalized rather than analyzed, there is reason to be alarmed. Exploring how genre can be used as a tool of propaganda, then, is a type of ideological criticism that can help "to understand and expose how 'obvious' or 'commonsense' assumptions about society and the individual's role in it operate to obscure realities of power and solidify social order" (Bjork 214).

Furthermore, the way the legislative process is described in the *Contract* reveals something troublesome about the relationship the *Contract* was proposing to have with the people of the United States. The *Contract*'s assumption that an election vote gave Republican legislators a mandate to push its policy undermined the ongoing citizen-representative communication that should take place between election cycles. Especially problematic was the pace by which the *Contract* explained legislation to the people and the pace by which legislation was to be passed by Congress. Citizens had little time to process what was happening. While the *Contract* promised that each bill would "be given full and open debate, each to be given a clear and fair vote, and each to be immediately available this day for public inspection and scrutiny" (9), it moved through the information much too quickly and was much too subjective in the information it chose to present to allow such inspection and debate. In addition to ignoring voters' capacity to assess information, the *Contract* also denied the voice of voters who were represented by Democratic legislators by undermining bipartisan deliberation and failing to acknowledge that some of the best policies evolve when the process is complicated by many views before they are signed into law.

Finally, this analysis suggests that the *Contract with America* was more than a name; it was a multilevel contractual, generic, and rhetorical device. While the *Contract*'s message itself might not have been that convincing, the levels of form on which it performed its speech act added a depth and stability it otherwise might not have had. As such, this analysis demonstrates not only the interrelatedness of form and message but also how the blending of different genres and forms can be used to add impact and casing to a single speech act. The legal contractual genre became the basis of the *Contract*'s legitimacy, purpose, and relationship with the people of the United States. At the same time, the *Contract* built a social contract, promising to respect the individual rights of the people and asking that they respect and support the Republican legislators' duty to implement the *Contract*. In addition, the *Contract* created an outer casing of narrative form, within which the message was intertwined and disseminated, that protected the relationship the *Contract* had created between the people and their representatives. Thus, the *Contract* used a mutually reinforcing rhetorical packaging of form and message to pull readers in and provide them with multiple layers of "protection" from the cynicism, uncertainty, and ambiguity of electoral politics and to assure them that Republicans were committed to and united in the *Contract*.

Notes

1. Public opinion polls throughout the year indicated that less than 30 percent of the public approved of congressional performance, a record-breaking low (Benedetto, "Congress" and "Voters"; Welch; Merida, "Polishing").

2. Haley Barbour, Republican National Chairman, was also convinced that the party needed a renewed vision and sent out surveys to see what the people of the United States wanted from their government. He received back 20 percent of the surveys instead of the 5 percent he had expected. Barbour states that the response showed that "people [were] dying to participate" and agreed with many core GOP issues (qtd. in Garrett 58). Polling and focus groups were also conducted to test the key ideas of the contract (Gimpel 6, 18; Garrett 73–78, 94–97; Bader 184–88), and Gingrich insisted that every issue have at least 60–70 percent public approval ratings (Bader 187–88).

3. Many media outlets and Democratic politicians, however, quickly argued otherwise; the contract was branded as a gimmick. Democrats attacked the contract on many grounds (Jones; Garrett; Priest; Merida, "Challenger").

4. By design, the contract's main architects avoided divisive issues, instead choosing to focus on items of more general appeal (Garrett). See also n. 2 above.

5. Three refrained because of philosophical objections to parts of the contract, and the other four generally endorsed the contract but did not attend the signing ceremony (Gimpel 27–28).

6. Democrats also turned over their majority in the Senate, losing eight seats. Also, for the first time in 140 years, the sitting Democratic Speaker of the House, Tom Foley, was ousted and later replaced by Gingrich.

7. As this analysis proceeds, subsequent references to the *Contract*, unless noted, refer to the actual book published in 1994 rather than to the Republican plan in general.

8. Other important works on genre include Aichele and Jamieson and Campbell.

9. See Hillman (9) and Blum (10) for further discussion of how contract law rests on the liberal ideas of individualism, autonomy, and laissez-faire economics.

10. Moreover, Leff and Sachs state, "Iconicity is a regularly occurring phenomenon of language-use that reveals a cooperative interaction between form and meaning" (260). Burke makes a similar argument in *Counter-Statement*, maintaining that "form is the creation of an appetite in the mind of the auditor, and the adequate satisfying of that appetite" (31). McGee also problematizes the text/context split, using the concept of fragmentation to "collapse 'context' into 'text'" (283). See also Condit for a critique of McGee's and Leff's critical arguments. See also Short and Leech for an interesting discussion on iconicity.

Works Cited

Aichele, George, Jr. "Genre and Reality." *The Limits of Story*. Minneapolis: Fortress, 1985. 77–102. Print.

Bader, John B. *Taking the Initiative: Leadership Agendas in Congress and the "Contract with America."* Washington, D.C.: Georgetown UP, 2007. Print.

Bawarshi, Anis S. *Genre and the Invention of the Writer: Reconsidering the Place of Invention in Composition*. Logan: Utah State UP, 2003. Print.

Benedetto, Richard. "Congress Knows It's 'Show-Me Time' to Voters." *USA Today* 7 March 1994: A11. Print.

———. "Voters 'in a Stoning Kind of Mood.'" *USA Today* 11 October 1994: A1. Print.

Bernays, Edward L. *Propaganda*. 1928. Brooklyn: Ig, 2005. Print.

Bjork, Rebecca S. "Public Policy Argumentation and Colonialist Ideology in the Post–Cold War Era." *Warranting Assent: Case Studies in Argument Evaluation*. Ed. Edward Schiappa. Albany: State U of New York P, 1995. 211–36. Print.

Bloomfield, Morton W. "Stylistics and the Theory of Literature." *New Literary History* 7.2 (1976): 271–311. Print.

Blum, Brian. *Contracts: Examples and Explanations*. New York: Aspen Law and Business, 1998. Print.

Burke, Kenneth. *Counter-Statement*. Chicago: U of Chicago P, 1931. Print.

Campbell, Karlyn Kohrs, and Kathleen Hall Jamieson. "Form and Genre in Rhetorical Criticism: An Introduction." *Form and Genre Shaping Rhetorical Action*. Falls Church, Va.: Speech Communication Assn., 1978. 9–32. Print.

Chirelstein, Marvin A. *Concepts and Case Analysis in the Law of Contracts.* New York: Foundation, 1998. Print.

Cohen, Morris. "The Basis of Contract." *Harvard Law Review* 46.4 (1933): 553–92. Print.

Condit, Celeste M. "Rhetorical Criticism and Audiences: The Extremes of McGee and Leff." *Western Journal of Speech Communication* 54.3 (1990): 330–45. Print.

Contract with America: The Bold Plan by Rep. Newt Gingrich, Rep. Dick Armey and the House Republicans to Change the Nation. Ed. Ed Gillespie and Bob Schellhas. New York: Times Books, 1994. Print.

"Democrats Recover but GOP's Turnout Edge Looms Large." *Times Mirror Center for the People and the Press.* 28 October 1994. Web. 28 February 2012.

Fairclough, Norman. *Critical Discourse Analysis.* Essex, Eng.: Longman, 1995. Print.

Fried, Charles. *Contract as Promise: A Theory of Contractual Obligation.* Cambridge, Mass.: Harvard UP, 1981. Print.

Friedman, Lawrence M. *Contract Law in America: A Social and Economic Case Study.* Madison: U of Wisconsin P, 1965. Print.

Gardner, George K. "An Inquiry into the Principles of the Law of Contracts." *Harvard Law Review* 46.1 (1932): 1–43. Print.

Garrett, Major. *The Enduring Revolution: How the Contract with America Continues to Shape the Nation.* New York: Crown Forum, 2005. Print.

Gimpel, James. *Fulfilling the Contract: The First 100 Days.* Needham Heights, Mass.: Allyn and Bacon, 1996. Print.

Gingrich, Newt. "Rep. Newt Gingrich: Washington Research Group Symposium, 11 Nov. 1994, Washington, D.C." *Contract with America: The Bold Plan by Rep. Newt Gingrich, Rep. Dick Armey and the House Republicans to Change the Nation.* Ed. Ed Gillespie and Bob Schellhas. New York: Times Books, 1994. 181–96. Print.

Hillman, Robert A. *The Richness of Contract Law: An Analysis and Critique of Contemporary Theories of Contract Law.* Dordrecht, the Netherlands: Kluwer, 1997. Print.

Jamieson, Kathleen Hall, and Karlyn Kohrs Campbell. "Rhetorical Hybrids: Fusions of Generic Elements." *Quarterly Journal of Speech* 68.2 (1982): 146–57. Print.

Jones, Charles O. *Clinton and Congress, 1993–1996: Risk, Restoration, and Reelection.* Norman: U of Oklahoma P, 1999. Print.

Joseph, Joel, and Jeffrey Hiller. *Legal Arrangements in Plain English.* Chicago: Contemporary, 1982. Print.

Leff, Michael. "Things Made by Words: Reflections on Textual Criticism." *Quarterly Journal of Speech* 78.2 (1992): 223–31. Print.

Leff, Michael, and Andrew Sachs. "Words the Most Like Things: Iconicity and the Rhetorical Text." *Western Journal of Speech Communication* 54.3 (1990): 252–73. Print.

Lucaites, John L., and Celeste M. Condit. "Re-constructing Narrative Theory: A Functional Perspective." *Journal of Communication* 35.4 (1985): 90–108. Print.

McGee, Michael C. "Text, Context, and the Fragmentation of Contemporary Culture." *Western Journal of Speech Communication* 54.3 (1990): 274–89. Print.

Merida, Kevin. "Challenger Burned Learning the Ropes; Sound Bites Can Bite Back." *Washington Post* 5 October 1994: A1. Print.

———. "Polishing Congress's Tarnished Image; Lawmakers Struggle to Counter Public's Distrust of the Institution." *Washington Post* 25 January 1994: A1. Print.

Miller, Carolyn R. "Genre as Social Action." *Quarterly Journal of Speech* 70.2 (1984): 151–67. Print.

Priest, Dana. "A Mostly Clinton Family Gathering; President Can't Draw Voters to Brother-in-Law's Senate Campaign Rally." *Washington Post* 16 October 1994: A7. Print.

Rousseau, Jean-Jacques. "The Social Contract." *Democracy: A Reader.* Ed. Ricardo Blaug and John Schwarzmantel. Irvington, NY: Columbia UP, 2001. 44–52. Print.

Short, Michael H., and Geoffrey N. Leech. "The Rhetoric of Text." *Style in Fiction: A Linguistic Introduction to English Fictional Prose.* London: Longman, 2007. 209–56. Print.

Welch, William M. "Congress Held in Record-Low Esteem." *USA Today* 29 September 1994: A4. Print.

PROPAGANDIST MANAGEMENT: "SUSTAINABILITY" IN THE CORPORATIZED PUBLIC UNIVERSITY

LAURAL LEA ADAMS

> What is sauce for the journalistic goose is sauce for the academic gander. . . . Just as journalists have mostly internalised the liberal myth of the objective media, so such academics have mostly internalised the liberal myth of objective academia. —Eric Herring and Piers Robinson, "Too Polemical or Too Critical? Chomsky on the Study of the News Media and US Foreign Policy"

In their 1988 book, *Manufacturing Consent: The Political Economy of the Mass Media*, Edward S. Herman and Noam Chomsky argue that many factors impinge upon the range of choice that media personnel have in news production and that these factors serve as "filters" through which current events are reported, characterizing the news as a mode of propaganda. Herman and Chomsky's propaganda model (PM) asserts that the media, which necessarily court economic backers, such as producers, advertisers, and other investors, are unable to achieve journalistic objectivity and slant current events to reflect moneyed interests. "News," arising largely from mass media's pool of elite economic backers, is repackaged by broadcasters who have adopted their ideological lenses through their memberships in media firms. Further, the information produced by media personnel is subject to a second round of scrutiny by the very same institutional forces that generated this news to begin with. Any media outlet or personnel within such an outlet who attempt to produce news that violates the norms and expectations of media's moneyed constituents are subject to "flak," as when advertisers withdraw their patronage in response to news they dislike; this process brings reporting back into alignment with moneyed interests. Herman and Chomsky identify these characteristics among the interlocked set of institutions that shape the news. However, the same dynamics also describe the corporatized public university's participation in the knowledge economy.

This chapter couples the PM with cultural-historical activity theory (CHAT) to argue that the same factors that constrain the media also constrain academia: like the media, the academy participates in a sector of society purposed for producing information and knowledge, and, like the media, it is constrained by a similar set of factors that functions to filter intellectual work produced there. Ultimately, like the media, the academy also produces propagandist discourse that serves the interests of its most powerful constituents. In accordance with the model, such propaganda can emanate from any "broadcasting" point within the institution—administrators, boards of trustees, staff, faculty, or students. It can be directed toward any constituent inside or outside of higher education, and, consistent with the model, most actors producing propaganda are largely unaware their discursive activities reflect neoliberal ideology. This broad scope leaves open the possibility for extensive analysis of propaganda produced in higher education, particularly regarding how it is used to shape faculty's research and teaching agendas to serve corporate interests. However, this chapter focuses largely on the propaganda that arises from administrators via university websites, arguing that websites are to universities what news broadcasts are to mass media, sites from which to disseminate propagandistic messages. While these websites are designed to reach broader publics, they are also intended for faculty audiences and are characterized by specific persuasive aims that arise out of neoliberal underpinnings.

Neoliberal aims have saturated the corporatized university and its discursive activities, producing distinct bodies of propagandized communiqué. One of these is the discourse on "sustainability," which has been appropriated from ecology and reformulated to conceal economic motives under the ideological guise of mutuality, conservation, and community. Using a critical discourse approach, I examined the discourse on university websites. As Teun A. van Dijk notes, critical discourse analysis aims not merely to describe discourse but also to explain it in terms of social interaction and institutional dynamics by focusing on "the ways discourse structures enact, confirm, legitimate, reproduce, or challenge relations of *power* and *dominance*" (353). This approach takes systems into account and makes the method compatible with both the PM and CHAT. I reviewed numerous websites for a holistic sense of the genre's features and rhetorical strategies; I then focused on eight websites that foreground sustainability in their organizational identity. This process revealed a neoliberal ideology veiled beneath the claim that universities enact sustainability initiatives to serve the public good.

While Herman and Chomsky identified anticommunist ideology as the formative ideological force shaping the media's production of news in 1988, Chomsky later asserted that this force had shifted to neoliberalism. The PM recognizes that, at their core, these ideological interests have always been economic. However, despite refiguring the PM to reflect contemporary ideological forces, the model continues to be criticized by some academic audiences as conspiracist and overly determinist. In fact, numerous articles have questioned why the model, and Chomsky generally, are not more commonly cited by some academic audiences.[1] Eric Herring and Piers Robinson, who explore the absence of the PM from relevant published work and share their own experiences of reviewers' negative responses to the inclusion of references to Chomksy, argue that the marginalization of the PM from scholars' research agendas is evidence of the same filtering factors functioning in the academy (555). Their assertion warrants further exploration in the context of the recently corporatized academy and its discourses. However, in order to address criticisms of the PM, it is helpful to couple it with a CHAT perspective.

HOW ACTIVITY THEORY EXTENDS THE PROPAGANDA MODEL

The PM is criticized by some academics who believe the model posits a ruling class responsible for the coordinated, premeditated use of mass media for propagandist aims. Critics point to the obvious dissent that plays out in media as proof that Herman and Chomsky's model either overstates this cohesiveness or lapses into conspiracy claims (Herring and Robinson 560). Herman and Chomsky's model remains susceptible to these criticisms because, fundamentally, while the PM exemplifies a systems perspective, some of its components are underdeveloped, leaving its capacity to account for certain phenomena in question. Specifically, the model does not fully account for how the powerful can act in decentralized capacities as members of organizations and institutions to affect central-ized efforts directing the course of social policy through propaganda. Nor does it provide a satisfactory explanation for how less powerful members of institutions take on the ideologies and goals of the more powerful in the absence of obvious coercion. Instead, the PM's strength resides in its ability to reveal how institutions are constituted by interlocked systems and how power functions to shape them. More comprehensive systems models, such as CHAT, are less likely to privilege interrelationships between systems and more likely to thoroughly explain the interrelationships between individuals and systems.

Founded by Russian psychologists Lev Vygotsky and A. N. Leont'ev in the 1920s, CHAT is a descriptive framework for explaining systems and accounts for the recursive manner in which the social shapes the individual and the individual shapes the social. Central is the notion that individual action is mediated by cultural means, tools, and signs and is goal-driven. CHAT's account of individual behavior as shaped through artifacts helps address the criticisms of the PM by enabling us to understand how members of the system align themselves to the goals and values inherent in material artifacts. This emphasis helps clarify how decentralized actors affect unified pressures and constraints on interlocked systems without resorting to conspiracist or determinist explanations. However, in order to understand when discourse becomes propaganda, we must to turn to propaganda as it is theorized more generally, beyond the confines of the knowledge economy.

Through CHAT's lens, propagandist writing operates on both social and cognitive levels and can be regarded as a communicative act intended to conceal or manage contradiction in order to maintain or change the system's goals and objectives: "Institutions have their goals, and propaganda contributes to the achievement of such goals. For example, propaganda may help the institution to maintain the existing status quo. . . . [It makes] little sense to try and understand propaganda on its own, outside goals that the institution is trying to achieve" (Marková 39). As with the PM, from a CHAT perspective, actors need not be aware they are internalizing and reproducing ideological content through textual artifacts; instead, their attention may be focused on actualizing their own aims and subgoals, which are tied to (and crucial for maintaining) membership in the institution. As Chomsky notes, "Those who choose to conform, hence to remain within the system, will soon find that they internalize the beliefs and attitudes that they express and that shape their work; it is a rare individual who can believe one thing and say another on a regular basis" (qtd. in Klaehn 151). This "naturalization" of institutional ideology occurs through the meditational role of textual artifacts in the process of enculturation. The discourse that results lends the impression that there is no dissent. As critical discourse theorists are quick to point out, the strategy of omitting dissent prevents audiences from becoming aware that alternative perspectives are possible and from questioning the ideological ground from which the discourse arises.

In higher educational institutions, propaganda is used at junctures of contradiction to construct organizational identities that help fulfill aims and goals forged by the neoliberal climate in which they operate. At this historical moment, higher education is straddled between its new role as a participant in the knowledge economy and its traditional role as a public sector institution with a mission to serve the "public good." While higher education has traditionally justified its public funding with its mission to serve the public good and constructed its identity accordingly, public funding has dwindled, and institutions have shifted their missions to accommodate financial stakeholders situated in the private arena. As a result, institutions of higher education are increasingly responsive to neoliberal economic policies and practices framed on the assumption that market forces best regulate the public sector. According to Mark Olssen and Michael Peters, in a global neoliberal climate

> the traditional professional culture of open intellectual enquiry and debate has been replaced with an institutional stress on performativity, as evidenced by the emergence of an emphasis on measured outputs: on strategic planning, performance indicators, quality assurance measures and academic audits. . . . Universities are seen as a key driver in the knowledge economy and as a consequence higher education institutions have been encouraged to develop links with industry and business. . . . The recognition of the economic importance of higher education and the necessity for economic viability has [led to the promotion of] greater entrepreneurial skills as well as . . . measures to enhance output and to establish and achieve targets. (313)

Sustainability is the newest of such "performativity measures" that educational institutions have adopted, and they expend considerable effort discursively formulating the construct and their embodiment of it as they respond to and operationalize neoliberal approaches to valuing and solving social problems. Today, a "market discourse" increasingly saturates the discursive formulations of U.S. public research universities, often reflecting an agenda of economic globalization (Chaput 174). Now institutions of higher education work to discursively embody entrepreneurialism and managerialism in order to construe the organizational legitimacy that appeals to their economic backers. The contradiction between the traditional university and the privatized one requires discursive formations that refigure and then maintain the corporatized institution's values, goals, and practices.

Evidence suggests that the academic and administrative cultures residing in universities are quite distinct. Academics tend to endorse the value of intellectual freedom, autonomy, and the legitimacy of specialists' expertise, and they believe that management lacks an understanding of the significance of these features in the production of knowledge and teaching. Academics also generally equate the strategic move to a corporate culture as interference with the right to work autonomously, a shift toward excessive supervision, and an increase in the use of intrusive "quality processes" (Ramsden 27). On the other hand, the culture of academic management reflects a concern with accountability, efficiency, cost-benefit analyses, and return on investments; administrators characterize faculty as self-indulgent, lacking relevance, unappreciative of the need for managerial competence, and lacking an entrepreneurial spirit (27). Clearly, contradiction abounds. However, the most prominent discursive representations of contemporary institutions of higher education, namely their websites, offer almost no evidence of this plurality.

Instead, the university website serves as a discursive field occupied by administrative interests that functions to eclipse other discourses and structure stakeholders' perceptions of the institution. This site participates in a discursive system that seeks to align members of the organization with its goals and objectives. An examination of sustainability discourse there reveals that these pages are not simply intended to report on environmental initiatives, nor to function solely as part of marketing strategies appealing only to external stakeholders. This discourse also functions to circulate propagandist rhetoric intended to persuade faculty to adopt neoliberal values and practices in their work-related aims and activities. To put it in terms of both the PM and CHAT, university websites are mediational tools that disseminate neoliberal ideology serving "elite" corporatized interests, and the discourse surrounding sustainability in higher educational institutions is propagandistic because it uses framing devices that conceal its economic motives and ideological underpinnings. Universities frame their identities in terms of "social responsibility" in order to legitimize their aims, which include globalizing their operations and transforming faculty values and practices in order to align them with the institutional

goals. Further, this approach mirrors corporate entities' strategies to manipulate their own stakeholders through corporate social responsibility
reporting, reemphasizing the reality that public universities fully operate
as corporatized organizations. The "feel-good discourse" of sustainability
functions to hide the reality that even when public universities seem to
be at their best, as when they advocate for environmental approaches to
their own roles, they are not doing so to serve the public interest but to
capitalize on a strategy that appeals to their audience's desire to cling to
a traditional educational mission.

SUSTAINABILITY AND SUSTAINABLE
DEVELOPMENT, COMPLEX CONSTRUCTS

Managerial discourse on sustainability appears in the university in discursive fields as diverse as operations management, curriculum development, and strategic planning. However, websites are especially significant
for organizational legitimacy. As Craig Deegan notes, "There is a good
deal of . . . evidence that corporate social and environmental reporting
is motivated by a desire, by management, to legitimize various aspects of
their respective organizations" (282). The notion of sustainability confers
legitimacy to the idea that an organization operates in a socially responsible way in relation to the environment, an image that appeals to higher
education's many stakeholders.

Sustainable development was defined by the Brundtland Commission in
1987 as "development which meets the needs of the present without compromising the ability of future generations to meet their own needs" (Brundtland Commission). However, as Stephen Gough and William Scott describe
in Sustainable Development and Learning: Framing the Issues, stakeholders
in higher education define it variously (15–18). But a variety of stakeholder
perspectives is not evident in the monologic perspective appearing on most
university websites. Instead of reflecting an academy actively engaged in
the dialogic or dialectical process of exploring what constitutes "knowledge" about sustainability, these websites feature a form of "greenwash"
where the term sustainability is used as a catchall. However, this omission
dismisses alternate discourses on sustainability that, according to M. Peterson, Markus J. Peterson, and Tarla Rai Peterson in "Conservation and the
Myth of Consensus," has detrimental effects: "Ironically, efforts to isolate
a single meaning for sustainable development in a world of diverse social
constructions of reality render the term meaningless" (764). This greenwash

is particularly poignant in higher education, which has traditionally fostered diverse thinking. Nevertheless, academic explorations into the complexities of sustainability, the socially constructed nature of these constructs, and the actuality of environmental crises remain largely cordoned off from public view on websites that function for alternative aims.[2]

Instead, university websites present uncontested views of sustainability through a technocratic lens, showcasing campus operations, curricula, and faculty research mostly predicated on technological solutions to sustainability. Technological innovations are represented either as active decisions to replace components of facilities or operations with eco-efficient devices and processes or as creative solutions arising from faculty research in uncomplicated ways. For example, Boston University's sustainability web pages describe a collaborative project with MIT in techno-utopian terms:

> The research team envisions equipping individual buildings with the capability to integrate production and consumption of electric energy via a smart micro-grid capable of monitoring and controlling smart appliances, plug-in hybrid electric vehicles (PHEVs) and other grid-friendly devices, [such as] photovoltaic panels and wind turbines. Each building would . . . exchange electric energy with external energy markets, enabling it . . . to sell some of its own power to the grid. (Dwortzan)

The page foregrounds a $2 million grant from the National Science Foundation and the project's potential to respond to environmental issues by "creat[ing] a virtual energy market," but it does not raise any of the potential impediments to such a project nor the larger concerns that a critical perspective would yield. For example, the page mentions engaging various stakeholders, including unspecified "private interests," to "determine the optimal use of energy, transportation, food, water and green space" but does not suggest a method for doing so or that these determinations are likely to be highly contested.

Often depictions of technological sustainability initiatives feature student efforts as they simultaneously gain valuable job skills. Grand Valley State University features a digital "Sustainability Guide" on its website, and the cover includes a quote by Martin Luther King Jr. ("The time is always right to do what is right") as well as photos of students engaged in activities such as collecting samples off the side of a small boat, picking up trash, and working the soil in a garden plot. By framing students' environmental work as activist and coupling it with the suggestion that these efforts prepare them for future jobs doing socially responsible "good work," websites appeal to students' and parents' tripartite anxieties about whether an investment in college degrees will yield jobs, whether an environmental crisis is overtaking the globe, and whether the course of world events is decided through competition and exploitation by multinational corporatized interests possessing no ethical or moral bearings.

Universities are well aware of the power of these appeals. According to surveys by the *Princeton Review*, more than 60 percent of both parents and students said that knowing a university was committed to the environment would positively affect their decision to attend ("College Hopes"). The websites provide their viewers with assurances on sustainability that construe universities not as corporate entities but as institutions still in alignment with traditional models to serve the "public good." In fact, Grand Valley State University's digital "Sustainability Guide" notes that its "liberal education . . . fosters a commitment to economic, social, and environmental sustainability and an inclusive campus that values diversity. Through its forward thinking education, students are empowered to affect the global community now and in the future" (7). Linking sustainability to a liberal education is a maneuver that attempts to forcibly situate sustainability initiatives into the traditional university.

Further, these websites reflect an environmental crisis uncritically in neo-Malthusian terms that assume "the Earth's resources are finite and . . . if we go on as we are its 'carrying capacity' must be exceeded" (Gough and Scott 18). The result is often a narrow conservationist approach to environmental problems. Websites tend to tout the investment and installation of new physical plant technologies or student and staff efforts to recycle cans or save energy by reducing thermostats in dorm rooms, in contrast to, for example, collective approaches to sustainability that call for anti-expansionist public policies. The cost savings these sustainability initiatives represent to the university take a backseat to the narratives about individuals' impact on the environment. For example, Ball State's "University Sustainability Statement" mentions economic motivations once, in a final bullet that promises to "consider the social, economic and environmental impacts of . . . operational policies and foster a participatory process in developing these policies." Yet, buried in a press release elsewhere is the fact that Ball State University's "geothermal heating and cooling system . . . will save the university an estimated $2 million per year in operating costs" (Richards). From a less critical vantage, it would seem that universities are only secondarily motivated by such savings, or that an approach that "kills two birds with one stone"—particularly in difficult economic times—is a windfall and should not warrant such interrogation. Yet, the pattern is consistent: university websites deemphasize economic motives, such as cost savings and development opportunities, in more altruistic frames. This practice is a convention borrowed from the discourse of corporate social responsibility where it is a "grand taboo" to mention continuous economic growth, the political nature of corporate social responsibility, or the amoral nature of business entities (Kallio).

Narratives of campus initiatives often include supporting images of young adults smiling as they engage in environmentally focused activities against sunlit backdrops, such as planting seedlings, and web page backgrounds are frequently populated with images of green leaves, stylized illustrations of trees, and close-up shots of industrious hands at work. The narratives make it is extremely difficult to criticize sustainability efforts or resist the urge to champion the resilient and optimistic spirit of the single individual juxtaposed against the magnitude of global environmental issues, as it is discursively framed. King's University College, located in Canada, features an "ECO Initiative" web page that includes an announcement for an annual event wherein volunteers donate slips from their perennials to raise money for campus gardens, a picture of a dozen people behind a sizable pile of trash collected in a twenty-minute town "makeover," and endearing photos of sweater-clad students attempting to raise awareness of environmental issues on "Ugly Sweater Day" ("King's ECO Initiative"). On websites such as these, conservationist efforts by individuals are personalized and celebrated. These individually enacted eco-efficiency approaches appeal to their audiences by persuading them to regard themselves as efficacious and by encouraging them to view each act of conservation as a meaningful contribution to an important cause that accretes over time, especially in concert with the actions of others. This propagandist appeal draws attention away from the magnitude of agency that institutions possess, both economically and culturally, and it occludes universities' economic motivations for sustainability initiatives.

In fact, many of the websites make a clear distinction between what the institution does and what individuals *can* do, a grammatical modality that intends to frame the institution as fulfilled and the individual's potential for environmental activism as causally attributable to and *only in relation to* the institution. Boston University's sustainability pages contain a header with links that read "What We're Doing" and "What You Can Do." The effect is to appropriate individual activities by rendering them creditable to higher education's advocacy role. Ways by which individuals can "help save the environment" are presented with the register of activist imperatives as calls for "action" rather than as suggestions. For example, the University of Kansas invites students to pledge via an electronic signature to "make KU a better place for myself and future Jayahwks [*sic*] by living more sustainably. I will strive to make decisions that protect our natural ecosystems, create economic prosperity and treat all people with equality and respect" (Center for Sustainability). The cover page under which this opportunity appears contains twenty-two suggestions for conservation, including "Use a cloth napkin and save 350 paper napkins a year" and "On hot days close blinds to keep the heat out." Eco-efficiency suggestions are interspersed with others that clearly do not yield cost savings to the university, such as "Buy and sell used items at thrift stores," which distracts viewers from seeing the attempts to structure individual activities for economic gains. Messages like this persuade viewers that the institution is so thoroughly committed to sustainability as to give over some of its web space, its virtual territory. However, research has shown that universities that provide "useful information" to their users as part of a dialogic approach to website design also experience higher alumni giving and retention rates (Gordon and Berhow). Constructing discursive formations that construe universities as responsive and altruistic pays well.

Most universities feature a figurehead group on their sites, such as a council, committee, or organizational unit designated to spearhead initiatives. These smaller groups usually comprise representatives from various campus stakeholder groups who are tasked to operationalize sustainability on campus, which creates the impression that the process is democratic rather than managerially dictated. The term *sustainability* is more prevalent than *sustainable development*, a strategic omission, since its oxymoronic and expansionist connotation risks inviting dissent. Further, institutional commitments are discursively demonstrated by public signatories, usually presidents, whose endorsements are framed as heroic "pledges," actions that take the university into technologically innovative and socially responsible directions. By alluding and linking to environmentalist or sustainability-related associations and organizations, universities use their websites to aggrandize their own institutions while simultaneously doing the same for what are largely symbolic entities.

The websites frequently refer to planning activities, formal assessments, and reporting. Dining services, waste reduction, and campus transportation alternatives are often mentioned, as well as green events, conferences on campus, greenhouse gas emissions, and Leadership in Energy and

Environmental Design (LEED)–certified buildings. When biodiversity is discussed, it is usually in a local context. *Community* is usually locally defined, though it is often linked to the global arena with vague assurances that local efforts are tied to broader national and international efforts to "make a difference." For example, Pennsylvania State University grandly assures its website viewers that

> we have a responsibility to our students, our institution, and our greater society to teach, embody, and communicate a world view that allows the collective "we" to prosper, both now and in the future . . . with humility, responsibility, openness, commitment, and a profound belief in the power of "we." It is with a charge to do better, to think and act anew, that the University has created the Sustainability Institute. (Sustainability Institute)

Sustainability initiatives are framed as work in progress, since the task of saving the environment is never complete; this strategic approach persuades viewers to believe the institution is relentless in its advocacy and provides a justification for continued investment into additional initiatives. The economic and political aims that motivate corporations to depict themselves as socially responsible also propel universities to do the same, and these depictions are constructed in part through a system of certification that extends well beyond the institution.

DISCURSIVE ECONOMIES OF GREEN CERTIFICATION IN HIGHER EDUCATION

Sustainability initiatives provide various economic and political opportunities, and the university carefully crafts descriptions of them in order to veil its aims and take advantage. These discursive formations are part of a complex economy of legitimacy that is commercially bought and sold. One of the most prominent mechanisms by which universities discursively construct an organizational identity founded on social responsibility is through the mechanism of sustainability certification. For example, the Association for the Advancement of Sustainability in Higher Education (AASHE) markets its "Sustainability, Tracking, Assessment and Rating System" to more than three hundred universities that have provided data in a multifaceted "reporting framework" spanning their curricula, operations, and other initiatives. In return for a fee, universities earn the designation of bronze, silver, gold, or platinum participant. Evidence is self-reported and usually includes links to web pages; however, these are frequently dead ends or present tenuous evidence. For example, one university with a "gold" rating answered yes to the prompt that asked if it had an outdoor program that followed "Leave No Trace" principles; the supporting evidence was a link to a Facebook group that included six members contributing a handful of posts and pictures each year with no mention of Leave No Trace principles. Another university's "excessive idling policy" attested that car owners were prohibited from idling their vehicles for more than sixty seconds when outside temperatures were "reasonably warm," yet the link to the policy indicated "Page Not Found," calling the existence of the policy into question. A careful examination of these certification processes reveals they are transactional and symbolic as universities buy the right to display the insignia that attests to their commitment to sustainability. This certification adds legitimacy while also enabling the university to veil its aims toward the performativity that Olssen and Peters note. Particularly, it allows universities to adopt the accounting and accountability practices employed in corporations, which track and monitor employee activities via productivity and cost assessments, by packaging these measures as ethically and morally motivated. Further, the certification itself is a valuable marker of legitimacy.

While most of AASHE's website contains carefully crafted messages about its goal to enable universities to fulfill a social responsibility role through sustainability, a closer examination evidences the dynamics of a process of commercialization that accompanies universities' discursive claims about their own sustainability initiatives. For example, the AASHE site features a blatantly manipulative message to students, but one that faculty, staff, and administrators are invited to use for their own purposes. In a blog post titled "Create the Green Economy You Want BEFORE You Graduate!" the author notes,

> Higher education purchases a share of nearly everything consumed by the greater society . . . includ[ing] vehicles, cleaning services, food, apparel, lab equipment, televisions, whole buildings, financial services . . . *you name it!* . . . When higher education makes sustainability a key part of its purchasing decisions, it has the opportunity to influence what is sold to everyone else. *That is why getting involved in how your institution buys products and services will give you a hand in creating the green economy you want!* . . . It isn't . . . easy to insert sustainability criteria into purchasing decisions. . . . You can let that discourage you, or you can see that as an opportunity to influence the hundreds of billions annually spent through state contracts! (Hummel)

The blog encourages students to contact vendors and provides links to the *AASHE Business Member Product and Service Directory* and AASHE's annual business expo to further enlist students in commercial aims. As Chomsky might observe, the blog post, framed in terms of students' interests, functions to broadcast a call to action that is ultimately designed to aid the institution in fulfilling its economic aims.

Green certification is a central mechanism by which universities construct the environmentally conscious identity they feature on their websites, and there are numerous participants in this discursive system. The U.S. Green Building Council's (USGBC) LEED certification is yet another example. The council asserts that it "works toward its mission of market transformation through its LEED green building program, robust educational offerings, a nationwide network of chapters and affiliates, the annual Greenbuild International Conference & Expo, and advocacy in support of public policy that encourages and enables green buildings and communities" ("LEED™ Is Driving the Green Building Industry"). Not only does this organization sell its certification through membership and certification fees, but it also sells an online education program to certify those who have the signatory power to designate buildings as certified. LEED has not escaped scrutiny, however, as the term *LEEDwash* has come to be associated with efforts to attain certification for buildings that excessively overuse materials, with decisions that privilege publicly visible signs of greening over legitimate building features, and with green practices that end as soon as certification is bestowed. As LEED critic Henry Gifford notes, LEED has influenced the popularity of green buildings, making this a "valuable selling point that . . . is featured prominently in advertisements. . . . LEED certified buildings make headlines, attract tenants, and command higher prices . . . despite the fact that . . . [many] use *more* energy than comparable buildings. What has been created is the *image* of energy efficient buildings, but not actual energy efficiency" (1). Gifford suggests that the council's name is intended to create the perception it consists of independent environmental experts; however, "the USGBC is really the construction industry telling itself what it ought to do" (2).[3]

As this debate suggests, the "economies of green certification" at work in higher education parallel those in the corporate sector. Understanding their history in the corporate sector sheds light on their function in higher education. Multinational companies increasingly feature corporate social responsibility reports on company websites, particularly since the inception of "global reporting initiatives" and "sustainability reporting guidelines."

While the reporting is ostensibly voluntary, motives for doing so, as well as dubious certification practices, are strikingly similar to those in higher education. Paolo Perego and Ans Kolk note, "The voluntary demand of independent verification by [multinational companies] can be explained by their willingness to enhance a sustainability report's credibility vis-à-vis stakeholders. Organizational benefits from the assurance exercise may also arise in the form of improvements in internal information and reporting systems, resulting in better management of social and environmental performance" (174). In other words, corporations use third-party certification to discursively construct a commitment to social responsibility that construes the corporation's sustainability initiatives as legitimate evidence for "corporate caring" while simultaneously enabling them to monitor employees' activities. The corporatized university mirrors corporate motives and goals when it too uses third-party certification of its sustainability initiatives.

These economies of certification and the discursive trading of legitimacy are evident in the tendency of web pages to allude to organizations such as the American College and University Presidents Climate Commitment, the International Sustainable Campus Network, the *Princeton Review*'s list of "green colleges," and the Talloires Declaration. In "U.S. Progress Toward Sustainability in Higher Education," Wynn Calder and Richard M. Clugston offer recommendations to universities who have signed the Talloires Declaration, and they suggest that substantial potential economic affordances motivate universities to construct organizational legitimacy through certification: federal government agencies, such as the Department of Education, the Department of Energy, and the National Science Foundation, "could make sustainability a major focus of higher education if those agencies made sustainability a research priority. Organizations such as NCSE [National Council for Science and the Environment], which is positioned to leverage support for sustainability teaching and research through federal agencies, should aggressively do so" (644). That agents on behalf of higher education should mobilize to effect public policy suggests there are numerous external stakeholders to whom declarations about being an institution with an environmental focus can substantially pay off.

However, as with corporate assurance practices, the discursive formations begin to "project a . . . symbolic image of accountability through assurance, thereby undermining the credibility of these verification practices" (Perego and Kolk 173). The result is that sustainability is becoming a "rational myth," mainly ceremonial and superficial. Moreover, verification practices are actually decoupled from operational practices and are "subject to 'capture' by powerful managerial and professional interests [who] take control of . . . sustainability policy and practices by appropriating the language and processes of traditional financial auditing in order to meet their own . . . objectives." Likewise, assurance providers are primarily motivated to promote their own agendas, including limiting their potential liability if their assessments are called into question. "The practical outcome," say Perego and Kolk, "is that third-party assurance does not add credibility to sustainability reporting" (176). Even the university's dining facilities participate in the certification business. For example, the Green Restaurant Association's logo attests to green operations and purchasing. The association's website features a helpful list of vendors whose products meet the green standards. However, several layers down, one finds web pages that reveal these products require upwards of $12,000–$18,000 for their endorsements, depending on the length of contract ("Endorsement Contract").

Ultimately, there is money to be made in sustainability initiatives, in appealing to the public's need to be reassured that someone is responding to the global environmental crisis, a public that includes university faculty in its ranks. Universities take advantage of this by constructing propagandistic messages to veil economic motives with images of social responsibility and by crafting the impression they still function in accord with a traditional mission to safeguard the public good. Additionally, these mechanisms structure employee activities, including faculty's, by cloaking productivism in moral and ethical discourses of conservation and eco-efficiency. The corporatized business model is so rampant in higher education that even the production of these propagandistic messages has been commercialized in a complicated system for buying and selling organizational legitimacy.

Herman and Chomsky's observations about the mass media aptly describe higher education's role in the knowledge economy:

> The mass media serve as a system to communicate messages and symbols to the general populace. It is their function to amuse, entertain, and inform, and to inculcate individuals with the values, beliefs, and codes of behavior that will integrate them into the larger institutional structures of society. In a world of concentrated wealth and major conflicts of class interest, to fulfill this role requires systematic propaganda. (1)

In "Neo-liberalism and Marketisation: The Implications for Higher Education," Kathleen Lynch points out that "in most countries in the world the universities have remained relatively elite institutions. What has come to pass in the early 21st century is that that elitism is being reinvigorated as marketisation and commercialisation have taken hold" (3). This process is intimately tied to higher education's increasing focus on globalization. Norman Fairclough, in *Language and Globalization,* points to the materiality of power-relations through this discourse evident in the standard definition used in business and economics: "a process (or set of processes) which embodies a transformation in the spatial organization of social relations and transactions . . . generating transcontinental or interregional flows of networks and activity, interaction, and the exercise of power" (2). Catherine Chaput, in examining the discourse of globalization in *Inside the Teaching Machine,* calls on faculty to critically examine "globalization" in university mission statements, asserting that "something as apparently trivial, inconsequential, or mundane as a mission statement . . . produces power-effects—rhetorically constructed enclosures within which material reality can be acceptably designed" (176). So too faculty must recognize that the ordinary university website participates in managerial discourses that effectively restructure the ways faculty work, channeling that work toward corporatized and commercial aims. The burgeoning presence of sustainability is not a benign depiction of higher education's social consciousness or an awareness of its role in the global ecology but evidence that it is operating out of a neoliberal stance wherein free market systems can and should regulate social spheres. As Richard Alexander stresses in *Framing Discourse on the Environment: A Critical Discourse Approach,* so long as corporate interests claim to operate toward human rights and welfare but are in fact worsening them "for reasons of state or in the name of protection of jobs, national security, free trade, 'shareholder values,' democracy, or whatever other excuses are given . . . [language scholars must] mediate in this evident mismatch between saying and meaning" (6).

The discourse of sustainability, like that of globalization, veils the corporatized university's aims. Faculty must interrogate this discourse and work to interject dissenting views into public spaces "captured" by administration. We must draw attention to the reality that faculty still function in the relative comfort of disciplinary silos, vaguely unsettled but assured we are safely housed on the hallowed grounds of a traditional university working fervently to protect the environment, create jobs that enable students to do the same, and manage the university in fiscally and environmentally sustainable ways. Meanwhile, despite the alarms that populate the academic research, administrative discourses continue to enable the best-kept secret in higher education: the corporatization of higher education is all but complete.

Notes

1. See, for example, Woods.

2. Occasionally, working documents belie the notion that sustainability is a "no-brainer" about which everyone agrees. For example, "Climate Action Plan: Promoting Sustainability at Frostburg State University" includes a brief section called "Defining Sustainability" that notes that although "committee members agree with the EPA [Brundtland] definition, many feel that it may suggest a 'maintenance' mentality. There is also some confusion over the breadth and depth of the term 'sustainability,' with a concern that it is strictly limited to environmental issues" (Learning Green). The passage suggests anxieties about constraints to a wider institutional development strategy from some members and failures to consider sustainability's complexity from others, but these concerns remain unaddressed and hint at undercurrents of difference and dissent that are generally disallowed from administratively controlled spaces.

3. The testimony of Gifford, the well-known designer of heating, cooling, and ventilation systems, is not sponsored by a mainstream publishing venue but is available on his personal website, along with pictures of him clad in a T-shirt and working among pipes and ducts. The class action suit that Gifford brought against the USGBC for false advertising was eventually dismissed, but questions about the legitimacy of LEED certification persist among many architects advocating for environmentally sound building practices.

Works Cited

Alexander, Richard. *Framing Discourse on the Environment: A Critical Discourse Approach.* London: Routledge, 2008. Print.

Boston University. "Sustainability@BU." Boston University Sustainability. Trustees of Boston U, 2010. Web. 3 June 2013.

Brundtland Commission. *Our Common Future: Report of the World Commission on Environment and Development.* Oslo: United Nations, 1987. Print.

Calder, Wynn, and Richard M. Clugston. "Higher Education." *Stumbling Toward Sustainability.* Ed. John C. Dernbach. Washington: Environmental Law Inst., 2002. 625–46. Print.

Center for Sustainability. "Programs and Projects." KU Center for Sustainability. U of Kansas, n.d. Web. 3 June 2013.

Chaput, Catherine. *Inside the Teaching Machine: Rhetoric and the Globalization of the US Public Research University.* Tuscaloosa: U of Alabama P, 2008. Print.

Chomsky, Noam. *Profit Over People: Neoliberalism and Global Order.* New York: Seven Stories, 1999. Print.

"College Hopes and Worries Results." *Princeton Review.* The Princeton Review, 10 April 2013. Web. 3 June 2013.

Deegan, Craig. "The Legitimising Effect of Social and Environmental Disclosures: A Theoretical Foundation." *Accounting, Auditing and Accountability Journal* 15.3 (2002): 282–311. Print.

Dwortzan, Mark. "NSF Greenlights Sustainable Building Project." Boston University Sustainability. Trustees of Boston U, n.d. Web. 3 June 2013.

"Endorsement Contract." Green Restaurant Association. Green Restaurant Assoc., n.d. Web. 3 June 2013.

Fairclough, Norman. *Language and Globalization.* London: Routledge, 2006. Print.

Gifford, Henry. "Building Measuring Systems." EnergySavingScience.com. Google Sites, 11 September 2008. Web. 3 June 2013.

Gordon, Joye, and Susan Berhow. "University Websites and Dialogic Features for Building Relationships with Potential Students." *Public Relations Review* 35.2 (2009): 150–52. Print.

Gough, Stephen, and William Scott. *Sustainable Development and Learning: Framing the Issues.* New York: Routledge, 2003. Print.

Grand Valley State University Sustainability Initiative. "Sustainability Guide." Grand Valley State University. Grand Valley St. U., n.d. Web. 3 June 2013.

Herman, Edward S., and Noam Chomsky. *Manufacturing Consent: The Political Economy of the Mass Media.* New York: Pantheon, 1988. Print.

Herring, Eric, and Piers Robinson. "Too Polemical or Too Critical? Chomsky on the Study of the News Media and US Foreign Policy." *Review of International Studies* 19.4 (2003): 553–68. Print.

Hummel, Sam. "Create the Green Economy You Want BEFORE You Graduate!" AASHE. Assoc. for the Advancement of Sustainability, 12 September 2011. Web. 3 June 2013.

Kallio, Tomi J. "Taboos in Corporate Social Responsibility Discourse." *Journal of Business Ethics* 74.2 (2007): 165–75. Print.

"King's ECO Initiative." King's Western University: Canada. King's UC, n.d. Web. 3 June 2013.

Klaehn, Jeffery. "A Critical Review and Assessment of Herman and Chomsky's Propaganda Model." *European Journal of Communication* 17.2 (2002): 147–82. Print.

Learning Green, Living Green Sustainability Committee. "Climate Action Plan: Promoting Sustainability at Frostburg State University." Frostburg State University. Frostburg State U, 15 September 2009. Web. 3 June 2013.

"LEED™ Is Driving the Green Building Industry." LEED. US Green Building Council, 2013. Web. 3 June 2013.

Lynch, Kathleen. "Neo-liberalism and Marketisation: The Implications for Higher Education." *European Educational Research Journal* 5.1 (2006): 1–17. Print.

Marková, Ivana. "Persuasion and Propaganda." *Diogenes* 55.1 (2008): 37–51. Print.

Olssen, Mark, and Michael A. Peters. "Neoliberalism, Higher Education and the Knowledge Economy: From the Free Market to Knowledge Capitalism." *Journal of Education Policy* 20.3 (2005): 313–45. Print.

Perego, Paolo, and Ans Kolk. "Multinationals' Accountability on Sustainability: The Evolution of Third-Party Assurance of Sustainability Reports." *Journal of Business Ethics* 110.2 (2012): 173–90. Print.

Peterson, M., Markus J. Peterson, and Tarla Rai Peterson. "Conservation and the Myth of Consensus." *Conservation Biology* 19.3 (2005): 762–67. Print.

Ramsden, Paul. *Learning to Lead in Higher Education*. London: Routledge, 1998. Print.

Richards, Chanel. "Ball State Recognized by Higher Education Group for Sustainability Efforts." Ball State University Education Redefined. Ball State U, 14 November 2012. Web. 2 June 2013.

"STARS: A Program of AASHE." Assoc. for the Advancement of Sustainability in Higher Educ., 2003. Web. 3 June 2013.

Sustainability Institute. "The Sustainability Institute." Sustainability.psu. edu. Pennsylvania State U, 2013. Web. 3 June 2013.

"University Sustainability Statement." Ball State University Education Redefined. Ball State U, 2013. Web. 3 June 2013.

"U.S. Progress toward Sustainability in Higher Education." ULSF. Assoc. of University Leaders for a Sustainable Future, 2011. Web. 3 June 2013.

Van Dijk, Teun A. "Critical Discourse Analysis." *The Handbook of Discourse Analysis*. Ed. Deborah Schiffrin, Deborah Tannen, and Heidi E. Hamilton. Hoboken: Wiley-Blackwell, 2003. 352–71. Print.

Woods, Lawrence T. "Where's Noam? On the Absence of References to Noam Chomsky in Introductory International Studies Textbooks." *New Political Science* 28.1 (2006): 65–79. Print.

CONCLUSION: WRITING DISSENT IN THE PROPAGANDA FLOOD

ROBERT JENSEN

> Have you thrown your senses to the war, or did you lose them in the flood?
> —Bruce Springsteen, "Lost in the Flood"

To supplement the systematic analysis of propaganda in this volume, I want to add a discussion of my ongoing struggle with propaganda. I want to take propaganda personally, as a path to confronting the depth of the political crisis we all face. So, I start with an inventory of my relationship to propaganda.

- A target of propaganda: I have lived my life in the United States, which means I am a member of the most intensely propagandized group in human history.
- A producer of propaganda: I have worked in mainstream corporate-commercial journalism, which means I have unwittingly helped distribute propaganda.
- A critic of propaganda: I teach about media and politics at a university, where I do my best to train students to identify and resist propaganda.
- A political activist: I work on a variety of progressive community-organizing projects, where I help create spaces for real democratic dialogue.

In political terms, my early experience was completely conventional. I was a predictably liberal kid in reaction to predictably conservative parents, growing up in a small midwestern city with no interesting political

264

conversations audible to me anywhere in the vicinity. A respectable but uninspired education in public schools and a public university left me unaware there were any serious political options outside the Democratic and Republican Parties. I spent my twenties working as a reporter and editor at a variety of mainstream corporate-commercial newspapers, where the political spectrum was just as narrow. And as I consumed advertising-supported, corporate-generated entertainment, I naively assumed that I was immune to the hucksterism of the commercial mass media.

As I edged toward the age of thirty, I was a competent news worker at a good regional daily newspaper where I could have settled into a reasonably secure professional life. The only problem was that I was bored. Though I had no clear understanding of what was missing from the world according to mainstream journalism, this vague restlessness led me to graduate school, with the hope that I might be able to teach at a college someday. Career concerns drove the process, but my underlying hope was that I would find ideas to reenergize myself.

That energy came from a wide array of radical approaches to politics, economics, and society—starting with radical feminism and critiques of white supremacy, moving through analyses of imperialism and capitalism, and eventually tackling crucial ecological issues. Although graduate school is not designed to radicalize students—and often has the opposite effect—I was lucky enough to meet some interesting people who helped me understand the power of radical ideas. Like most "ordinary" Americans, I had been trained to believe that radical politics was, by definition, crazy. But when I stopped accepting the culture's caricature of radicals and actually paid attention to what they had to say, a new world opened up for me.

Like any job, academic work has its downside, but I can say without hesitation that in twenty-eight years of study and teaching, I have never been bored. This state of intellectual excitement is a direct result of the radical writing I stumbled upon in my first years of graduate school, and one of the central steps in that process of expanding my intellectual and political horizons was reading Edward S. Herman and Noam Chomsky's book *Manufacturing Consent* and Herman's *Myth of the Liberal Media*, which helped me to understand the propaganda model. Fairly quickly, two things struck me about the model.

First, it was a compelling way to analyze the newsrooms in which I had worked. Much of the academic theorizing I was reading in graduate classes seemed pretty far removed from the world as I knew it, but Herman and Chomsky helped me understand my own experience. I always knew at some level that journalists' claims to neutrality and objectivity were obfuscation, but as a working journalist I had no framework to analyze my working life. Herman's model, identifying the filters through which news-of-the-world must pass to become news-in-the-media, provided me with a way to reflect on my journalism career and understand how effectively I had been socialized.

Second, surprisingly few folks around me in journalism education seemed interested in the model. That reason for the professorial neglect of the propaganda model wasn't difficult to understand: journalism schools in the United States at the time existed to produce students who were willing and able to take relatively low-paying jobs in a profitable journalism industry—which was not interested in hiring people schooled in such radical critique (Jensen, "Faculty Filter"). The collapse of the traditional business model for mainstream journalism in the first decade of the twenty-first century has meant the industry has far fewer jobs to offer our students, but the fundamental relationship of journalism schools to the journalism business hasn't changed much.

Prior to this course of study, I would have never thought of myself as either a target of propaganda (as a citizen) or a purveyor of propaganda (as a journalist). Whatever dissatisfaction I felt with the political and professional world in which I lived and worked, *propaganda* was a term I would have reserved for Nazi Germany, the Soviet Union, and other authoritarian societies. Propaganda, in other words, was something done to others by others.

These radical intellectual and political experiences left me with questions I would come back to regularly and with challenges I set for myself.

The questions: In a relatively free society, why do those in the intellectual professions (journalists, teachers, professors, scholars, clergy, and so on) so routinely fail to challenge the claims of the powerful or, more important, fail to critique the institutions within which the powerful operate (Jensen, "Myth")? How do the rewards and punishments of those professions so successfully induce conformity when intellectuals are relatively free from overt constraints? What are the mechanisms of social control?

The challenges: How effectively can I use the freedom that the system offers me? How critically self-reflective can I be in evaluating my choices? If the privileged position I've stumbled into gives me such extensive freedom, how do I tell the truth as I understand it as aggressively and effectively as possible?

CRACKING THE MAINSTREAM

As a junior professor whose career depended on successfully surviving my probation period (the six-year odyssey called "getting tenure"), I had to balance the institutional demands to produce scholarly work with my personal desire to be part of politics beyond the university. In reality, the balance usually tipped in favor of the institutional demands, which took up most of my time. But when that period was over, I vowed to lean the other way and chose to abandon scholarly writing aimed at fellow academics in order to devote myself to putting critical ideas in front of the widest audience possible.

One way I attempted to do that was in writing short political essays for newspapers—op-eds, in the parlance of journalism, which run on the two pages most daily newspapers reserve for openly opinionated writing. The vast majority of op-eds that appear in U.S. mainstream newspapers reflect the conventional Democratic/Republican spectrum of opinion, but editors can, and sometimes do, run the occasional piece that expresses more radical ideas. I decided to use my journalism training to place op-eds that presented radical critique, especially of capitalism and the United States' imperial foreign policy.

For several years I had a pretty good run of luck. I never cracked the big three (the *New York Times,* the *Washington Post,* and the *Wall Street Journal*), but I was able to place pieces in the daily papers in Los Angeles, San Francisco, Dallas, Houston, Atlanta, and a number of other U.S. cities. There's no way to know what effect any single piece of writing has on political conversations, but at least the placement of those essays in general circulation publications meant that some people who didn't already agree with me would be exposed to the arguments. Feedback from newspapers readers included lots of condemnations, which suggested the pieces were being read and taken seriously by a range of people. Left/progressive people also wrote to thank me for placing such blunt critiques in the mainstream, mentioning that what was most important wasn't the analysis I offered (which typically wasn't new to them) but the boost they felt from seeing their point of view taken seriously in such a venue.

Those experiences led to a book, *Writing Dissent: Taking Radical Ideas from the Margins to the Mainstream,* which offered tips to other radicals about how to shape ideas in a way that newspaper editors would accept. In my political organizing, I routinely heard from people who said that they had an op-ed rejected because mainstream journalists are scared of radical politics. That no doubt happens, but it's also true that many such pieces are rejected by mainstream editors because they are badly argued and/or badly written. I wanted to encourage fellow dissidents to write and to remind them that the goal of writing is to engage and persuade, not simply to rant and rave.

GOING AROUND THE FILTERS

I was writing those op-eds about the same time that the Internet was starting to become widely used by the general public. By the time my book was published in 2001, a number of websites (Common Dreams, ZNet, Counterpunch, Alternet) had established themselves as reliable places to find left/progressive news and commentary, offering a mix of original content and pieces taken from print publications.

The creation of these sites seemed like a particularly well-timed development after the terrorist attacks on 11 September 2001. In the hyperpatriotic atmosphere that followed 9/11, the mainstream news media offered little space to those questioning the mad rush to war. There were exceptions, including a piece of mine published by the *Houston Chronicle* (Jensen, "U.S. Just as Guilty") that generated lots of discussion, but critique of the dominant narrative of U.S. innocence and self-righteous indignation was pushed from its usual dimly perceptible place on the margin to almost complete invisibility.

I was grateful for those websites, which provided a place both to post my own essays and to read other critical voices. Given the rapidity of political developments and the sense of impending doom about the consequences of U.S. military action that many of us felt (presciently, it turned out), the near-instant dissemination of that writing seemed crucial. Those of us who identified as political dissidents needed a way to communicate quickly outside the mainstream, and these websites provided it.

In the decade-plus since 9/11, the number of websites has exploded, and more of them are supporting original journalism. As digital tools get less expensive and easier to use, citizen-journalism and citizen-advocacy expands. For those who know what they are looking for, it's easy to get outside the narrow political spectrum that mainstream politicians and journalists offer. Dissidents used to have to search for things that now flow freely on the Internet.

When people ask me which I think is more important—writing for a general audience to attempt to change the minds of political opponents or writing for one's dissident political cohort to help deepen knowledge and sharpen arguments—I say yes. Both are important, both are worth effort, and both require the same skills. The tips from *Writing Dissent* on how to present an effective argument apply to writing for the Web as much as to writing for a mainstream newspaper. Even if one is posting an op-ed on a website whose readers are mostly like-minded, thinking about how to persuade opponents is always a good exercise in critical thinking that strengthens one's writing. When we are writing only for others committed to the same cause, it becomes all too easy to leave our own assumptions unchallenged.

But we should remember that compelling political analysis, no matter how intelligently argued and smartly written, doesn't guarantee political progress, whether it's in or out of the mainstream. First-rate arguments mean little if they are yoked to second-rate organizing. Writing dissent, whether by cracking the mainstream or by going around the filters, is only one part of a political strategy.

As one who wants to counter the propaganda that is generated by the centers of power—primarily the government and the corporation—I hold onto a conviction that evidence and logic matter (Jensen, *Arguing for Our Lives*). In a fair fight, I am confident the positions of left/feminist radicals would gain greater acceptance. Even when the people defending the imperial nation-state and capitalism have at their disposal the immense resources of the institutions of those systems, I still believe the power of critical arguments can carry the day over time, if given some space to be heard and engaged.

But as commentators have been pointing out for decades, serious impediments to honest intellectual/political engagement come not only from repression but also from numbness. Legal scholars Ronald Collins and David Skover suggest that we face not just Orwellian but also Huxleyan threats to democratic dialogue. The former are rooted in the nightmare vision of the novel *1984*, in which thought and expression are constrained by the direct repression of the state and no meaningful freedom is permitted. The latter describe the equally nightmarish vision of *Brave New World*, in which people are flooded with a pacifying array of amusements so that freedom becomes irrelevant.

That framework is useful in broadening how we think about propaganda. It's tempting, no matter how much we know about the complexity of the world of political communication, to want to think of propaganda as the lies that others tell to manipulate "the masses"—something done to others by others. But if we really care about understanding the ways in which propaganda is an impediment to the honest and open dialogue required in democracy, then the definition we use has to deal not only with Orwell but also with Huxley.

PROPAGANDA WINS? ARE WE JUST LOST IN THE FLOOD?

"Discourse is dying in America," Collins and Skover proclaim, "yet everywhere free speech thrives" (xlix). In their explanation of that apparent paradox, they highlight the differences between

- the old principles of political speech (rational decision making, civic participation, meaningful dissent) and the new practices of an electronic entertainment culture (trivialization, passivity, pleasure);
- the informational principles of commercial speech (marketplace of economic ideas) and the imagistic practices of a mass commercial advertising culture (marketing of items);
- the lofty principles of artistic expression (self-realization) and the low practices of a pornographic culture (self-gratification). (202)

Transforming Bruce Springsteen's question "Have you thrown your senses to the war, or did you lose them in the flood?" into an assertion, the problem increasingly is not just that we've thrown our senses to the culture of war but that we've lost them in the commercial flood. The longer I work as a teacher and organizer, the more I think the greatest obstacles to critical thinking and progressive political change are not from state repression (though we can't ignore the ways in which the state is always refining its ability to use coercion and violence when needed to beat back challenges and how that violence is used against the most vulnerable people in society) but from that flood.

As this book demonstrates, *propaganda* can mean very different things at different times in different places. But we struggle to define the term as clearly as possible because we need to be able to distinguish between attempts to persuade that are consistent with good intellectual practice and democracy (what we might call democratic persuasion) and attempts to manipulate people that are inconsistent with good intellectual practice and democracy (what we might call undemocratic propaganda). The distinction is not as easy to make as we may wish it, but here are two tentative lists of features of systems that intuitively we think of as healthy persuasion and unhealthy propaganda.

Democratic persuasion involves a

- serious effort to create background conditions that give each person access to the resources needed to fully participate in discussion; and
- serious effort to create forums in which access to the discussion is based not on power or money but on a principle of equality; and
- commitment of all participants to intellectual honesty in presenting arguments and a willingness to respond to the arguments of others.

Undemocratic propaganda involves deliberate

- falsification of accounts of the world to support one's interests; and/or
- attempts to ignore or bury accurate accounts of the world that are in conflict with one's interests; and/or
- diversion of discussion away from questions that would produce accounts of the world in conflict with one's interests.

There is one disturbing implication of this framework: it suggests that virtually all commercial advertising and a significant portion of our political discourse is propaganda. From this perspective, the advertising, marketing, and public relations industries would be described collectively as the propaganda industries. When we consider how much our social environment is influenced by those industries, we would hesitate to speak glibly about living in a democratic political system and a free society. When journalists become the transmission vehicle for much of this material, we might hesitate to speak glibly about a free press.

What do we say about the state of our political discourse when a presidential campaign can win the advertising industry's "marketer of the year" award, as the Obama campaign did in 2008 (Creamer)? What do we say about a democracy in which a president's chief of staff, when asked why the Bush administration waited until after Labor Day to launch its campaign to convince the American public that military action against Iraq was necessary, said, "From a marketing point of view, you don't introduce new products in August" (Bumiller)?

The question we have to face is unsettling: To what degree have deception, distortion, and distraction become not perversions of an otherwise healthy public discourse but the perverse norm of that discourse? In such a world, whether we try to break into mainstream media outlets or go around the filters through independent media, we are not just swimming against the current but instead are lost in a flood.

This isn't an admission of defeat, though defeat may be inevitable. When human settlements are flooded, people continue to struggle to save what can be saved, rebuild what should be rebuilt. People keep on living. Many of us continue to teach dissent, to write dissent. But we should do that work fully aware that the problem is not that there is a lot of propaganda in the society but that society itself is propagandistic, in ways that are deeply woven into the fabric of everyday life. That means the task of fashioning a better world is more difficult than we may have once thought and more important than ever.

Works Cited

Bumiller, Elisabeth. "Traces of Terror: The Strategy; Bush Aides Set Strategy to Sell Policy on Iraq." *New York Times* 7 September 2002. Web. 20 April 2016.

Collins, Ronald K. L., and David M. Skover. *The Death of Discourse.* 2nd ed. Durham: Carolina Academic, 2005. Print.

Creamer, Matthew. "Obama Wins! . . . Ad Age's Marketer of the Year." *Advertising Age.* Crain Communications, 17 October 2008. Web. 20 April 2016.

Herman, Edward S. *The Myth of the Liberal Media.* New York: Peter Lang, 1999. Print.

Herman, Edward S., and Noam Chomsky. *Manufacturing Consent: The Political Economy of the Mass Media.* Rev. ed. New York: Pantheon, 2002. Print.

Jensen, Robert. *Arguing for Our Lives: A User's Guide to Constructive Dialog.* San Francisco: City Lights, 2013. Print.

———. "The Faculty Filter: Why the Propaganda Model Is Marginalized in U.S. Journalism Schools." *The Political Economy of Media and Power.* Ed. Jeffery Klaehn. New York: Peter Lang, 2010. 235–42. Print.

———. "The Myth of the Neutral Professional." *Bound by Power: Intended Consequences.* Ed. Jeffery Klaehn. Montreal: Black Rose Books, 2006. 64–71. Print.

———. "U.S. Just as Guilty of Committing Own Violent Acts." Editorial. *Houston Chronicle* 14 September 2001: A33. Print.

———. *Writing Dissent: Taking Radical Ideas from the Margins to the Mainstream.* New York: Peter Lang, 2001. Print.

Springsteen, Bruce. "Lost in the Flood." *Greetings from Asbury Park, N.J.* Columbia, 1973. CD.

CONTRIBUTORS

INDEX

CONTRIBUTORS

Laural Lea Adams teaches organizational and intercultural communication at Virginia Commonwealth University. Her research explores implications of meaningful work as a rhetorical construct and as a component of workplace literacy for millennials, as well as the enabling and constraining roles of mental models in knowledge ecologies, organizational change, and leadership. She has most recently published on using ecofeminism to sustain open educational resources in the university and on the role of writing practices in graduate education.

Charles Bazerman, a professor of education at the University of California, is the author of numerous research, theoretical, and practical books on academic writing and writing in society; his most recent are *A Rhetoric of Literate Action* and *A Theory of Literate Action*. He has been the chair of the Conference on College Composition and Communication and is the founding chair of the International Society for the Advancement of Writing Research.

M. J. Braun is a retired professor of rhetoric and composition. Over her career, she has taught a variety of courses, including first-year composition and upper-division and graduate courses in rhetoric. Her research interest is the intersection of rhetoric and political economy, and her publications include articles in *JAC* and chapters in *Writing Program Administration* and edited collections. She also coedited *Entertaining Fear: Rhetoric and the Political Economy of Social Control*.

Catherine Chaput is an associate professor in the English department at the University of Nevada, Reno, where she teaches courses in rhetoric, critical theory, and writing studies. She has published in *JAC, College English, CCC, WPA*, and *Philosophy and Rhetoric*, among others. She wrote *Inside the Teaching Machine* and is currently working on a book project titled *Capitalism and Our Affective Investments*.

Patricia Dunmire is a professor of English at Kent State University. Her research examines the linguistic and discursive means by which political discourse projects representations of the future and how these representations legitimate U.S. foreign policy. Her book *Projecting the Future through Political Discourse* examines this issue within the post-9/11 security environment. She is currently working on a project that situates post–Cold War foreign policy discourse within the tradition of the American jeremiad.

Lanette Grate is a senior lecturer at the University of Central Arkansas, where she teaches composition and serves as the assistant director of the writing center. Her previous publications include "Jane Addams: Citizen Writers and a 'Wider Justice,'" a chapter in *Jane Addams in the Classroom*, edited by David Schaafsma. In 2008 she received the Rachel Corrie Award for Courage in the Teaching of Writing.

Jayson Harsin is an associate professor of global communications and international and comparative politics at the American University of Paris. His comparative, critical, and theoretical work on the intersection of popular culture, media, and politics appears in such books and journals as *Communication, Culture, and Critique*; *Communication and Critical/Cultural Studies*; and *French Politics, Culture, and Society*.

Gae Lyn Henderson is an associate professor in the Department of English and Literature at Utah Valley University. She has published in *JAC*, *Present Tense*, *Open Words*, *Reflections*, and *Rhetoric Society Quarterly*. Her article "The Parrhesiastic Game: Textual Self-Justification in Spiritual Narratives of Early Modern Women" won *JAC*'s 2008 Elizabeth A. Flynn Award.

Thomas Huckin is an emeritus professor of English and writing at the University of Utah. His publications include *Genre Knowledge in Disciplinary Communication*, *The New Century Handbook*, *Technical Writing and Professional Communication*, some fifty scholarly papers, and many editorials and letters on current topics in Salt Lake City newspapers. He is now writing *Deception by Omission: How Silence Creates Propaganda*. He is a founding member of Rhetoricians for Peace.

Robert Jensen, professor in the School of Journalism at the University of Texas at Austin, is the author of *Plain Radical: Living, Loving, and Learning* *to Leave the Planet Gracefully, Arguing for Our Lives: A User's Guide to Constructive Dialogue,* and *All My Bones Shake: Seeking a Progressive Path to the Prophetic Voice.*

Sharon J. Kirsch is an associate professor of English and rhetorical studies in the New College at Arizona State University. She is the author of *Gertrude Stein and the Reinvention of Rhetoric* and a coeditor of *Primary Stein: Returning to the Writing of Gertrude Stein.* Her articles appear in *Rhetoric Review, Rhetoric Society Quarterly, Feminist Wire, Present Tense: A Journal of Rhetoric in Society,* and *Trivia: Voices of Feminism.*

Meg H. Kunde is an assistant professor of communication studies at Augustana College in Rock Island, Illinois, where she teaches rhetorical criticism, rhetorical theory, and political communication. In addition to her academic research, she collaborated on several published policy reports as a program evaluator for the North Carolina General Assembly from 2013 to 2015.

John Oddo is an assistant professor in the rhetoric program at Carnegie Mellon University. He has published several journal articles on call-to-arms discourse and is the author of *Intertextuality and the 24-Hour News Cycle,* a monograph that examines news coverage surrounding Colin Powell's 2003 UN address. Currently he is preparing a new book on American war propaganda.

Stefania Porcelli teaches Italian languages and literature at City University of New York and the Fashion Institute of Technology. Her research focuses on the intersection of political discourse, history, and literature. She has published on Elizabeth Bowen, Elsa Morante, and Hannah Arendt.

Gary Thompson is a professor of English and the department chair at Saginaw Valley State University, where he has taught since 1979. He is the author of articles on Thomas Pynchon's fiction and of a writing textbook, *Rhetoric through Media.* He taught for three years during the 1980s in then-Communist Poland, which sensitized him to the range of possibilities for propaganda and the need to be observant about its forms in the West.

INDEX

ABC, 181, 183, 185, 187, 194–96, 207
academics: and managed democracy,
  2, 42, 162–63, 165, 168, 244, 248–
  49, 251, 260; as social action 11–12,
  19, 265; and study of propaganda,
  8–10, 14, 55, 137–38, 245–46
academy, 19, 31, 152(n15), 245–46, 250
action, social, 83, 227
Addams, Jane: biography of, 52–54;
  ignored by propaganda studies, 54–
  56; as peace propagandist, 65–66;
  as propaganda analyst, 51–67; as
  subject of propaganda, 59–60
administration: Bush, 9, 11, 18, 40,
  127, 139, 181, 195–96, 199(n5), 208,
  213, 215, 217, 218(n3), 271; Clinton,
  213; political, 133; Republican, 133;
  university, 19, 245, 249, 256, 260,
  261(2); Wilson, 60–61
advertising: as bullshit, 137, 141, 143,
  145–46, 149; ethics of, 39, 244; and
  propaganda, 124, 132, 141, 145, 211,
  245, 257, 261(n3); as tool of capitalism, 82; and war, 104
affect: and analysis, 7, 159, 166, 182,
  199(n4); and biopolitics, 206; and
  economic propaganda, 165–73,
  175–77; and new media, 207, 215–
  17; techniques of, 217–18; theory of,
  18, 20(n3), 159–62, 166, 177(n3, n5),
  214, 216
agency, rhetorical, 9, 41, 48(n14), 102,
  135, 218, 237–38, 253
ambiguity, 79–80, 195, 205, 212, 236,
  240

American Tobacco Company, 33
antiwar, 67(n2), 195, 197–98, 203
appraisal theory, 182
Arbenz-Guzman, Jacobo, 43–44
Aristotle, 14, 87, 166
art: for art's sake, 80, 83; as propaganda, 96, 101; as rhetorical, 73,
  80, 83, 92(n7); as social action, 77,
  79, 82

Barber, Benjamin, 41, 48(n13)
BBC, 99, 104, 177(n6)
Bernays, Edward, 8, 16, 20(n5), 29,
  31–46, 46(n2), 47(nn6–9), 48(n17),
  77–78, 120–21, 128–29, 144, 159,
  203, 238
binaries, 80, 87, 234–36
blog, 131, 207–10, 215, 218, 218(n1),
  256–57
Booth, Wayne, 4, 9, 12–14
Bowen, Elizabeth, 96–113
British propaganda, 17, 65, 97–101,
  103–5, 108, 113, 119, 164
bullshit: definition of 137–39; as distinct from propaganda, 141–43; as
  propaganda, 138–41, 148–51
Burke, Kenneth, 1–2, 17, 72–90,
  178(n9); on capitalism and propaganda, 77–80; and concept of
  identification, 76–77, 86, 90, 91(n2);
  on propaganda analysis, 83–86; on
  psychology and rhetoric, 73–77; on
  symbolic action, 73, 87
Bush, George W., 18, 134, 148, 181–85,
  187–98, 199(5), 206(n2), 214–15, 224